"A compelling recounting of the unique way that women elementary teachers in Ontario struggled to achieve equity in education through their union."

— **Larry Kuehn**, past director of research and technology, British Columbia Teachers' Federation

"An essential contribution to scholarship on an increasingly significant part of the labour movement in Canada—elementary teachers. Hanson fills a huge gap in labour history and labour studies by documenting the process by which elementary teachers and their union, ETFO, have become one of the most important forces in Ontario politics and a key actor in the fight against neoliberalism in education. This is a must-read for anyone interested in understanding the central contributions of public sector workers like teachers to today's labour movement."

— **Dr. Stephanie Ross**, director and associate professor, School of Labour Studies, McMaster University

"*Class Action* provides important insight into the public school system, the struggles of teachers' unions, and class—both the social relations and the place where teachers work and students learn. Andy Hanson offers a valuable combination of research and theory and insights from his own experiences as teacher and unionist. It is well worth the read."

— **David Rapaport**, former OPSEU activist and author

"This book is a marvelous exploration of the history of two Ontario teacher unions, and how their long-term conflicts eventually ended up in their amalgamation. Extensive research and an analysis based on both gender and class provides us with a comprehensive picture of relations between teachers' organizations and the state during the twentieth century."

— **Harry Smaller**, associate professor emeritus, York University

# Class Action

**How Ontario's Elementary Teachers
Became a Political Force**

**Andy Hanson**

Between the Lines
Toronto

Class Action
© 2021 Andy Hanson

First published in 2021 by
Between the Lines
401 Richmond Street West, Studio 281
Toronto, Ontario, M5V 3A8, Canada
1-800-718-7201 · www.btlbooks.com

Every reasonable effort has been made to identify copyright holders. Between
the Lines would be pleased to have any errors or omissions brought to its
attention.

Library and Archives Canada Cataloguing in Publication

Title: Class action : how Ontario's elementary teachers became a political force
    / Andy Hanson.
Names: Hanson, Andy, author.
Description: Includes bibliographical references and index.
Identifiers: Canadiana (print) 20210241519 | Canadiana (ebook) 20210241608 |
    ISBN 9781771135689 (softcover) | ISBN 9781771135696 (EPUB) |
    ISBN 9781771135702 (PDF)
Subjects: LCSH: Elementary Teachers' Federation of Ontario—History. |
    LCSH: Teachers' unions—Ontario—History. | LCSH: Elementary school
    teachers—Political activity—Ontario.
Classification: LCC LB2844.53.C32 O57 2021 | DDC 331.88/113711009713—dc2

Cover design by Anna Kwan
Text design by DEEVE

Printed in Canada

We acknowledge for their financial support of our publishing activities: the
Government of Canada; the Canada Council for the Arts; and the Government
of Ontario through the Ontario Arts Council, the Ontario Book Publishers Tax
Credit program, and Ontario Creates.

*This book is dedicated to the many teachers I have known who understood the importance of their union, whose struggles achieved what today is taken for granted. And it is for my grandchildren, Nate, Sami, and Hannah, who will need unions to safeguard their futures.*

# Contents

# Acronym Legend

| | |
|---|---|
| AEFO | l'Association des enseignants franco-ontariens |
| AIB | Anti-Inflation Board (Canada) |
| BCTF | British Columbia Teachers' Federation |
| CLC | Canadian Labour Congress |
| CLRB | Canadian Labour Relations Board |
| CODE | Commission on Declining School Enrolments in Ontario |
| CTF | Canadian Teachers' Federation |
| CUPE | Canadian Union of Public Employees |
| EQAO | Education Quality and Accountability Office |
| ERC | Education Relations Commission |
| ETFO | Elementary Teachers' Federation of Ontario |
| ETFO-caa | Viewed at the ETFO offices, copies available from the author |
| ETFO CPS | ETFO Coordinator of Protective Services Christine Brown's office records |
| ETFO GRO | ETFO Government Relations Officer Vivian McCaffrey's office records |
| FWTAO | Federation of Women Teachers' Associations of Ontario |
| FOPSAT | Federation of Provincial Schools Authority Teachers |
| IPRC | Identification, Placement, and Review Committee |
| LEAF | Women's Legal and Education Action Fund |
| NDP | New Democratic Party |
| OEA | Ontario Educational Association |
| OECTA | Ontario English Catholic Teachers' Association |
| OFL | Ontario Federation of Labour |
| OISE | Ontario Institute for Studies in Education (University of Toronto) |

OPSBA   Ontario Public School Boards' Association

OPSEU   Ontario Public Service Employees Union

OPSMTF  Ontario Public School Men Teachers' Federation
        (later, OPSTF)

OPSTA   Ontario Public School Trustees' Association

OPSTF   Ontario Public School Teachers' Federation
        (previously, OPSMTF)

OSSTF   Ontario Secondary School Teachers' Federation

OTF     Ontario Teachers' Federation

PSAC    Public Service Alliance of Canada

QECO    Qualifications Evaluation Council of Ontario

SUB     supplemental unemployment benefit

TFC     Teachers' Federation of Carleton

YUCTA   York University, Clara Thomas Archives and Special
        Collections

# Preface

Late in the 2019–20 school year, the members of the Elementary Teachers' Federation of Ontario (ETFO) joined the other teachers' unions in work-to-rule restrictions and a series of rotating strikes. The teachers were opposed to the Doug Ford Progressive Conservative government's cuts to the education budget and a legislated 1 per cent limit on salary increases.[1]

The teachers kept up a sustained pressure that ended, not because of a negotiated settlement, but because of the COVID-19 pandemic, which forced both sides to retreat. Prior to their compliance with self-isolating at home, the teachers' unions had successfully fought the Ford government to a standstill. At the forefront was the ETFO, representing the elementary teachers, the largest teachers' union in Canada. Interestingly, prior to 1998, elementary teachers had belonged to two unions that were constantly at odds with each other. Both had salaries and working conditions well behind those of their secondary peers.

How did those people whose job it is to educate children to become good citizens become the front line of union activism? What happened to turn elementary teachers into a political force in Ontario? How did elementary teachers come to join the vanguard of resistance to the neo-liberal turn in government policy?

This book follows the making of the elementary teachers as a distinct class of white-collar, public sector workers who awoke to the power of their collective strength. I argue that their labour consciousness developed over time as they engaged with their employers and with the state. The strategies implemented against the Ford government in 2019–20 were distilled from over four decades of campaigns that included both wins and losses. Of these campaigns, two province-wide strikes stand out: in 1973 for one day, and in 1997 for two weeks.

The 1973 strike of all five teachers' unions achieved the right to strike for teachers in Ontario. It took place as the Keynesian welfare state was coming to an end in Canada. While the elementary teachers had previously been reticent to use labour tactics, once they achieved collective bargaining rights they began to experiment with them.

The 1997 strike began on Monday, 27 October. All of Ontario's teachers walked out of their classrooms. The combined forces of the five teachers' unions faced off against the Conservative government of Premier Mike Harris. It was regarded as the largest teachers' strike in North American history.[2] Some of the teachers patrolling their picket lines had participated in the Days of Action in Hamilton, where they had been greeted by the Ontario Provincial Police in full riot gear. Other teachers could recall parading down Toronto's University Avenue to the provincial legislature at Queen's Park a year earlier. Teachers marching down the main streets of towns and cities across the province had become labour's front line against the neo-liberal policies of the Harris government. Their numbers, and their position of caring for children, provided a critical intensity to the struggle with their political masters. The 2019–20 strikes against the Ford government had parallels with those of the Harris years.

In 1997, five unions represented teachers who worked in the publicly funded schools across Ontario. Teachers were sorted by the language of instruction, the students' religion, the students' grade, and the teachers' sex.[3] The French-language teachers were represented by l'Association des enseignants franco-ontariens (AEFO). The Ontario English Catholic Teachers' Association (OECTA) acted for the Roman Catholic separate school teachers. The secondary school teachers in the public system belonged to the Ontario Secondary School Teachers' Federation (OSSTF).

The elementary teachers in the public system were divided into two unions based on their sex. Women elementary teachers were members of the women-only Federation of Women Teachers' Associations of Ontario (FWTAO). The men elementary teachers belonged to the Ontario Public School Teachers' Federation (OPSTF), which, until 1982, had been called the Ontario Public School Men Teachers' Federation (OPSMTF).[4] For their entire history these two unions were at odds over whether or not to amalgamate. The men's union wanted one organization; the women's union preferred its independence. The amalgamation debate came to an end eight months after the 1997 strike with the formation of one union, the Elementary Teachers' Federation of Ontario, creating four teachers' unions in Ontario.

I will make four arguments as to how Ontario teachers rose to the forefront of resistance to neo-liberal/populist provincial governments. The first, that certain conditions inside and outside their unions had to exist before teachers would engage in labour activism.

Next, their unique union configuration had a fundamental influence on the trajectory of the elementary teachers' labour activity. The feminism of the mid to late twentieth century was a driving force in the women's union, which drew a reactionary response from the men's union. While having separate labour organizations delivered tangible gains for women teachers, it dampened militancy in both unions.

Moreover, teachers eventually appropriated the narrow professionalism imposed on them by Egerton Ryerson, the designer of the public school system in what was then Canada West. Teachers ultimately integrated professionalism as a demand for improving their work lives while developing a sense of themselves as a group of workers whose interests were opposed to those over them. This occurred in parallel with, and partly because of, the rise of neo-liberalism on the Canadian political landscape.

Finally, I argue that gendered and classed social structures defined labour relations in the classroom. By "gendered," I mean something that was done to and by individuals and social groups to assign them their place in society, and that reproduced men's privilege through systemic patriarchy. As a social process, gender was intrinsic to the formation of two elementary teachers' unions. It must be noted that, although ableism, racism, and homophobia have been deeply ingrained in the Ontario education system as well, the two unions did not comprehensively address these issues before their 1998 amalgamation.[5]

In order to trace the historical contours from the formation of the FWTAO and the OPSMTF, in 1918 and 1920 respectively, to the formation of the ETFO, this study relies primarily on the fonds of the two teachers' unions. That information is given support through media reports, other histories of the period, and quantitative data from Statistics Canada and the Canadian Teachers' Federation (CTF). A number of interviews with union members, staff, and elected officials, both local and provincial, present at times a more personalized viewpoint.

Those writers who have examined teachers' labour organizations have most often done so from a political economy standpoint, although there are some exceptions.[6] This study holds a labour feminist lens, asking who performs the work, who has the power, who benefits, and where the contradictions are.

In this investigation of two teachers' unions, class differences are considered in the context of power differentials. Class, as a social distinction, has had its primacy downgraded over the final quarter of the twentieth century, partly due to the emergence of competing identities, notably gender, race, ethnicity, and sexual orientation. While identity politics has secured essential, fundamental rights for identified groups, the enormous economic disparities of the twenty-first century have reaffirmed the class distinctions that are at the heart of union activity.[7] Those intersections between class and identity have brought activists from all camps together. As American political writer Bhaskar Sunkara has said, "class is the underlying thing that conditions other oppressions."[8]

Certainly, class was at the forefront of Doug Ford's 2019–20 efforts to reduce the salaries of teachers by half the increase in the cost of living and to end supports and programs for vulnerable students. The teachers were facing an entrenched neo-liberal orthodoxy in the Ford government that demanded suppressing the wages of public sector workers. Their response once again made them front-page news.

## A Note on the Research

The primary data for this book was provided from the records of the two unions, the Federation of Women Teachers' Associations of Ontario and the Ontario Public School Teachers' Federation. Supporting materials have come from the electronic archives of various newspapers and government websites. The British Columbia Teachers' Federation (BCTF) provided copies of the Canadian Teachers' Federation records of teacher strike actions across Canada. The few interviews undertaken with former teachers' union members and staff provided personal reflections on the events of their time and helped to clarify some of the ambiguities contained in the primary documents.

The FWTAO records are archived at York University in Toronto, Ontario. The women's union had made a habit of storing its records, with the result that a large collection of material was available for research. The sheer volume of documents was more than could be read. The FWTAO archives are identified as they appear in the catalogue of York University, Clara Thomas Archives and Special Collections (YUCTA). Whenever possible, the relevant file is listed.

The material from the OPSTF posed some difficulty when it came to organizing and recording. As of my reading those records, they had not yet been archived or catalogued and were stored in the ETFO offices. After I completed my research, the ETFO transferred the OPSTF material to York University, where it was reorganized and catalogued. While I was able to track down most of the documents in the new location, some were impossible to find without reviewing the entirety of the records. For the OPSTF documents I was unable to find, I have referenced them as "Viewed at the ETFO offices, copies available from the author" (ETFO-caa).

**Archival material:**
Federation of Women Teachers' Associations of Ontario (FWTAO) Archive, York University, Clara Thomas Archives and Special Collections (YUCTA), Toronto.
Ontario Public School Teachers' Federation (OPSTF) Archive, YUCTA, Toronto.

**Personal records that were made available to me:**
ETFO Coordinator of Protective Services Christine Brown's office records (ETFO CPS).
ETFO Government Relations Officer Vivian McCaffrey's office records (ETFO GRO).

## Organizational Structures in the Two Unions

### FWTAO elected positions
- Provincial president and executive
- Regional directors
- Association presidents and executives
- Representatives to the annual meeting

### FWTAO administrative positions
- Executive secretary
- Staff

### OPSTF elected positions
- Provincial president and executive
- District presidents and executives
- Representatives to the provincial assembly

### OPSTF administrative positions
- General secretary
- Staff

The central offices for both unions were in Toronto. The provincial president and the executive were elected at the respective annual general meetings, which were held at the same time in different venues.

The FWTAO had a structure of independent locals, called associations. Each local had an elected president and an executive. The local had the authority to negotiate collective agreements while the provincial body provided support.

Similarly, the OPSTF locals, called districts, elected a president and an executive, with the authority to negotiate collective agreements. Some of the OPSTF locals also had branches, which were another layer to local authority.

The OPSTF regularly brought its local presidents together in a council of local presidents. The FWTAO would bring its local presidents together from time to time in a presidents' conference.

The FWTAO achieved local representation through regional directors, who were elected from the locals and met in Toronto regularly. The directors received their direction from the provincial executive but met as a body to make financial decisions.

## Acknowledgements

First, I need to thank Professor Bryan Palmer for guidance, continued support, and unwavering faith in the project. Also, Professor Joan Sangster for interceding when I needed it. A special thanks to Suzanne Dubeau, Michael Moir, and the staff at the Clara Thomas Archives and Special Collections at York University. Without their dedication to archival records, this research would not have been possible.

Thanks to the Elementary Teachers' Federation of Ontario and to Gene Lewis, general secretary, for generously permitting me access to the OPSTF materials. I am eternally grateful to Olesia Romanko, ETFO manager of information and records services, who provided the advice and guidance I required to make my way through the many boxes. Her assistance was invaluable. An additional thanks to Vivian McCaffrey, coordinator of communications and political action services, and Christine Brown, coordinator of protective services, for providing me with their personal collections from the predecessor organizations.

I received a copy of the CTF booklet "Teacher Strikes and Sanctions in Canada, 1919–1992" from Lesley Harrington of the British Columbia Teachers' Federation. Kathie Waterhouse at Collective Bargaining Information Services, Ministry of Labour, Toronto, provided me with updates to the booklet. Thanks to them both for an essential reference piece.

Thanks to Glen Tunney at the Ontario Teachers' Pension Plan for the statistical information on retirements. As well, thanks to Scott Perkin for his references regarding the relationship between the Ontario Teachers' Federation (OTF) and the Ontario Teachers' Pension Plan.

Friends and family, too numerous to mention here, supported me throughout the project. To the friends who listened to me through the many walks, bicycle rides, canoe trips, lunches, and dinners, thank you for being there. Thank you to my family: to my mother and father, who believed in teachers; to Garth and Sandra for their many meals and a bed; and to Emily and Dan for the weekends and the jazz. Most particularly to my partner, Gwen Schauerte, who provided me with much-needed prodding and support to get it finished.

# CHAPTER 1
# Constructing Public Education

Today, the vast majority of Ontario's children pass through the public school system. But that was not always the case. In Canada, as in most Western countries, the requirement for all children to gain a basic education became social policy during the mid-nineteenth century. To achieve that goal, the school system was envisioned in a form that was palatable to the elites, politically designed and materially constructed.

Public education served a variety of purposes, from developing a workforce to assimilating or punishing marginalized groups. Ontario began its public education project some 170 years ago to provide more than the skills of numeracy and literacy. It was to be a moral enterprise that would transform individuals by reforming behaviours and social practices.[1]

A distinction has to be made between residential schools for First Nation children and the provincially funded day schools provided for the general population. Egerton Ryerson, the first superintendent of education for Canada West, recommended residential schools for Indigenous children. A recent plaque at Ryerson University specifies that he participated "in the establishment of the residential school system in Canada and the harm that was caused by the system that robbed many Indigenous Peoples of their culture and left them with psychological, emotional and physical damage."[2] In the words of Canadian historian James Miller, the purpose of the residential school system was to "eliminate Indians by assimilating them. . . . In other words, the extinction of the Indians *as Indians* is the ultimate end."[3] Examples of this goal were repeatedly brought forward in 2015 by the Truth and Reconciliation Commission.[4] Provincial public education systems in Canada, while colonizing in their broad intent, served a different purpose from the residential schools.

The white, anglophone elite openly stated that cultural continuity and uniformity were the most important elements of education.[5] The value of paying taxes for an education system for the working class was that it would inhibit social unrest while training a homogenous workforce.[6] Although Canada's Industrial Revolution would not fully engage until the 1880s, by the 1840s there were indications of what could be expected from early forms of industrial capitalism and the infrastructure supporting it.[7] Teachers' work, then, was designed to be twofold: the development of a moral citizenry and skills training.

The passage of the Common School Act of 1846 in Canada West and the appointment of Ryerson, a staunch supporter of the governor general, to the position of superintendent of education began the public education project. Ryerson designed his public schools as an arm of the British state, where teachers would instill appropriate bourgeois conduct in their charges.[8] English was to be the language of instruction and British loyalties were to be assured. The education system's most vital purpose was the development of a shared "common sense," which would govern social behaviour and validate the dominant ideology as the obvious, irrefutable understanding of how the world operated from bottom to top.[9]

Labour groups also wanted the benefits education would bring. Success at school promised to expand children's life chances.

Education was viewed as a contributing factor to employability, income level, and a broader world view.

The homogenization of the educating process began with state control of the training facilities for teachers and the requirement that teachers attend. County model schools were created across the province to provide apprenticeship training under the stern eye of a principal and the guiding hand of an experienced teacher.[10] While the effectiveness of the training was disputed, the model school system claimed to produce an elementary teacher in thirteen weeks.[11] Model schools were a pragmatic choice for single women with little access to their own resources.[12] Teachers who passed through the model schools could progress to the more formalized training in one of the normal schools at a later date, if they found the financial means to do so.[13]

Normal schools were the academic institutions for training teachers. They instructed applicants in a common, or "normal," teaching practice. The first such school was established in Toronto in 1847.[14] Standardized academic qualifications (which were quickly lowered), a character reference from a religious official, a requisite interview, often undertaken by Ryerson himself, and strict adherence to the regulations governing the separation of the sexes filtered applicants.[15] The normal schools trained teachers in the application of state-approved pedagogy, curricula, and morality.[16]

Normal schools would continue to function until the mid-twentieth century.[17] In 1907, another layer would be added to the qualifications available to teachers, as degree-granting faculties of education were established at the University of Toronto and Queen's University. In time, more would follow. In 1953, "normal school" would be changed to "teachers' college."[18] In the mid-1970s, the Conservative government of Bill Davis would absorb the teachers' colleges into the faculties of education.

To ensure ongoing control of what went on in the classroom, Ryerson devised a disciplining bureaucracy that could reach into the farthest corners of the province.[19] After the School Act of 1871 was passed, teachers were routinely observed and evaluated by a cadre of provincial inspectors who visited each of the schools in their district on a regular basis to ensure that students were receiving appropriate instruction and that teachers were fulfilling their duties.[20] Nonetheless, Canadian historian John Abbot's examination of the harsh treatment of women teachers by the inspectors, who were almost always male, is disturbing.[21] Other writers report on the trivial minutia inspectors deemed to be important.[22] These inspections were a feature of teachers' lives from Ryerson's day through to 1967.[23]

Ryerson predicted that the normal schools would professionalize teaching and attract married men of British background to lucrative careers in education.[24] His prediction neglected to take into account the funding model imposed on local boards.[25] Education was controlled by the legislature, but funding had to be raised locally. Limits on teachers' salaries were set by locally elected trustees, who were required to finance education through the levying of property taxes.[26] Their parsimonious inclination directed them toward women teachers.[27]

Women were not accepted into universities in the mid-nineteenth century, but the teachers' training facilities had been kept separate from the universities.[28] They were one of the few avenues of academia open to women. By the late nineteenth century, women were half to two-thirds of those enrolled.[29] Teaching offered young women a livelihood independent of their fathers and husbands.

Women could free themselves of immediate male control, but that did not leave them unbound. Morality, gender, and hiring practices soon intersected when it came to employing an increasingly feminized workforce. Any evidence of women's sexual activity was incompatible with British moral standards and deemed unacceptable for the classroom. Marriage, with its declaration of a shared bed, ended a woman's teaching career.[30] Trustees continued to hire women and pay them half of what a man would receive, but they did so with monastic vengeance.[31] For over a hundred years, women teachers in the Canada West / Ontario public school system could be denied their livelihood if they chose to have sexual relationships of any sort.

Despite having to make such choices, women would be nearly half of the rural teachers in the province and over 70 per cent of the teachers in urban Ontario by 1871.[32] Of those, nearly half were under the age of twenty-five, while only 16 per cent were over thirty years of age, a reversal of the statistics for men. Many more women than men would enter teaching, but if a woman desired her own family, she was forced out of her classroom as soon as she married unless the board was in dire need of teachers.

The 1871 legislation also imposed additional training requirements on teachers. As well as the prerequisite thirteen weeks at a county model school or a passing grade at a normal school, teachers had to attend teachers' institute conferences twice a year to take part in professional training, at their own expense and on their own time.[33] The institutes were overseen by the local school inspector and included an obligatory membership fee. If teachers failed to attend, they could be suspended. By the early twentieth century, regular and compulsory state-mandated professional upgrading was a constant feature of teachers' lives, ensuring that teachers would not move beyond the pedagogical boundaries set by the education bureaucracy.

## Organizing Teachers

In 1861, the Ontario Educational Association (OEA) formed as a voluntary gathering of educators.[34] Designed to reflect professional objectives, membership was open to elementary teachers, secondary teachers, students from the normal schools, school trustees, provincial superintendents, and retired teachers. The OEA provided a venue for professional upgrading and networking, but it also served to awaken a rudimentary labour consciousness in teachers. It provided a space where general grievances could be articulated and a common identity could be forged between teachers who were very often isolated from one another.

The first teachers in Ontario to recognize the need for collective strength were women teaching in urban centres. In the 1880s, Toronto was a centre of suffragist activity. Educated urban women were calling for social reforms that included workplace safety, child labour laws, and prohibition, along with the right to full enfranchisement.[35] Feminists, such as Dr. Emily Stowe, Canada's first woman doctor, were leading campaigns to politicize women. In 1885, the women teachers of Toronto organized themselves to demand a salary schedule based on length of service rather than on the grade taught.[36] They won their case before the trustees. The success of their campaign encouraged these women to formally launch the Lady Teachers' Association of Toronto in 1888 (changed four years later to the Women Teachers' Association). Despite the effectiveness of their collective action, they rejected membership in the Trades and Labour Council for fear they might be required to go on strike. Other cities and regions would form Women Teachers' Associations (WTAs), but they would remain independent from one another into the twentieth century.

The WTAs were a response to a range of challenges women teachers faced. Reports of country schools having classes of up to seventy-five students varying in age from young children to adult learners were not uncommon.[37] Most rural schools consisted of one room.[38] Teachers working in city schools reported class sizes of up to a hundred students in one room.

Not only did school boards hire too few teachers, but the family wage, the accepted standard paid to a man to support his family, worked against women teachers. Although exceptions were occasionally made for widows or for women who were the sole support for their families, generally a woman had to be unmarried to teach. But when it came to salary, she was punished for not being married. She could be paid less because, as an unmarried woman, she did not have to support a family.[39] It was much more difficult for women to save the money to advance in the education hierarchy. By the close of the nineteenth century, two streams of teachers existed: university-educated men in positions of authority and less-educated women teaching in classrooms.[40]

At the end of the First World War, women teachers who had been organizing seized the opportunity to expand their influence. The official history of the Toronto WTA describes their intentions:

> In May 1917 a proposal from the London Women Teachers' Guild suggested a formation of a Federation of Women Teachers to include all the women teachers in the province, and a representative was sent to London to discuss the matter. That union means strength had been clearly demonstrated in Toronto, London and a few other centres. . . . The Federation of all women teachers would, it was hoped, give to the isolated teacher the strength of a large professional organization and tend to stabilize and improve the salary and standing of all women teachers.[41]

On 3 April 1918, at the instigation of the London Women Teachers' Guild and the Toronto Women Teachers' Association, women teachers from the nine cities of Hamilton, North Bay, Port Arthur, Prescott, Ottawa, Chatham, Galt, London, and Toronto met during the OEA's annual meeting to amalgamate their local associations into the Federation of Women Teachers' Associations of Ontario.[42] The FWTAO was the first of the five teachers' unions that would eventually represent the interests of teachers in Ontario.

The handwritten minutes of the 1920 FWTAO annual general meeting record that a motion was carried to add to the objects of the organization, "that we have separate Federations of men and women teachers and that we co-operate by means of a central committee."[43] It was a bold move at time when male authority extended in all directions. At that point in time, women had only recently won the right to vote in federal elections. The women teachers of the FWTAO declared that they were shouldering the responsibilities of their own labour relations without having a man speak for them.

A year after the women teachers formed their union, the secondary teachers organized as the Ontario Secondary School Teachers' Federation, representing both men and women. The men elementary teachers did not want to become a unique body and approached the FWTAO to form a single organization. The women refused. On 8 April 1920, the OEA Public School Section took time out from its meeting to permit the men teachers to form the Ontario Public School Men Teachers' Federation.[44]

The other two teachers' unions would form later. L'Association des enseignants franco-ontariens was organized in 1939 to represent teachers in French-language schools after Regulation 17 was modified to permit bilingual schools. That notorious regulation had been issued by Premier James Whitney's Conservative government in 1912 to limit instruction in French to Grades 1 and 2. The Ontario English Catholic Teachers' Association formed in 1944 in response to the passage of the Ontario Teaching Profession Act, which required a teacher to belong to a teachers' union.[45]

The Ontario Teaching Profession Act of 1944 brought the five teachers' unions together under the Ontario Teachers' Federation as the joint body of the teachers' unions that would interact with the state.[46] At the same time, the act granted teachers a closed shop.[47] As education professor Harry Smaller notes, while it and similar legislation across Canada provided union security, these statutes significantly increased state control over teachers and their unions.[48] While the state decided that every teacher had to belong to one of the unions in order to teach in the public schools of Ontario (a closed shop), it also required that the unions establish and operate a discipline committee to punish unprofessional behaviour.[49] The teachers were granted the right to have union dues collected by their employer and passed on to the union (two years before the Rand formula required the same of all employers under collective agreements), but in exchange, constraints were placed upon their ability to negotiate with their employer.[50]

## The Postwar Context

Between the wars, the wider use of psychology as a lens through which to view human behaviour was gaining acceptance.[51] Education historian Jason Ellis recounts, "Beginning in 1931, Ottawa public schools tested the I.Q. of every single one of the system's Grade 5 pupils. In 1942, the board grew the program and tested, twice per year, every child in Grades 1, 3, 4 and 6."[52] The postwar education system became the seat of psychological discourses that defined the attributes of the "normal." This new moral order dramatically altered the discourse concerning who would be permitted to teach in the schools.

The increase in the number of children born in the two decades after the war became known as the baby boom.[53] As new schools were built, the supply of unmarried women teachers was soon depleted. Boards of education shifted their gaze to young, married woman with children.[54]

For decades, women teachers had been required to remain unmarried and sexually abstemious, but by 1951, 28 per cent of women teachers were married.[55] By the 1960s, women were being asked to continue teaching even during their pregnancies, a momentous change from a generation earlier. A 1962 FWTAO survey of rural women teachers reported that 51 per cent were married.[56] Six years later, the FWTAO established the Young Married

Women Teachers Committee to focus on the problems of teachers who were balancing career and family, a new issue for the union.[57] By the late 1960s, the FWTAO was advocating for a woman's right to retain her job after marriage, to teach during pregnancy, and to return to her position after giving birth.[58]

As the image of the woman teacher was remodelled, the union found its more recent arguments in support of married women being turned against its older members who had not had those options when they began their careers.[59] Canadian feminist writer Sheila Cavanagh reports:

> The spinster image, once celebrated by early advocates of teacher professionalism, seemed to be unhealthy and associated with latent homosexuality. . . . An article on why women teach, published in the Ontario elementary school teachers' magazine, attempted to differentiate the modern teacher from the spinster now seen as a social outcast. . . . Never before had the construction of the spinster been recognized as an embodiment of sexual- and gender-identity transgression. . . . Women teachers' federations refused to speak outwardly in support of the unmarried teacher in both the postwar Canadian and the British context.[60]

Society's retreat from a celibate professionalism for women in the classroom placed a veil of suspicion over older, single women who had been forced to choose between marriage and career when they began their teaching. Despite an emerging feminism, the FWTAO did not engage in a debate that included same-sex sexuality.

The concerns of women who had little chance of promotion and felt trapped in subordinate positions to male principals found expression in the revitalized feminist movement that appeared in the late 1960s, often called second-wave feminism. Feminists' objection to men's privileged position threatened to undo long-standing imbalances that had rewarded masculinity with money, power, and improved quality of life. It was a time of excitement and hope for women. United under the banner of feminism, the FWTAO joined other women's organizations to push at the boundaries of what was permissible.

Parallel assumptions of masculinity's place in education were slower to shift. There was no need for the men of the OPSMTF to press for change. They maintained their hold on administrative positions and the senior grades, where higher pay scales were a common feature at the time.[61] Male teachers had been able to marry and raise children with impunity since the first days of public education. For those who benefited from the status quo, breaking down the doors that guarded privilege had little attraction. In the fall of 1970, John Fielder, editor of the *OPSMTF News*, wrote, "Our president, Al Robb, has gone on record as supporting FWTAO in its fight to end promotion discrimination against women—just because they are women. . . . For it must be our position that principals are chosen on the basis of merit."[62] There is little in the editorial to indicate a recognition that merit had long been equated with those traits that were traditionally viewed as male.

The historical salary differential in elementary teaching was a fundamental issue that divided the FWTAO and the OPSMTF. In 1946 the OTF Board of Governors, consisting of representatives from all five teachers' union, had proposed a resolution supporting "equal opportunity and equal pay for equal qualifications and responsibilities between men and women."[63] But well into the 1950s, men teachers were content with their better salaries. In 1954, Tom Alcorn, the retiring OPSMTF president, reflected on the ambiguity within the union regarding one salary schedule. "It has become quite common now for the two Federations to negotiate jointly . . . when arranging a salary set-up with a board of trustees. Many OPSMTF members *still do not agree* with this policy and feel there should be a differential based on sex."[64]

In October 1955, the FWTAO and the OPSMTF established a joint committee on salaries. By the summer of 1957 the FWTAO executive reported "that OPSMTF have pretty well closed all doors on active cooperation on salary policy with FWTAO, but we felt that we could put in a request for a meeting and see what happens."[65] Surprisingly, a joint meeting held that November did produce a draft for a single salary policy for collective bargaining.[66] That raised the ire of men teachers who were against one salary grid. One OPSMTF member, W.J. Redford, stated, "The women want the men to fight their battles and to have a 'me too' attitude re salaries . . . men teachers should be in a position to 'go it alone' . . . I am willing to cooperate with the women but not by one salary policy."[67] At the time, a woman in the same position with the same qualifications and seniority in the same board would earn less than half of what a man was paid. The February 1962 OPSMTF newsletter reported that a male teacher who had finished high school had an average salary of $4,638, while the average for a woman teacher with the same education was $2,016.[68]

Despite the reactionary rhetoric of some of the OPSMTF members, the 1957 decision of the two unions to negotiate one salary schedule would hold firm. It would bind the two unions together for the purposes of collective bargaining for the next four decades.

In 1969, the FWTAO, OPSMTF, OECTA, and AEFO established the Qualifications Evaluation Council (later, the Qualifications Evaluation Council of Ontario, known as QECO) to develop standards for harmonizing teachers' salaries and their qualifications.[69] It was an arms-length body of representatives from the four unions with responsibility "to establish and review policies on which an evaluation program should be based."[70] When the Department of Education proposed introducing a single Ontario School Teachers' Certificate, the unions met with the Ontario School Trustees' Council and the Department to advocate for QECO.[71] By the summer of 1972, the trustees were accepting QECO ranking as the standard for placement of teachers on their salary grids.[72] The priority QECO gave to formal qualifications made pay equity even more urgent for women teachers who did not hold additional credentials.

Equal pay for work of equal value was one of the prime objectives of the new feminism penetrating the Canadian consciousness. As women teachers became more vocal in demanding an equal place in the school system, the men of the OPSMTF intensified their efforts to convince FWTAO members of the need for one union of elementary teachers. At the local level, the men were able to convince some FWTAO locals to amalgamate with them to create one local of men and women.[73]

The FWTAO response to the OPSMTF was equally vigorous. "Co-operation NOT Amalgamation" read the title of a special newsletter being prepared by the FWTAO in January 1970.[74] The reasons for a woman-only union were listed. Five arguments were made that would frame the discourse for the next twenty-eight years. The first was that the OPSMTF was an organization ruled largely by principals and vice-principals, who did not have the interests of the classroom teacher at heart.

> The men are oriented toward promotion to administrative positions, and they try to ensure that they will become able principals and vice-principals, and that working conditions in the system will be such that they will be able to run their schools smoothly and competently. . . . On the other hand, women in the school systems, being predominantly classroom teachers, are oriented toward the education of the child, and consequently toward measures which will improve their effectiveness in their day-to-day duties.[75]

The second point was that women did not have an equal voice in any of the other teachers' unions where both men and women were members.

> All one has to do is take a look at other teacher organizations where both men and women compose the membership. . . . Women hardly ever are elected to their Executives and it is the exception to employ any to the executive positions on their large male office staffs.

The third argument, and one of the strongest, was that women in the FWTAO were given a chance to be leaders. "We need to give women as many opportunities as possible to find out if they are good leaders." This third point tied directly to a campaign the FWTAO was initiating to train women to assume leadership positions.

Fourth, women were discriminated against and the men had not made any effort to rectify that situation. "We cannot rely on men to champion the cause of women, despite the fact that many men are both fair and honest in their assessments." None of the Ontario teachers' unions had made pay equity a deal breaker during any negotiations.

The final point challenged women to take charge of their professional lives.

> We need a strong educational programme to overcome certain preconceptions about women, particularly the prejudices which lead men to see only "stereotypes" and not individuals. But these attitudes aren't restricted to men by any means. While we need to educate men, we need a programme equally strong to change the attitudes of women to women. Women are naturally conservative, and we need to bring them out of a limited orbit.[76]

This point rankled some. Many of those women in the FWTAO who supported the OPSMTF campaign for one union found too patronizing the claim that women needed the guidance and hand-holding of the FWTAO to be equal.

The FWTAO had the resources to support a range of campaigns for women's rights. The Committee for the Equality of Women in Canada, the most prominent group of feminists in the country, operated almost entirely out of the offices of the FWTAO.[77] Such commitment reflected the willingness of Ontario's largest teachers' union to develop alliances with groups that supported women's equality. As a conduit into every community in the province, the FWTAO became important to building capacity within feminist organizations.

In all but a few instances, the OPSMTF would not align with the negotiating goals of the FWTAO to further the cause of equity.[78] Joint bargaining did not work for the FWTAO in matters of gender. Representing only women, the FWTAO chose to bring the class issues it shared with the men to contract negotiations and to advocate for gender issues through its relationship with the state. An early example of the success of the latter was the release of the green paper *Equal Opportunity for Women in Ontario: A Plan for Action* in 1973.[79]

In seeking to improve conditions for themselves, FWTAO members became actively engaged in the larger feminist movement. Among other initiatives, they approved funding for activities promoting the United Nations International Women's Year in 1975.[80] And of particular importance to education, the FWTAO argued for the removal of sex bias and sex discrimination in curriculum and textbooks.[81]

## Robarts and Hall-Dennis

In the 1960s, Ontario began to invest in "human capital." Minister of Education John Robarts took advantage of federal funding to expand education. Under what became known as the Robarts Plan, a raft of larger and more expensive elementary and secondary schools were constructed. In 1950, the Hope Commission had tabled its report recommending improvements to the training of teachers.[82] After becoming premier in 1961, Robarts established training facilities at Queen's University and the University of Western Ontario to produce university-educated teachers for the new schools.[83] By the 1970s, parents had come to view education as a gateway to achieving material security for their children. For governments, the politics of education became critical to their survival.

The rapid expansion of the school system in the 1950s and 1960s had created tensions between teachers and their employers. Larger schools provided opportunities for teachers to share grievances and to develop collective responses. Equally significant was the change in the relationship between teachers and trustees that took place in the late 1960s. Approximately two thousand small community school boards were reconfigured into 190 county-sized boards of education.[84] The disappearance of the small boards broke down long-standing paternalistic relationships that had previously governed negotiations.[85] Teachers became conscious of themselves collectively as a unique group of professional workers, no longer under the eye of trustees who lived in the same community.

At the same moment, teaching, particularly elementary teaching, was turned on its head. The Provincial Committee on Aims and Objectives of Education report was released in 1968.[86] Known as the Hall-Dennis Report after the chairs of the committee, it attempted to establish a child-centred pedagogy in the Ontario education system, a major change from the prevailing curriculum focus in elementary education.[87] Australian educator Nadeem Memon sums up the subtler influence of the Hall-Dennis Report:

> In the years following the publication there was an increase in educational experimentation. . . . Individual schools and school boards proved open to all sorts of new approaches in school structure, classroom management, and approaches to learning. . . . And the humanistic philosophy underlying the

individualized system initially found "widespread appeal among Ontario teachers."[88]

Despite the initial enthusiasm with which Hall-Dennis was greeted, wholesale adoption proved difficult. Memon gives one example:

> One day teachers were told about open classrooms and the next day they walked into schools with no walls. . . . Ill-equipped and untrained to implement a student-centred approach in their classrooms, many teachers simply refused to cooperate and began to campaign against reform.[89]

The foundation of the Hall-Dennis Report was that children came to the classroom with innate abilities, including the ability to learn, that the teacher had to draw out and direct by providing an experiential environment. This flew in the face of an education system that had been based on filling the minds of students with prescribed subject matter. The new emphasis was on the individual student. Teachers would not only have to develop lessons and teach the concepts, but they would have to accommodate individual differences. Pedagogically this was sound teaching, but at the time, teachers had no experience of how to manage this kind of classroom. Most of the report's 258 recommendations fell directly on teachers' shoulders.

The Hall-Dennis Report was delivered in 1968, but just as important to classroom teachers had been the 1967 release by the Department of Education of Curriculum P1J1, the policy document that would guide education in the primary and junior levels, Kindergarten to Grade 6.[90] While Curriculum P1J1, the Hall-Dennis Report, and the curriculum documents that came out later made much of teachers' freedom to choose their materials and approaches, that lack of definition required teachers to take on the responsibility to produce curriculum, integrate new teaching styles, and undertake professional retraining, mostly at their own expense.[91]

Eunice Saari from Nipissing had been an FWTAO representative on the committee that had met with Department of Education officials following the release of the documents. Eight years later, she expressed teachers' frustration when she confronted the representative of the renamed Ministry of Education, Doug Penny, at the 1975 FWTAO Annual General Meeting:[92]

> As you probably know, the main thrust is left to the individual principal and staff. . . . Of course, the P-1 J-1 is to involve teachers and this was produced because the Ministry did not wish to impose too rigid guide lines. I assured [Deputy Minister of Education] Mr. Waldrum that he need not fear the imposition of any rigid guide lines, even at the local level, because I doubt it whether the teachers would even have time to formulate some guide lines to impose. . . .We see in many local areas groups of teachers going in circles; duplicating each other's efforts; trying to formulate some type of curriculum. The result is exhaustion, with few curriculum units being produced . . . with teachers already working trying to individualize programs . . . now they have the mammoth job of curriculum building. In the name of flexibility and being involved, this is quite something, a new responsibility to assume.[93]

On behalf of classroom teachers, Saari went on to plead for some "relief time, so that they won't be doing this after 12 [midnight], when they are exhausted."[94]

### Not Waiting for Permission: Activist Professionalism

The Canadian Teachers' Federation records indicate that sanctions imposed by the elementary teachers in Deseronto in 1953 were the first example of militancy by any teachers' union in the province.[95] The FWTAO and the OPSMTF had issued a "grey letter," also known as "pink listing" against the trustees.[96] The letter advised teachers outside of the Deseronto board to refrain from applying for jobs there. Without the means of bringing in new teachers, the trustees were forced to negotiate. The Deseronto teachers won improvements in their salaries.

The next attempt by the elementary teachers was not as successful. Ten years after the Deseronto settlement, most of the FWTAO and the OPSMTF members in the Lakefield board resigned over salaries. At the end of the school year, the Lakefield board hired replacements for those teachers who had not returned to their classrooms.[97] The failure of the Lakefield action demonstrated both the weakness of the teachers' unions and the limitations of mass resignations as a strike tactic. In her study of the nurses' union, Linda Briskin makes the point that mass resignations are an effective strategy only when the entire sector is united and mobilized.[98] That was not the case with the small local strike at Lakefield.

The provincial legislation that governed education in the 1960s required individual teachers to sign a personal contract with their board of education. Teachers worked under a two-tiered employment agreement; the collective agreement set wages and entitlement to benefits in each board, while individual contracts assured each teacher of having a job.

By the late 1960s, the teachers' unions had devised a means of using resignations to initiate a strike. Because teachers were not under the Ontario Labour Relations Act or any other labour legislation, they did not have the legal right to strike. To circumvent that constraint, they would each provide their local president with their resignation letter. In the event that contract negotiations stalled, the resignation letters would be presented to the trustees. Even at that, teachers had only two dates upon which they could resign, 31 January and the end of June, making the timing of negotiations and sanctions crucial. Resignations in June were ineffectual because the boards could hire new teachers as replacements for those who did not show up in September. So January was the only effective date for teachers to initiate strike action.

The negotiation process was also cumbersome. The local, through its joint negotiating team, the Economic Policy Committee, bargained with the board. Although the provincial offices of both unions offered assistance, they did not have the legal authority to demand conditions from the locals, making it difficult to achieve province-wide improvements. The teachers' federations were essentially coalitions of locals. The local held the authority to sign the collective agreement, a thin document that contained little more than salary and benefits terms.

In 1967, the FWTAO and the OPSMTF issued a grey letter in a month-long dispute in North York.[99] However, without the legal right to strike, the elementary teachers were reluctant to force the issue. They settled without further sanctions.

In 1971, the country was going through a period of double-digit inflation and teachers were chafing against expenditure ceilings the provincial Davis government had imposed on boards of education.[100] That year the OECTA, OSSTF, and AEFO, influenced by militant union activity in other sectors, began to use strikes, or the threat of strikes, as a remedy to address their declining earning power.[101] Teachers had begun to imagine how labour tactics could be used to enhance their lives. To do so, they had to redefine their historical understanding of professionalism that equated the welfare of students with keeping the schools open, a viewpoint that suppressed collective action and kept all the power with the trustees.

Canadian historian Rennie Warburton states, "professionalism must not be seen as a fixed concept for labelling teachers and distinguishing them from other non-professional groups, but as a dynamic element in their situation which both they and the state exploit as part of [a] dialectic of control and resistance."[102]

Like nurses and members of the civil service who have required university qualifications and specialized training, teachers and their employers grappled to define teacher professionalism.[103]

By 1971, elementary teachers' work lives had become more onerous and their relationship with their trustees more distant. By sitting on their hands, they were falling behind the gains made by their peers in the OSSTF, OECTA, and AEFO, who were taking strike votes.[104]

The emerging militancy of three of the teachers' unions provoked indignation from both Liberal and Conservative members of the provincial legislature.[105] In 1970, Bill Davis, as minister of education in the Robarts government, had established the Committee of Inquiry into Negotiation Procedures Concerning Elementary and Secondary Schools of Ontario, known as the Reville Committee.[106] In the spring of 1972, the committee released its findings, which attempted to set labour negotiations back a decade. The report recommended that teachers be denied the right to strike or to negotiate working conditions, that principals be encouraged to form their own negotiating entity, and that an adjudicative tribunal be established to settle disagreements between trustees and teachers through binding arbitration.

The Reville Report was ridiculed in the legislature and in the press. As Bryan Downie, the future head of the Education Relations Commission (ERC), would put it, it was "totally discredited."[107] The teachers hated it.[108]

The OSSTF, OECTA, and AEFO continued to call for mass resignations throughout 1972.[109] In response, Minister of Education Tom Wells sat down with the teachers to develop a labour regime that would not require teachers to resign. For fifteen months during 1972 and 1973, he negotiated with all five of the unions under the OTF umbrella.

The teachers were politicized by reacting to the Reville Report.[110] On 14 May 1973, the five unions called the first protest march ever undertaken by teachers in Ontario.[111] Over five thousand teachers gathered on short notice to oppose the loss of 1,145 teaching jobs in Metropolitan Toronto. Ron Poste, the OPSMTF president at the time, would recall the excitement of seeing hundreds of teachers marching for the first time.[112] In organizing the Metropolitan Toronto campaign, the unions developed the capacity to bring teachers together in a large body in one location.[113] The Reville Report had hardened the position of the unions.[114]

In her speech to the 1973 FWTAO annual meeting, president Lenore Graham called on her members to reject the report:

> Teachers must be allowed the broadest possible scope of negotiation, including the right to negotiate working conditions. . . .
> In the event there is an impasse, we propose that the difference between teachers and trustees may follow any one of two routes: Arbitration, on the one hand; or, conciliation—voluntary arbitration and imposition of sanctions, including strikes.[115]

Immediately following her speech, and with little debate, the FWTAO assembly passed a resolution supporting their right to strike.[116]

That same week, the OPSMTF was holding its annual general meeting in another part of Toronto. OPSMTF president Ron Poste had moved the recommendation in favour of strikes that had been received through the Report of the Committee on the Advantage and Disadvantage of Strike Action.[117] He was defending his motion when one of the delegates pointed out that the FWTAO had already adopted the position he was advocating. Hearing that news, the men quickly passed Poste's motion. Both unions went into the fall of 1973 with the majority support of their members firmly in hand.

In December, the leaders of the five affiliates were meeting with representatives of the Ministry of Education under the auspices of the OTF. They were expecting that some legislation on collective bargaining would be introduced prior to the legislature being dissolved for the Christmas break.[118] It would give the Conservative government an opportunity to demonstrate to its constituency that it was dealing with the issue of teacher strikes. As the teachers understood it, the fall session of the legislature was about to end, so the bill would be tabled and then allowed to die on the order paper.

On 10 December 1973, as the representatives of the unions were preparing to leave the OTF talks with ministry officials, they were asked to remain in the room to hear an announcement from the minister on a piece of emergency legislation he would introduce that same day. Wells then informed them that he would be making unilateral changes to what had been agreed upon over the previous fifteen months. After delivering his message, Wells left the room.

Later the same day, the minister presented Bill 274, An Act to Amend the Ministry of Education Act, to the legislature.[119] It nullified any of the mid-year resignations that teachers had put in the hands of their local presidents. That effectively removed whatever leverage teachers had in collective bargaining for the 1972–73 school year.

Then Wells introduced Bill 275, An Act to Amend the Schools Administration Act.[120] This second piece of legislation required teachers to submit to compulsory arbitration, conclusively closing the door on future strikes in any form, including mass resignations.[121] The minister had reversed himself completely and sent a very strong message that he agreed with the much-maligned Reville Report; teachers would not be granted the right to collective bargaining.[122]

The teachers were shocked and angered by the unexpected turn of events. School board trustees and board administrators were also displeased with the proposed bill.[123] They believed government-appointed arbitrators undermined the power of local boards to manage costs.

The OTF president offered up his own claim to the members of the legislature:

> The teachers of Ontario have since 1944, when the Teaching
> Profession Act was established, negotiated thousands of collec-
> tive agreements with school boards, and in all that time schools
> have been closed in only three communities—for 17 days in one,
> and for 3 days in another, and 2 days in another.[124]

With the legislature days away from closing for the holidays,
Wells rushed to squeeze in the two bills at the last minute. The first
piece of legislation, Bill 274, if passed, was scheduled to take effect
on 18 December 1973, just before the Christmas holidays.

Despite the distraction of Christmas, teachers had been paying attention. Preparations for mobilization had been going on for
months. The reaction of teachers to the introduction of the emergency legislation was swift, emotional, and furious. Every afternoon
during the debates, irate teachers stood in the public gallery shout-
ing at Conservative members. The angry confrontations moved
the issue of collective bargaining for teachers to the front page. On
11 December, fifteen hundred teachers from Metro Toronto and the
surrounding area staged a rally at Queen's Park.

Other organizations expressed their outrage at the actions of
the government. The Ontario Medical Association president, Dr.
Wilson, stated, "If the free movement of teachers in and out of
employment can be restricted by legislation, no one in society is
safe from arbitrary government control."[125] The Canadian Labour
Congress (CLC) president, Donald MacDonald, made the connection between the right to strike and other fundamental rights by
declaring Bill 274 "a blatant denial of human rights."[126] It would be
from this demand for rights that the teachers' unions could mount
an effective counterattack.

Wells understood teachers' concerns; he had been negotiating
with them for almost a year and a half. In response to their protes-
tations, he offered them a carrot along with the big stick of compulsory arbitration. When he tabled Bill 275, he included in it the right

to negotiate working conditions,[127] a small concession that would legitimize the principle of working conditions being included in future collective agreements. That was a provision that teachers in some of the other provinces would come to envy.[128]

The unions had not been entirely guileless about the possible outcomes of their discussions with the minister. Each of the five unions had established protocols for mobilizing a province-wide walkout in the event it was needed. As soon as the two offensive bills were tabled, the unions sent telegrams to all of the three thousand schools they represented.[129] They had expanded the model that had been developed the previous year for the march on behalf of Toronto teachers. It took them only eight days to connect with every one of their members, advising them of a province-wide strike.[130]

The FWTAO decided to bring its local presidents together on Saturday, 15 December. The FWTAO president, Florence Henderson, explained some of the most serious aspects of the legislation:

> With the passage of this bill, those teachers [who had handed in their resignations to become effective at the end of December] are not allowed to resign, but must continue their duties until the end of August—in other words, the school year must be completed. That is one of the basic things to which we have objected—that this human right should be denied.[131]

Henderson also drew attention to the section of the bill that made a teacher's mid-year resignation a criminal offence for the 1973–74 school year. As she spoke to the local presidents about how to deliver their message to their members, she repeatedly referred to the legislation as "a denial of human rights."

The seriousness of the situation drew Premier Bill Davis into the fray.[132] As the teachers prepared to gather in Toronto, Davis and

Wells met with the five unions to negotiate a resolution. At that point neither of the two offensive bills had been enacted, so both sides had some room to manoeuvre.

Davis's exertions came too late. On 18 December 1973, all the teachers in Ontario walked out of their classrooms.[133] They shut down almost every school in the province. Teachers came in the thousands to rally at Maple Leaf Gardens and then marched as a body on Queen's Park.

The teachers' first political strike was a success. Davis agreed to reopen negotiations for a collective bargaining process. Bill 274 would be allowed to die on the order paper at the Christmas recess.[134] The teachers agreed to push back the date of the resignations, making them effective 31 January. The additional month was to provide adequate time for contract negotiations to be successfully completed between trustees and the locals. Davis conceded that teachers would be permitted to resign if they so chose. In the new year, all sides would discuss the alternatives to compulsory arbitration. The unions were promised ample time to work out the details. With Bill 274 dead and Bill 275 open for discussion, local presidents left their members' resignations in the drawer. Teachers went back to their classrooms, local negotiating teams picked up contract deliberations where they had left off, and the minister and the unions prepared to return to the table.

At the annual general meeting the following year, FWTAO Executive Secretary Florence Henderson commented on the "agony of the heart" that teachers had suffered in the decision to walk out on 18 December.[135] In her speech, she assured the delegates that they had indeed remained true to their professionalism:

> December 18th and Bill 275, which is dealing with legislation concerned with collective bargaining, may appear to us as being not unimportant, but we may at times question whether it is truly of a highly professional nature. I would like to suggest to you

that every one of those issues [collective bargaining, provincial grants, and women's rights] is of a highly professional nature. Everything that touches you as a woman elementary teacher affects the job you are doing and the vocation to which you have dedicated your life.[136]

Henderson's defence of the one-day strike merged professional responsibility with collective power. In the future, the unions would continue to identify teachers' interests as professional concerns, embedding collective action into the union structures. Most importantly, they would have war chests that would enable them to sustain a strike, something the FWTAO leadership had begun to consider immediately after the province-wide strike.[137]

The success of the teachers' 1973 strike was in large part due to the agreement of all five teachers' unions to hold together as a coalition of independent organizations. Virtually every teacher in the education system walked out. The outcome could have been different if the teachers had been required to co-operate for a longer period, or if even one union had hesitated.

CHAPTER 2

# Structuring Collective Action

"**U**nity is strength. That's what we learned," wrote Garth McMillan, the OPSMTF newsletter editor.

> Suddenly teachers learned what so many other groups have known and practiced for so long. Suddenly teachers learned that with unity on any issue their power was enormous. . . . Suddenly teachers were transformed. They were angry, upset, threatened, confused and frightened. But they were transformed.[1]

McMillan's editorial in the January 1974 edition of the *OPSMTF News* summed up the politicization process that teachers had undergone by participating in the 18 December strike.

The one-day strike was illegal by legislation, by teachers' personal contracts, and by the collective agreements they had negotiated. Although the unions had called for teachers across the province to write their letters of resignation, the resignations would not have come into effect until 31 December. Boards of education could have disciplined teachers for their actions, but no group of trustees chose that route.[2]

Trustees agreed with the teachers' position. They were against the Conservative government closing off teachers' right to strike.[3]

The Toronto Board of Education, reported the *Toronto Star*, "unanimously approved a motion expressing opposition to the labor and educational implications of the bill."[4] Trustees viewed the binding arbitration process that the government was recommending as an assault on their authority.[5] Their tacit approval gave legitimacy to the teachers' collective action.[6]

For eighteen months, between January 1974 and July 1975, the five affiliates of the Ontario Teachers' Federation met with the minister to design a labour relations regime for teachers. The result of those negotiations was a unique piece of legislation, the School Boards and Teachers Collective Negotiations Act, generally known as Bill 100.[7] It came into effect in July 1975. Bill 100 was the education sector's equivalent of the Ontario Labour Relations Act. In addition to granting teachers the right to strike, it gave them access to a grievance procedure and provided them with a labour relations board of their own, the Education Relations Commission.[8] At a time when 80 per cent of the workers in Ontario's public service were denied the right to strike, it was a remarkable victory.[9]

Bill 100 opened by naming each of the affiliates of the OTF, giving each of them legal standing.[10] It granted two or more affiliates, such as the FWTAO and the OPSMTF, the authority to act together for negotiations as long as the affiliates and the boards involved agreed. The new legislation also permitted any other party at the table, including union staff or legal advisers, a contentious issue in the past.

Under Bill 100, either side could give notice to bargain when the current collective agreement expired, or they could do so in January of the year in which the agreement would expire. No longer would the January date for resignations determine the course of negotiations.

The legislation made an arbitration system available and provided for mediation, but both sides had to agree before either could take place. If an impasse was reached, the ERC had the authority to assign a fact finder whose report would be released to the public fifteen days from when it was received by the minister, something neither side would want.

Part IV of Bill 100 contained a detailed process for interest arbitrations to resolve issues during negotiations. Part VI included access to rights arbitration when there were differences in interpretation of the collective agreement once it was ratified. Agreements had to be for a minimum of one year, taking effect on 1 September, and no strike or lockout could take place during the life of the contract.

The ERC had the sole duty of tracking and facilitating negotiations between trustees and teachers, and keeping the government informed of them. It was the ERC that would recommend back-to-work legislation if, in its view, the students' year was in jeopardy.

Initiating a strike (or lockout) was a drawn-out process.[11] Teachers could not take a strike vote until fifteen days after the fact finder's report was made public and the members of the local had voted on the trustees' final offer. All votes had to be by secret ballot. Then the teachers had to give the school board at least five days' notice of the strike date.

Teachers could not be terminated for participating in a legal strike, a consideration the Lakefield teachers had not had available in 1963. Principals and vice-principals were to remain in their schools during a strike or lockout, even though they were included in the union. While Bill 100 was very clear on the penalties for counselling an unlawful strike, it gave the authority for collective bargaining, including calling a strike, to the local, not to the provincial body. Despite its limitations, teachers were proud of the legislation that they had achieved as a result of their one-day strike.[12]

Shortly after Bill 100 came into effect, the FWTAO and the OPSMTF found time for a discussion on co-operation. At that meeting they reached agreement on a policy of joint negotiations with mutual participation in any strikes and joint arbitrations.[13] Each union retained the right to grieve violations of the collective agreement on its own.

The OPSMTF's declared intention of one union of elementary teachers and its aversion to independent gains being made by the women kept it in the partnership. But for the FWTAO, joint negotiations would prove to be a weak link in its labour relations. Some issues, such as salary, were the same for women and men, but some other needs were unique to women. At the level that matters the most in labour, the materiality of salaries, benefits, and working conditions, the FWTAO and the OPSMTF were one body. Women's unique needs remained on the back burner of joint negotiations for the very reasons the FWTAO argued for its own existence, because men would not support them.

## Paving the Way for Neo-liberalism in Canada

In the fall of 1975, the federal government was dealing with a serious inflation problem. It turned to controlling workers' wages as the most expedient political solution. Conservative leader Robert Stanfield had fought the 1974 federal election on a platform that included wage and price controls. The Liberals under Pierre Trudeau had opposed controls and won. In one of the most famous (some would say dishonest) Canadian bait-and-switch election campaigns, Prime Minister Trudeau brought in the Anti-Inflation Act on Thanksgiving Day 1975.

Canada, like most Western states at the time, was beginning to adopt the theories of Milton Friedman and the Chicago School. To this way of thinking, disrupting collective bargaining and suppressing unions was seen as strategic to the ability of the marketplace to operate freely.[14] While Trudeau's wage and price controls were not classic neo-liberalism, it was this response to the financial crisis of the state that precipitated the rise of the new right in Canada and its embrace of neo-liberalism.[15] Similar initiatives would take a more classical neo-liberal form in the future.[16]

Trudeau's attacks on unions and on workers' wages set the tone for the country.[17] He left no doubt of his feelings about unions. "We'll put a few union leaders in jail for three years and others will get the message," Trudeau said.[18] Wage and price controls, in their various incarnations, would prove to be the vanguard of the neo-liberal state.

The Ontario government's 1970 spending ceilings on the boards of education had been a blunt instrument that put the onus on trustees to contain costs. Trudeau's wage and price controls offered a sharper weapon that directly attacked collective agreements. The Anti-Inflation Board (AIB) was the enforcement apparatus. Trudeau appointed Jean-Luc Pepin, a retired politician who had served in the cabinets of both Lester Pearson and Trudeau, to chair the board. Under Pepin's leadership, the AIB enforced wage controls of 8 per cent the first year, 6 per cent the second year, and 4 per cent the third.[19] Referred to by Pepin himself as "rough justice," the AIB had a free hand in investigating any agreements between employers and their employees and making its own decisions on their legitimacy.[20] The Essex County elementary teachers were first; the AIB rolled their salaries back 10 per cent.[21]

As the AIB came into effect, ideological paralysis overwhelmed the elementary teachers' unions. In their interviews for this book, former OSSTF president Margaret Wilson and former OPSTF president Dave Lennox both mentioned that, at this early stage, no one knew if teachers would walk out at critical moments; teacher militancy was still too new.[22] The teachers had won one battle; they chose not to test their members with a second province-wide campaign.

The labour movement's resistance to Trudeau's anti-inflation program culminated in a one-day general strike on 14 October 1976, the first anniversary of wage and price controls coming into effect.[23]

Despite their criticism of the arbitrary nature of AIB decisions and the instances of AIB rollbacks of teachers' salary increases, the elementary teachers did not join the affiliates of the CLC.[24] The FWTAO, at its August annual general meeting, recommended that the OTF send a letter of moral support to the CLC, but did not send one itself.[25]

Canada lost 11.5 million person-days to strikes in 1976, the highest number in the second half of the twentieth century.[26] Over the three years of the federal AIB, Ontario teachers would undertake thirty-two workplace sanctions, but none of them would involve the elementary teachers.[27] While the FWTAO and the OPSMTF had the minimum organizational structures needed to mobilize their members for one day in 1973, they had not developed the deep structures and the financial resources necessary to sustain anything longer. Nor had they abandoned their attachment to an altruistic professionalism.

## Affirmative Action

The genesis of affirmative action in Ontario's public education system had come early in 1973 when Minister of Education Tom Wells drafted a memorandum on Equal Employment and Promotion Opportunities for Women.[28] It was a weak document that lacked the teeth of legislation, but it provided a platform from which women could advance their efforts in support of affirmative action. By the end of the decade, the Ontario Women's Directorate and the Ministry of Education would be working with the FWTAO to develop affirmative action programs in the school system.[29]

The FWTAO became involved with other organizations advocating for universal equity programs. Some of the best work done by the women teachers' union on behalf of Canadian women occurred at this time. The FWTAO provided office space and labour power for the National Action Committee on the Status of

Women, which had been formed in 1972. It worked with the Ontario Status of Women Council and with the Advisory Council on Equal Opportunity for Women,[30] gave financial support and office space to the Women's Legal and Education Action Fund (LEAF),[31] and participated in Organized Working Women.[32]

The OPSMTF reacted to the FWTAO's push for affirmative action with a strong anti-feminist position. Four years after Wells's memorandum encouraging the promotion of women, OPSMTF president Ron Stephen's editorial in the January 1977 newsletter, ironically titled "My Brother's Keeper," stated:

> We constantly read about the plight of women in the work force. They make less money, have less job security and there appear to be fewer avenues open for upward mobility. . . . Let us examine, however, the field of education. Nowhere does a woman teacher, working for a board in Ontario, make less money than a man teacher, provided their qualifications, positions and years of experience are the same.[33]

Even though the OPSMTF was the men's union, Stephen's statement revealed an unusual level of chauvinism that was dated even by the standards of the time; his provisos ignored the reality for most women teachers. Male teachers may have felt that their entitlement to managerial positions within the education hierarchy was being threatened by women's demands, but the country was already moving toward greater gender equity.[34]

Before Stephen's comments appeared in the newsletter, the opportunity for the OPSMTF to demonstrate solidarity with the women had never been more accessible. Had the OPSMTF executive been willing to take even a mildly pro-feminist position, it would have made the men's union more palatable to the women of the FWTAO at a time when they were still debating amalgamation as a viable alternative to the two-unions model. The reactionary stance of the men's union to affirmative action ran counter to the direction the education system was taking, leaving the OPSMTF well behind other unions and bearing the flag of flagrant self-interest.

In the spring of 1979, Education Minister Dr. Bette Stephenson required boards of education to adopt formal affirmative action plans for the 1979–80 school year.[35] The FWTAO responded with a motion at its 1980 annual general meeting declaring, "our major target in the next five years [will be] the establishment of affirmative action policies in every school board jurisdiction in Ontario in order to achieve equal opportunity for women."[36]

The next year, Stephenson issued an attachment to the original memorandum. It focused on sex-role stereotyping in Grades 7 and 8 and required school boards to ensure that their learning materials portrayed women in non-stereotypical roles. Stephenson's willingness to address sex-role stereotyping would become entrenched in the education system. By 1990, the Ministry of Education would acknowledge that gender stereotyping contributed to violence against women and girls.[37]

Feminist campaigns offered women teachers material benefits beyond opening the door for a few women to become school administrators. Those campaigns were able to achieve improvements that matched or exceeded what collective bargaining was able to deliver during the years when federal and provincial wage controls were a brake on workers' advances.

The OPSMTF continued to react to the FWTAO's campaigns. Its 1981 annual general meeting demanded "that advocacy of any form of preferential treatment or quota system be opposed; that any board program which discriminates against present members of the profession for perceived grievances that occurred in the past be opposed in the strongest possible manner."[38]

In April 1984, the OPSTF's Dave Lennox wrote about the FWTAO's efforts to set targets for women in administrative positions, "targets are only a euphemism for quotas. In the target model, affirmative action really becomes a form of reverse discrimination . . . programmes which discriminate against men and result in the promotion of underqualified women to fill numerical requirements."[39] "Underqualified women" was a slap in the face to every woman teacher with ambitions to become a principal.

## Closing Off Dissent

Some women teachers did believe that an amalgamated union was their best chance to succeed in bringing gender equity to education. There were FWTAO locals from Red Rock to Hamilton that had amalgamated with the OPSMTF local in their area.[40]

At the 1976 annual general meeting, some of the women in the amalgamated locals had appealed to the members' democratic sensibilities by calling for a polling of the FWTAO membership to determine support for uniting with the men's union. Two-thirds of the representatives present at the meeting agreed the poll should go ahead.[41]

The FWTAO chose Canadian Inter-mark to conduct a poll by mailing a questionnaire to every member.[42] The provincial executive immediately began a campaign urging members to reject the amalgamation option, a contentious effort to undermine an annual general meeting decision.[43] Anti-amalgamation workshops were developed for local executive members. At the fall presidents' conference, small-group sessions were dedicated to a discussion of the value of a separate women's union.[44] An article was included in the newsletter in which the reasons for supporting separate unions of men and women were detailed.[45]

While the pro-amalgamation forces did not have the same resources or opportunities to deliver workshops across the province, they did have the support of the OPSMTF, and its majority of principals and vice-principals in the system provided a pipeline to classroom teachers.[46] That gave them access to most schools and added the weight of in situ authority to the pro-amalgamation arguments.

Canadian Inter-mark delivered its report, *A Research Survey on Attitudes of FWTAO Members Toward Amalgamation*, in July 1977, just ahead of the annual general meetings.[47] The results were highly ambiguous, due in part to the design of the survey. Only 18 per cent of respondents preferred to keep the FWTAO as it was.[48]

The FWTAO executive highlighted the statement in the report, "Almost *three quarters* (72%) of all members replying to the survey *do not want any provincial form of amalgamation*."[49] That was a misrepresentation. In drawing their conclusion, Inter-mark had taken the sum of the first four results, all of which referred to maintaining the FWTAO as an organization but doing so with some changes. The survey indicated that up to 40 per cent of members did support some form of amalgamation. Up to 28 per cent of the respondents were in favour of doing away with FWTAO entirely. The membership appeared to be interested in further discussions between the amalgamation and anti-amalgamation camps and a re-examination of their relationship with the men's union.

That was not how president Jeanne Frolick presented the report to the annual general meeting in August: "Only 14 per cent of those who replied are in favour [of amalgamation]. That means that the overwhelming majority—86 per cent do not want provincial amalgamation with the OPSMTF and chose some other option."[50]

The OPSMTF drew a different conclusion. President George Meek combined the results of the last three questions, each of which supported some kind of closer ties, with the 35 per cent of the FWTAO members who wanted to develop greater co-operation between the two unions without amalgamation, and declared, "FWTAO has received a clear mandate from 75% of respondents to their survey to expand cooperation with OPSMTF at the local and provincial levels."[51] The OPSMTF had taken a poll concurrently with the FWTAO survey in which 88 per cent of its respondents supported full amalgamation. The surprise was that 12 per cent did not.

Within the FWTAO, the Inter-mark research survey had the effect of entrenching the two sides of the amalgamation debates. After the survey had been received, the Board of Directors recommended to the annual general meeting that a moratorium be placed on further debate of the amalgamation issue.[52] The support shown for moving closer to the men's union, despite the aggressive anti-amalgamation campaign, had shaken the FWTAO executive.[53] The motion for a moratorium was passed. Renewed annually for nearly two decades, the moratorium marginalized those women who were in the twelve locals that had some form of amalgamation with their OPSMTF counterparts and silenced those women who supported the idea of one union. It was not the FWTAO's finest hour.

The amalgamation fight would continue to divide the FWTAO. Because of the moratorium, the legitimate questions and concerns of committed FWTAO members about an amalgamated union would not be given a hearing. By silencing dissenting views and closing debate on an issue that split the membership, the union pushed women who wanted to consider alternatives into more extreme positions and forced them to look elsewhere for that conversation. The FWTAO would become locked in to fighting a rearguard action for the loyalties of many of its own members, a position no union wants to find itself in.

The OPSMTF looked at the results and realized that a significant percentage of women teachers were interested in some sort of amalgamation. In order to make the men's union more attractive to women, the 1977 annual general meeting reversed a number of the union's historical positions. Past-president Poste's resolution to begin the process of legally removing "Men" from the name of the organization was accepted.[54] The representatives adopted a Statement on Women's Rights that included this passage:

The Ontario Public School Men Teachers' Federation . . . deplores discrimination on the basis of sex . . . the subtle and invidious practices which tend to stereotype people must also be met with persistent action. . . . [It] strongly encourages all of its members to support all activities in their community which are designed to redress the legitimate grievances of women . . . eliminate such discriminatory practise as . . . the use of instructional materials in ways which reinforce sex-role stereotypes; the use of sexist language . . . [and] in particular, promotion policies should be reviewed to ensure that women teachers have equal access to positions of added responsibility.[55]

It was a dramatic turnaround for the men's union and one the originators of the Inter-mark survey could not have predicted.

## Preparing to Strike

In early 1974, the elementary teachers had still not begun to put together a strike fund. At the annual general meetings following the 18 December 1973 strike, the leaders of both the FWTAO and the OPSMTF attempted to correct the lack of funds available for collective bargaining by asking delegates to endorse an increase in their dues.[56] Delegates refused. It was de facto a decision to reject a strike fund. Trustees across the province must have breathed a sigh of relief.

Efforts to develop a war chest then teetered into the realm of the absurd. In the fall of 1975, a desperate OPSMTF executive asked members to sign a promissory note that would commit individuals to donate to the union's strike fund in the event of a strike.[57] Very few teachers signed on.

The FWTAO effort fared no better. Early in 1974, it made a request to all its members to voluntarily contribute thirty dollars per year.[58] The hope was to build a strike fund of $1 million.[59]

Contributions stalled at $33,000.[60] As Florence Henderson put it, "People don't want to go out on a limb with this $30.00 if someone else isn't going to do it."[61] At the 1974 FWTAO annual general meeting, attempts were made to establish a special "civil rights fund" for negotiations.[62] Those motions were ruled out of order.[63] The delegates from the locals were not about to give the provincial body control over their collective bargaining strategy.[64]

The FWTAO executive was the first to solve the impasse.[65] They moved $1 million from their Professional Services Fund to establish a new Collective Negotiations Dispute Fund.[66] That fund offered support to the locals by establishing a line in the budget to cover the costs of grievances, arbitrations, managing strikes, and strike pay.

The next summer, the 1975 FWTAO annual general meeting passed a resolution increasing their dues by fifty dollars to enlarge the Collective Negotiations Dispute Fund.[67] President Marie Myers's speech in support of the increase spoke to the new sense the teachers were developing of the power relations involved in collective bargaining. "How are we going to enter into this negotiation process? and How are we going to enter a field that is based on the use of power? You need to have real power!"[68]

The OPSMTF followed the FWTAO lead. In August 1976 the representatives at the OPSMTF annual general meeting established a Special Emergency Fund to pay for strikes and arbitrations.[69]

Those two decisions put the provincial executives of both unions at the centre of strategic decisions involving collective bargaining. The provincial office now had the final say on spending.

There were those among the teaching membership, particularly in the administrator-heavy OPSMTF, who grumbled that principals and vice-principals should leave the union and create a "sixth affiliate" within the OTF.[70] In the September 1975 *OPSMTF News*, Neil Davis, the union president, suggested that principals and vice-principals might want to take that advice.[71] His interrogation of administrators in the union in a post–Bill 100 world created a furor that quickly turned into a test of loyalty. When rank-and-file members complained that "principal power" was being used to control the union, first vice-president and school principal Ron Stephen called on the men to shout down these "radical teachers."[72] The debate resulted in the OPSMTF commissioning a survey to study "Professionalism and Militancy in OPSMTF."

The survey reported, "Higher militancy . . . was associated with teaching personnel while lower militancy was associated more with persons in administrative positions."[73] The conclusions were not a surprise, but nothing more came of them. The OPSMTF's reluctance to undertake militant action left a cautious FWTAO to lead the charge, a position the women did not relish.

## Changes in Working Conditions

In 1976 wage and price controls were keeping teachers in check. The Ministry of Education took the opportunity to further centralize education by seizing control of curriculum development. Trustees, who had been charged with the responsibility of approving curricula for local use since the introduction of P1J1, were to be excluded from the new process. As the education minister stated in his response to the OTF's concerns, "We felt that the state of local curriculum development had not in general lived up to our earlier expectations."[74] Standardization had political appeal. Premier Davis emphasized "high standards," "systematic measurement" using "objective information" for "evaluation and testing of pupil achievement," and "accountability."[75] The die was cast.

The new approach would be by and through measures of literacy. Sociologist Alan Sears argues:

> Literacy is a crucial foundation of educational classifications, the
> organization of the student population around specific measures

and assessments. It tends to be valued as a credential, an externally imposed measure of the individual that conditions educational and life trajectories, rather than as a tool for the literate person to make sense of the world.[76]

The idealism of the 1960s that was reflected in the Hall-Dennis Report had provided education and teachers with new possibilities for liberating their work as educators.[77] A generation of new teachers had entered their careers trained in the child-centred pedagogy and teacher-developed curriculum that had been at the centre of Hall-Dennis. While the argument has been made that Hall-Dennis was never given a real chance at implementation, it had a progressive influence. That influence was still evident into the 1980s, with articles referencing radical educators such as Henry Giroux and Peter McLaren regularly appearing in the OPSTF News.[78]

The seven-year experiment in optimism that had been Hall-Dennis was smothered by uncertainties about the economy. Coming out in 1975, The Formative Years and Education in the Primary and Junior Divisions signalled the beginning of a change in how curriculum would be regarded.[79] This new pedagogy emphasized the need for detailed planning in classroom presentation. Teachers were expected to develop comprehensive lesson plans, often with input from the school administration. It was not only teachers' classrooms and teaching styles that were under scrutiny, but their routines for lesson preparation as well.

As the 1970s came to a close, the shrinking number of students in the elementary grades became a political issue. With the passing of the baby boom, the number of students registering for school began to decline. In 1977, Premier Davis appointed his friend Robert Jackson, the former director of the Ontario Institute for Studies in Education (OISE), to head the politically volatile Commission on Declining School Enrolments in Ontario (CODE).[80] Jackson had previously steered the amalgamation of the former Toronto teacher training facility with the University of Toronto to create OISE as an education research facility.[81] He characterized declining enrolment in such apocalyptic terms as "the gravest crisis in education that we have ever seen."[82]

Jackson's background at OISE permitted him to embrace a range of perspectives, some of which were quite contradictory. As well as writing a final report, the commission developed a series of smaller documents, authored by specialists and academics across the field of education. They examined the effects of the declining numbers of students on a range of education issues from school closures to teachers' pensions.[83]

Declining enrolment meant thousands of teachers across the province were being threatened with school closures and job losses. The elementary teachers, the first to be affected by declining enrolment, were demanding a fair process for establishing layoff criteria and recall rights. Although labour unions had agreed for generations that seniority was the only fair means of assuring job security, within the OPSMTF, many of the principals supported the trustees' arguments for a process based on the quality of a teacher's work, a meritocracy.

A joint committee of the FWTAO and the OPSMTF executives was established to hammer out a staffing proposal for upcoming negotiations. In January 1979 the "FWTAO and OPSMTF Policies and Procedures for Redundancy" was completed. It stated:

> That a teacher's redundancy be determined on the basis of seniority within the employed group covered by the collective agreement. . . . That neither merit nor qualifications be used in determination of redundancy. . . . Each collective agreement shall include clauses outlining the procedure to be used in determining each teachers' position on the seniority list.[84]

The proposed clauses also covered class sizes. They established a pupil/teacher ratio setting the minimum number of teachers a board was required to maintain. Although the pupil/teacher ratio was important to front-line teachers, seniority would be the first battleground.

While teachers were focused on preparing for collective bargaining when the AIB came to an end, Queen's Park had begun to recognize the power available through computerized information technology. Opposition leader Stuart Smith was quoted as recommending province-wide testing of students. "Taxpayers have no way of determining if they are getting value for the millions of tax dollars spent on education. . . . Examinations would be given at the end of Grade 3, Grade 6 and Grade 10."[85] Davis let the idea die.

Demands for increased accountability reignited calls for the upgrading and recertification of teachers. Released in 1978, the Jackson Report recommended a five-year teaching certificate that would oblige teachers to show evidence of regular upgrading of their qualifications.[86] The report also recommended that a college of teachers be established to police teacher qualifications. With her medical background, the new minister of education, Dr. Stephenson, advocated for the plan.[87] The FWTAO refused to get drawn into the debate.[88] The OPSMTF, top-heavy with school administrators, was fully supportive.[89] Jackson's idea of a college of teachers and a five-year teaching certificate met with increasing resistance from the unions. Eventually both initiatives were buried.

Qualifications had always been a divisive subject between the two unions. The men's union put greater weight on formal qualifications, while the women's union argued for crediting teaching experience. Nonetheless, in an attempt to remedy some of the disparities women faced, the FWTAO had set aside significant funds each year for its members who needed financial assistance to further their professional training.[90]

## A New Generation of Leadership

In the spring of 1978, the Jackson Commission was completing its work. Federal finance minister Jean Chrétien had announced a phasing out of wage and price controls beginning 14 April 1978.[91] That would permit teachers to negotiate their September collective agreements without the impediment of the controls.

Joan Westcott was elected president of the FWTAO for the 1978–79 year.[92] George Meek returned as the OPSMTF president for a second term.[93] Westcott and Meek would be the first of a new generation of union leadership in the elementary teachers' unions, a generation that had been politicized by the 1973 strike and that were willing to adopt a more militant style in collective bargaining.

The chief administrator for the FWTAO was still executive secretary Florence Henderson. She had assumed the position of acting executive secretary in 1973 in time for the one-day strike.[94] Betty Hawke from Dryden had received applause for her motion at the 1973 annual meeting to send a telegram to Education Minister Wells to notify him that the FWTAO "insist that legislation on teachers collective bargaining include full bargaining scope and all other rights enjoyed by other organized employees."[95] She was in line to be the next FWTAO president. Douglas McAndless sat on the OPSMTF executive as first vice-president. He was a strong advocate for contract language ensuring that seniority was the standard that boards would use for the layoffs that would be the inevitable outcome of declining enrolment.[96]

This group of leaders needed to take at least one local into their first legal strike under Bill 100. They were finally financially ready. The FWTAO strike fund alone exceeded $2 million.[97] But first, the two unions had to make some decisions on the structure of their negotiating team. With hostilities constantly simmering between them, it was difficult to imagine mutual solidarity.

In the fall of 1978, tenure was the top issue. Teachers were facing the threat of job losses with no seniority language to protect them.[98] Trustees were insisting that they, as employers, had the right to determine whom they would retain on staff when they had surplus teachers in their systems. When boards lost students, they also lost the provincial funding that was attached to them. That made it more attractive to hire new teachers with lower salaries. The unions would need to take a hard line on a staffing formula and seniority entitlements if they intended to push trustees beyond their shrinking budgets. It was yet to be determined whether having the right to strike would translate into organized, effective resistance.

As the provincial purse strings tightened, seniority rights continued to resonate as the critically important issue for teachers.[99] In his interim report, Jackson noted, "During the hearings of the Commission across this province I sensed among teachers a degree of despair, even hopelessness, in response to the initial shock of accepting the facts of declining enrolments, economic stagnation and inflation."[100] Good employer/employee relationships were being put aside as trustees cut jobs with an eye to keeping local education taxes in check.[101] Teachers needed seniority language in their collective agreements to prevent trustees from laying off senior teachers who occupied the higher pay scales and to force boards to rehire experienced teachers who had been laid off.

Trustees in some boards were writing an end date into the contracts of new hires. These were known as "exploding contracts."[102] In June, when the contract ended, the teacher was no longer considered an employee. In September a new round of temporary teachers were hired. Generally, the same teachers, now with an uncredited year of seniority, were rehired for the new school year, but without the salary increases they would be entitled to as permanent employees. Their salary would remain at the same level forever. The teachers were desperate to end a practice that institutionalized year-end layoffs and did away with salary grids.[103] On this issue there was no middle ground.

Bill 100 prevented teachers from conducting province-wide negotiations, even for such issues as seniority. Local negotiations were the structural reason why teachers were insisting on local seniority, rather than on province-wide seniority.[104] Local seniority based on experience in a single board ensured teachers were protected against incursions by teachers from outside their own board. It also worked for trustees by discouraging teachers from jumping ship when a nearby board made a more attractive offer.

The executives of the FWTAO and the OPSMTF met to settle on interim protocols for workplace sanctions in early 1979.[105] The members of the FWTAO delegation included Margaret Beckingham and Mary Hesser, both of whom had been prominent during the 1973 strike. The OPSMTF delegation included future presidents Duncan Jewell and Douglas McAndless, both advocates of a seniority system.

Under Bill 100, the first phase in mobilizing teachers involved an all-member vote in the local. A voting system, then, was the first thing the union leadership needed to develop.

They came up with a rather unorthodox proposal, a system of one ballot box with the members of both unions in the same room. Having the members of one union vote with the members of another union was unusual; labour organizations tended to jealously guard access to their membership. With a single ballot box, the teachers were able to present one count of the votes rather than two added together. A single ballot box presented a united front to the trustees and to the membership of both unions. It prevented one affiliate voting in support of a strike while the other affiliate voted to accept the trustees' offer. The division by gender into two organizations representing one body of workers was unusual in its own right, but the elementary teachers were also exceptional among labour unions for having their two unions behave as one for collective bargaining.[106] By choosing a one-ballot-box system the elementary teachers ensured that, as they went into their first legal strike, they would be speaking with one voice.

## CHAPTER 3

# First Strikes

By the late 1970s, the FWTAO and the OPSMTF had come to the point where, if they were going to maintain credibility with the trustees, they needed a robust show of strength. Their strike funds were topped up and they had a voting procedure in place that enabled joint job action. The unions chose the Lambton County board as their test case.

The issue there was straightforward. The trustees had taken advantage of the Anti-Inflation Board rulings to include in their calculations of total salary expenditures the amount paid to new teachers as "increments" on the salary grid. This was something no other boards were doing.

Increments were a dollar amount added to the salaries of new teachers per year of teaching in addition to the percentage increases that all teachers received as a result of collective bargaining.[1] Young teachers accepted poorly paid jobs in exchange for the promise of two-pronged increases to their salaries. The savings to the boards were substantial over the fifteen-year span of most salary grids. A new teacher's pay could be half of that of an experienced teacher at full salary.[2]

Funding for the increments had always been counted outside the percentage increases. When the Lambton board included the increments in their calculations, it reduced the monies available for the general percentage increase for the entire body of Lambton teachers. That pitted new teachers against senior teachers.

On 26 April 1978, the two unions put the tentative plan they had developed into action by bringing all the elementary teachers together for a strike vote. FWTAO president Marie MacGregor, herself a Lambton County teacher, spoke. She urged both her women teachers and the OPSMTF members to support a strike.[3]

That first vote resulted in 97.7 per cent support for a strike.[4] The unions could not have wished for a stronger showing.

Despite the vote, the Lambton teachers were anxious about how they would be seen in the community. Volunteers blanketed the county with thirty thousand brochures, delivering them by hand. It was an effective strategy. Hours before the strike was to begin, the board capitulated. The threat of a strike had been enough to convince the trustees to go back to using the same method of calculating salaries as the surrounding boards. The elementary teachers had their first successful strike vote under Bill 100 behind them.

The leadership of the two unions now had a strong indication of the direction collective bargaining could take. With contract negotiations in both Peel Region and Brant County appearing to be heading toward a strike vote, the FWTAO and the OPSMTF could continue to act as one body or dissolve the partnership and negotiate independently. Fresh off their success in Lambton County, representatives from the provincial bodies sat down to firm up their guidelines for a joint presence at the bargaining table.[5]

The difficulty was that the two unions held opposing positions on protocol. A FWTAO report to the executive read, "The impression was left with many OPS members that we (FW) were being 'sticky' about details. The general feeling seems to be that FW's attitude is one of prompt attention to a problem whereas OPS attitude is one of 'time will take care of it.'"[6] The men's union, 20 per cent of whose members were school administrators, was content with the flexibility inherent in broad-stroke policies. The women's union, almost all classroom teachers, wanted to enshrine formal protections in the bargaining process.

The FWTAO was also clear that the joint sessions for collective bargaining were not to be misrepresented by the OPSMTF as some precursor to declaring a single organization. A later report to the FWTAO executive stated, "There is no 'joint organization' as such. The two executives met for matters of common concern. The presidents alternate in chairing these meetings. Administration meets with *both* presidents. Each executive meeting separately ratifies decisions made in joint session."[7] The women wanted to make sure that the constant efforts of the OPSMTF to amalgamate were not being encouraged by their mutual participation in one negotiating committee. By insisting that any collective bargaining processes developed by the joint committee had to be presented separately to each of the executives for approval, they kept the authority of the joint committee to an advisory one.

While joint bargaining did prevent competition between the elementary unions for diminishing resources, a problem that plagued the relationship between the elementary and secondary teachers, the single bargaining committee had some serious drawbacks. Consultations between the two unions slowed the negotiating process with the trustees. They became a natural brake on militancy.

Briskin has pointed out that being at the table was not enough for the FWTAO.[8] "Equity bargaining" is what she calls the processes of having women and other marginalized groups active at the bargaining table. Bringing equity issues to the table, Briskin calls "bargaining equity." The intransigence of the men impeded bargaining equity.

The other serious shortcoming to joint bargaining for the FWTAO was that the approach used amalgamation for its success.

Although the November report to the executive was a counter-point, if one negotiating team was the most desirable solution for collective bargaining, then a single union for elementary teachers was easily imaginable.

Maintaining control of the collective bargaining process required one voice at the bargaining table. The two unions agreed to give the authority to speak for both memberships to a single chief negotiator selected from either the FWTAO or the OPSMTF negotiating teams. Although they had no history of speaking on each other's behalf, if they were going to share a joint bargaining process, then both of the unions needed to affirm and build support for a negotiator who might come from the other organization. The transfer of loyalties appeared to have worked in Lambton County.

An issue that had been raised by the FWTAO in advance of the Lambton County strike vote was the ambiguous position that school administrators occupied, most of whom were OPSMTF members. Because the principals and vice-principals were not permitted to strike under the legislated terms of Bill 100, they were to remain in their schools and collect their full salaries. This thorny issue had to be settled before they could address the more general concern of maintaining picket-line discipline.

In April 1978, while preparing for the Lambton County strike, the joint negotiating committee had decided that during a strike school administrators would pay 100 per cent of their salaries to their union.[9] That appeared to be a fair resolution, since down the road principals would receive any benefit that came out of the strike. While collecting the pay of school administrators would prove challenging, a policy requiring principals and vice-principals to give up their salaries during a strike was enough to satisfy the rank and file.[10]

Opposite the problem of collecting principals' salaries was strike pay. At the same meeting, the two unions agreed to a provisional procedure on strike pay. It was set at twenty-five dollars a day to commence on the eleventh working day. The unions would continue to pay for benefits plans and to make pension contributions for those teachers in their critical last seven years, which were used to calculate the teachers' pension benefits.[11]

Once those structural issues had been worked out, the unions turned their sights on job security. Both the unions had new leaders who were committed to full collective bargaining: Betty Hawke was at the helm of the FWTAO, and Douglas McAndless was leading the OPSMTF.[12] They turned first to the Peel Region board, adjacent to Toronto.

Peel was a growing board that offered a variety of opportunities for teachers, yet problems were arising as new families moved into the newly built housing developments.[13] Teachers were being forced to move from schools with fewer students to schools with growing populations, and the Peel Region trustees would not recognize seniority in determining which teachers were transferred. Job reassignments, often to other schools some distance away, were determined solely at the discretion of administrators. Teachers were shuffled and dealt like trading cards passed between principals in closed-door meetings. The arbitrariness of the decisions angered mid-career and senior teachers who believed that they had earned entitlement to their jobs in their particular school, but Peel's trustees alienated even their newest teachers by insisting on the odious "exploding contracts."

The teachers may have voted to strike on those issues alone, but there was a fourth assault in the trustees' bargaining proposal. Like most boards across the province, Peel Region had developed a "retirement gratuity" plan to encourage teachers to make a long-term commitment to their board. The retirement gratuity plans compiled unused sick days over the span of a teacher's career up to a maximum number of days. The teacher could then redeem a percentage of them upon retirement.

The gratuity plans had been created at a time when the education system consisted of two hundred boards checkered across the province. The small size of these boards permitted poaching of trained teachers between neighbouring boards.[14] Originally, the retirement gratuity plans had been a way to retain staff, but with the 1967 amalgamation to larger boards, they no longer served their original purpose. Instead, they had become an attendance management system and a reward for long service.

The gratuity plans also generated significant savings for boards by encouraging teachers not to use their sick days. The savings to the board accrued because they had to pay double when a teacher was absent, the wages of a "supply teacher" to cover classes as well as the regular teacher's salary. Trustees, however, tended to view the retirement payout as a liability and to ignore the cost of absenteeism.[15]

The Peel Region trustees wanted to leave new teachers out of the plan. That would have created a two-tiered system that not only undermined any long-term support for the gratuity plan but also damaged new member loyalty at the stage in their careers when they were least familiar with the benefits of unionization. This threat demanded an immediate response from the unions.

Minister of Education Wells had set the wheels in motion three years earlier with a study entitled *Sick Leave Gratuities and Resultant Liabilities*.[16] In response to the ministry report, the OPSMTF commissioned its own study. It concluded that, on average, teachers were absent fewer than four days per year.[17] For their efforts to be at work in all but the most dire circumstances, teachers wanted the right to bank their sick days.

With the Peel Region trustees demanding that teachers concede on all four issues, the unions requested arbitration.[18] Arbitration was recognized as a means for both sides to get something of what they wanted. The trustees refused. The message was clear; they did not want to give the teachers anything. The unions were left with only two options. They could accept the boards' proposal or prepare for a strike.

On 2 October 1979, the 2,630 members of the Peel locals of the FWTAO and the OPSMTF began the first legally sanctioned strike by elementary teachers in the province of Ontario.[19] As they left their classrooms, Peel Region teachers strode onto the public stage, a new venue for them. They remained out for thirteen days.[20] By the third day of the strike, parents were picketing the board of education office demanding that the trustees accept the arbitration they had earlier refused.[21]

On 16 October the negotiators for the teachers' unions agreed to accept the report from the ERC's three-member mediation team.[22] The trustees would not accept the mediators' report without changes. Five days later they capitulated.[23] The teachers voted 89 per cent to accept a new contract with a 13 per cent increase in salary and a teacher-trustee committee to develop a seniority system for dealing with layoffs and recalls. The elementary teachers had won their first strike.[24]

The possibility of a second front opening up in Brant County persuaded the unions to establish a definitive set of strike protocols, now that they had some experience of how they worked in practice. On 3 November 1979, the two union executives again met and agreed to maintain the provisional protocols that they had put in place for the Peel strike while they developed permanent policies.[25] That was enough for Hawke and McAndless to entertain another strike.

The issue in Brant County was a staffing formula. The trustees refused to include in the collective agreement a 19.9 to 1 pupil/teacher ratio as the basis for staffing allocations.[26] The ratio would prevent trustees from making arbitrary cuts to the number of teachers on staff. Increasing class sizes had always been a favoured remedy for solving financial difficulties.

The Brant County board consisted of a mix of rural and urban schools with one-fifth of the number of teachers of the much larger, urban Peel Region board. Many of the parents worked in the Massey Ferguson, White's, and Pullman Trailmobile manufacturing plants. They were members of the United Auto Workers union and openly supportive of the teachers.[27]

On 14 November 1979, the *Toronto Star* reported, "The 540 elementary teachers of the Brant County board of education went on strike this morning, after talks broke off last night, leaving the 41 schools and 11,200 pupils without teachers."[28] The strike lasted twenty-two working days.[29] The Brant teachers achieved parity with their secondary colleagues with 7.5 and 8.5 per cent salary increases over two years. They retained their retirement gratuity, and most importantly, seniority would be used for redundancies and recalls. Their success enabled negotiating teams in other locals to pressure trustees into including seniority clauses in their collective agreements to govern layoffs and recalls, the effect known as "whipsaw."[30]

Once teachers had gone on strike to achieve improvements in their collective agreements, they took a more serious look at protecting the language that was in them. In November 1979 the FWTAO held its first training program for a new position, the local grievance officer.[31] The OPSMTF began to develop its "policy and procedures on grievances" in January 1980.[32] Grievance officers at the local and provincial level would monitor the actions of board officials through the lens of the collective agreement. The process of rights arbitrations to resolve differences began to build interpretations of negotiated language that could be applied to all boards without the need for the disruption and expense of strikes.

The strikes had given the teachers confidence, but the Davis government was ready to push back. Teachers' right to full collective bargaining had never been, and never would become, an absolute right. Labour rights remained subordinate to the state. While the teachers had been focused on the Peel and Brant strikes, Minister of Education Stephenson had appointed the Matthews

Commission to examine collective bargaining in education. After front-page stories of teachers on picket lines, threatening to remove the right of teachers to strike made for good press.

In the summer of 1980, the Matthews Commission released its report. Since Bill 100, teachers had engaged in 18 work stoppages divided between 5 bargaining units in 126 school boards in the province. With a total of 811 collective agreements negotiated, 2 per cent involved strikes.[33] As expected, the commission concluded that Bill 100 favoured the unions and needed to be balanced. It suggested some tinkering with the process and the granting of some additional powers to the trustees. But the final recommendation was to continue with free collective bargaining for the education sector. The unions breathed a sigh of relief. The Davis government accepted the Matthews Report as vindication of its framing of Bill 100 and maintained its relationship with teachers' unions.

By 1980, the elementary teachers' unions had achieved a strike vote on three occasions and twice tested their capacity to mount a work stoppage. Nevertheless, they had had their taste of labour militancy, and their brief engagement with it was enough for the moment. As though shocked by their own audacity, they did not take a strike vote for the next seven years.[34] In that time, the opportunity to build a culture of resistance would pass. The elementary teachers banked their successes and returned to a more conciliatory style of negotiations. The militancy that had invigorated them evaporated.

One more significant task faced the first generation of union leaders to engage with the full scope of collective bargaining: how to discipline members who broke ranks during strikes. Member discipline confounded both unions. The Teaching Profession Act stated that individuals needed to be members of the Ontario Teachers' Federation before they could teach. Belonging to the OTF required a membership in one of the unions.

The FWTAO consulted its legal counsel to examine their options regarding disciplining errant members. The response was cautionary. The outcome of wrongfully accusing a member of the offence of crossing a picket line was summed up eloquently in the lawyers' response:

> To accuse wrongly a person of being a scab in a strike situation is a serious matter and could result in a claim for substantial damages against the Federation. . . . Moreover, to follow the accusation by expelling a person so accused from membership of the Federation with the attendant notoriety would undoubtedly affect the individual's standing in the profession and cause her severe pecuniary loss and damages for which she could also have a claim.[35]

After hearing that, the FWTAO executive heeded their lawyer's advice and adopted a wait-and-see attitude to what OPSMTF might decide.[36]

The men's union took a more punitive and staged approach to disciplining its members. It started the discipline process with a letter to the member, then escalated to publishing the person's name in the newsletter, and ended with the ultimate penalty of revoking the membership of the offender for a "stated time."[37]

Although the OPSMTF appeared to have a more rigorous discipline process, few teachers were called to account and, by far, the majority of these were principals and vice-principals who had withheld their salaries.[38] No member is on record as having been expelled.

Bill 100 had provided a grievance process, but grievances, like strike votes, were not common occurrences in the elementary teachers' unions. The FWTAO reported, with some pride, that it had initiated over one hundred grievances during the 1981–82 school year.[39] That averaged a mere one grievance per local per year. Still, the FWTAO was open about its use of grievances. The OPSMTF, with principals in its ranks, was more guarded and did not report on grievances or publish the outcome.

Coming out of the Brant County strike, the elementary unions were very different organizations than they had been four years earlier. They now had well-funded strike funds and budget lines for grievances and arbitrations. They had demonstrated their potential for militant action and, in the process, coalesced much of the authority they had been granted under Bill 100 into the central organization. They had bloodied the trustees and put them on notice that they would have to at least ponder the possibility of strike action during future negotiations. As well, they had raised the spectre of grievances for violations of collective agreements, if only in the most egregious circumstances.

## Women Teachers in the OPSMTF

Amalgamation of the two unions had always been the OPSMTF's goal, but ten years earlier it had put aside its efforts to convince the FWTAO executive to willingly unite the two unions and began to make its appeal directly to the individual members of the women's union. At their 1972 annual general meeting, the delegates had amended the OPSMTF constitution to admit women as "voluntary members."[40] Mary Hill, the president of the amalgamated Teachers' Federation of Carleton at the time, was there to immediately sign up as the first woman to become a voluntary member of the men's union.[41]

Two years later, voluntary delegates to the OPSMTF annual general meeting were given the right to hold office in the union, clearing the way for a woman to occupy a seat on the executive.[42] In 1977, Hill appeared in the OPSMTF newsletter with other members of the Teachers' Federation of Carleton arm in arm with visiting members of the provincial executive.[43] She would continue to advance her career in the men's union. In 1982, Hill became the second vice-president and began raising her profile with regular contributions to the newsletter.[44] The first edition of the *OPSMTF*

*News* in the 1982–83 school year reprinted an *Ottawa Citizen* article congratulating Hill on her election. The *Citizen* derided the
FWTAO for its "Victorian attitude" toward single-sex membership
while applauding Hill for joining the OPSMTF.[45] Hill became the
poster child for amalgamation. In 1984, she was elected OPSTF
president (the union had dropped the M two years earlier) while
still being legally required to continue her membership in the
FWTAO.[46]

As president of one of the strongest locals advocating for amalgamation of the two unions, Hill had been silenced by the FWTAO
moratorium. Yet she would lead the union to which she could not
legally belong. Her presence would change policy in the OPSTF and
bring other women into the men's union.

## Wage and Price Controls II

On 4 August 1982, Pierre Trudeau's government enacted a second
round of national wage controls.[47] Like the first round, the controls
were widely endorsed by business interests as the means of reining
in inflation by curbing the strength of unions.[48] Supported by the
rhetoric of inflation fighting and the deification of "productivity,"
the Canadian state, at all levels, put a priority on reducing wages
for workers. Although inflation spiked in 1981, again due to high
oil prices, by 1983 the inflation rate would be lower than it had
been in a decade.[49] Nonetheless, Trudeau's finance minister, Allan
MacEachen, announced the introduction of the Public Sector
Compensation Restraint Act in June 1982.[50] This cavalier piece of
legislation abandoned any pretense of controlling prices.

The new controls set wage limits of 6 per cent and 5 per cent
applied only to the federal civil service. Journalist Ed Finn commented, "Even for the Trudeau government, this is a new low
in anti-union and undemocratic conduct."[51] The Public Sector
Compensation Restraint Act was a ready template available to other

levels of government. The Canadian Teachers' Federation prepared a national campaign to fight the controls, putting teachers' unions on notice as to the severity of the wage restraints.[52]

When the provincial legislature returned from its summer recess, Premier Davis was quick to enact his own version of wage controls, even more restrictive than the federal controls. On 21 September 1982, he announced Bill 179, the Ontario Inflation Restraint Act.[53] The act set a limit of 5 per cent on salary increases and extended public service collective agreements for one year.[54] Minister of Education Stephenson promised that the restraint program would continue into 1984 regardless of the rate of inflation.[55] Since Ontario's labour legislation prevented unions from calling a strike during the life of a collective agreement, extending collective agreements ended negotiations.[56]

The provincial Inflation Restraint Board was created to enforce the new rules. It was chaired by Jack Biddell, the president of a Toronto accounting firm.[57] He had been a member of the federal Anti-Inflation Board with its autocratic decision-making process.[58] Again, there would be no appeal process.[59]

As the teachers' unions prepared for this second round of wage controls, they received an unanticipated gift in the form of a report commissioned by the Ontario Public School Trustees' Association (OPSTA). In June 1982, the report, written by Professor D.A.L. Auld, was released. The OPSTA had expected it to show that public sector wages were higher than those in the private sector and that they were an important contributor to the rate of inflation. Instead, the report revealed that public sector wage increases were below those of the private sector and they were not a significant cause of inflation. The Auld Report stated:

> The conclusion we reach about trends in school board settlements in Ontario is as follows: Wage increase in this division of the public sector have fallen short of wage gains in the Ontario

private sector. School board settlements in Ontario lag behind those in the rest of Canada.[60]

While the Auld Report was a gift to the teachers' unions, they had been preparing their opposition to Bill 179 even before the report was released.[61] The 1982 FWTAO annual meeting had moved to send a telegram to the premier a month before the bill was enacted.[62] The delegates were concerned that the legislation would be a drag on women's efforts for equal pay. The September *FWTAO Bulletin* quoted Margot Trevelyan of the Equal Pay Coalition. "Wage controls simply freeze the gap between men and women," she said. "They leave women no tool with which to fight that gap."[63]

In addition to a wage freeze, Bill 179 limited the salary increments for new teachers, a flashpoint for the teachers.[64] In an effort to prevent strikes, Biddell devised what became known as the "$35,000 rule."[65] Teachers earning less than $35,000 would receive the increments; those earning over $35,000 would not.[66] The measure negatively affected only those teachers in mid-career who were not yet at the top of their multi-year salary grids but who were earning over $35,000.

The elementary teachers' response to Bill 179 began as a telegram sent to the premier and grew into a province-wide campaign, often co-ordinated with other unions. As a first step, the FWTAO and the newly renamed Ontario Public School Teachers' Federation (OPSTF) joined the other OTF affiliates on the steps of Queen's Park on 21 September.[67]

On the evening of 26 October 1982, the FWTAO and the OSSTF took the lead in co-ordinating a protest that took place in Hamilton.[68] It was one of a series of rallies organized by the OTF.[69] Teachers marched with members of the Public Sector Coalition in Windsor, London, Thunder Bay, and Ottawa.[70] Although it was to be a short-lived alliance, for the first time in their history the elementary teachers united with other public sector unions in organizing large-scale resistance to a government.[71] Still, despite their newfound common ground, they would not affiliate with the Ontario Federation of Labour (OFL).

The two elementary teachers' unions also expressed an uncharacteristic level of solidarity with each other. The FWTAO president, Sue Hildreth, and the OPSTF president, Dave Lennox, issued a joint appeal that carried the logos of both unions asking elementary teachers to sign petitions condemning the wage controls.[72] Hildreth wrote to Robert Welch, minister for women's issues, "As you will know from recently published studies . . . women are getting poorer, for the very obvious reason that percentage increases hurt lower paid workers most, and women are disproportionately the lower paid."[73]

Lennox wrote to Larry Grossman, treasurer:

> You fully comprehend the unfair discrimination brought about by the "magic" $35,000 figure. Teachers are being displaced and, for the first time in several decades, teachers with equal experience and equal qualifications do not receive equal pay. This does absolutely nothing to resolve inflation![74]

Trustees across the province took advantage of the Ontario Inflation Restraint Act to treat with contempt and indifference the teachers' attempts to bargain issues other than salary.[75] In the Peel Region board, the teachers' representatives called off negotiations when it was apparent they would be getting nothing from board negotiators. In Geraldton, the trustees changed the dates on the old collective agreement and handed it back to the teachers, declaring negotiations over. In Atikokan and East Parry Sound, the Inflation Restraint Board ordered the board to roll back negotiated salary increases in their new collective agreement to the level of the previous collective agreement plus 5 per cent. Each of these decisions cost teachers in salaries, benefits, and stagnant working conditions.

Shortly before the Ontario Inflation Restraint Act was tabled, the unions did manage to resolve one long-festering sore, the use of the "exploding contracts," the fixed term of employment that kept new teachers perpetually at the bottom of the seniority list. The particular case under discussion was the Peterborough board. After a meeting with the FWTAO's Florence Henderson, the Ministry of Education informed the trustees that they needed to stop using contracts that included an end date.[76] The board reversed its direction and corrected their calculations of seniority. The need to involve the minister pointed to the weakness of the ERC. It was an oversight body on the unions that had little authority over trustees.

At the end of 1983, new legislation was introduced. The Public Sector Prices and Compensation Review Act, 1983, Bill 111, renewed the cap of 5 per cent on salary increases.[77] It would stay in effect through 1984, at which point it would expire.

A decade after teachers had marched in the streets of Toronto for the right to strike, legislative restrictions had suppressed workers' activity for six of those ten years. The pressure on workers was mounting as corporate interests imagined new means of closing off unions. Despite their involvement with the Public Sector Coalition, the elementary teachers ended their participation in co-ordinated campaigns with other unions after wage controls ended. They then returned to a more cosseted politics.

## Teachers and Class Relations

In the last quarter of the twentieth century, employers in Canada were demanding a more precarious, flexible workplace as a means of ensuring profitability.[78] Right-wing political actors, who had been seeking a means of reforming the social contract, aligned with corporate interests to begin the construction of the neo-liberal state. This new economic regime was introduced to Canada by B.C. Social Credit Premier Bill Bennett. In May 1983, he simultaneously delivered twenty-six bills to the legislature launching the first neo-liberal government in Canada.[79] The premier seemed indifferent to the chaos he caused. Among other things, the legislation allowed trustees to lay off teachers without just cause, a situation that would allow school administrators to rid themselves of union activists.

Teachers were caught in the neo-liberal net on multiple levels. If neo-liberalism was going to be successfully established as state policy, workers would need to be trained to accept the ideological underpinnings of an economy that promised low pay, precarious jobs, the absence of benefits, and no union protections.[80] Students needed to be habituated to a view of themselves as the beneficiaries of personal responsibility for life choices, the entitlements of a meritocracy, and the logic of the marketplace. For that ideological shift to take place, education needed to be reconfigured. Because teachers were at the endpoint of institutionalized worker/citizen training, they were necessary targets of the new state regime.

Although the ideological shift in the classroom would be toward workplace training and individualism as curricular and pedagogical approaches, when teachers came together as union members, they entered an ideological space that advanced collective benefit. Teachers' work lives in the classroom and their lives as union members ideologically conflicted. This contradiction made teachers' work vulnerable to attacks from the right, but it also meant that teachers could defend themselves on ideological terrain through their unions.

Trudeau's strategy for undermining collective bargaining had opened a new space for governments to unilaterally reverse negotiated language. Demonizing workers' organizations was a strategy that allowed political actors to strip workers of long-established rights and pursue an aggressive strategy of systematically shrinking the obligations of employers toward their employees. In the process of pushing back, teachers developed a consciousness of themselves as a particular class of white-collar worker.

E.P. Thompson, a British historian, explains the phenomenon of class as something that happens within specific human relationships. He wrote:

> I do not see class as a "structure" or even as a "category," but as something which in fact happens (and can be shown to have happened) in human relationships. . . . The relationship must always be embodied in real people and in a real context . . . class happens when some men, as a result of common experiences (inherited or shared), feel and articulate the identity of their interests as between themselves, and as against other men whose interests are different from (and usually opposed to) theirs.[81]

While his comments were unusually gendered for the time they were written, they are relevant to the teachers' experience of white-collar unionism and the rise of class consciousness that was a unifying force in their labour relations. Although private-industry unions were in decline, and labour was weakened as a result, the size and institutional location of the teachers' unions as public service workers gave them a unique position from which they were able to make gains.[82]

## CHAPTER 4

# Defining Priorities

As the children of the baby boom became parents themselves, albeit of much smaller families than their parents had produced, the focus of education shifted from providing students the opportunity for their own learning, à la Hall-Dennis, to lifting the individual student to a higher standard. Employers were demanding academic qualifications for the simplest of jobs, and in the more competitive job market of the 1980s, those children who were experiencing problems learning to read, write, and calculate became a focus of the education system.

Doctors and psychologists, having entered the debates on schooling during the 1960s, had imbedded the terms "learning disabilities," "dyslexia," and "attention deficit disorder" into the jargon of education.[1] The development of "special education" inserted another layer of professionals between teachers and their students, forcing teachers to give up authority over certain aspects of the education process in the classroom. The experienced eye of the teacher was supplanted by assessment and instructional technologies developed by educational psychologists who claimed mastery in the fields of human development and cognitive testing. This transfer of authority from experience to external expertise became an educational form of scientific management. The skills of psychologists, important as they were for understanding human behaviour, were used to deskill teaching by dividing it into discrete, interchangeable packages that soon became available on the market. Commercially produced, individual learning packages did not create in students a burning interest to learn more about a particular topic and develop their academic skills in doing so, but they did provide a measurable outcome for specific skill sets.

Thousands of teachers, in an effort to secure their jobs, responded to the demands for special education. In the 1978–79 school year, some 4,875 teachers across the province enrolled in training courses for special education, more than double the number of six years earlier.[2] The availability of trained special education teachers allowed for new policy initiatives from the Ministry of Education.

In 1980, Dr. Stephenson, Minister of Education, bowed to pressure from parents of children with disabilities and formally introduced special education into the school system. Bill 82 provided a full schedule of legal requirements that boards were obliged to meet in order to address the needs of students who were diagnosed with a disability, including those with "learning disabilities."[3] Parents, trustees, and teachers' unions welcomed the additional funding and the much lower teacher/pupil ratio. Special education classes promised a partial solution to declining enrolment and the dire warnings of the Jackson Report.[4]

For many children with limitations who had floundered, additional funding and smaller classes meant a more accessible education. The FWTAO submission to the Social Development Committee on Bill 82 complimented the Ministry of Education for having pledged $75 million over five years for special education and an additional $7.5 million as start-up for the first year of the program.[5]

Bill 82 was very narrow in its scope.[6] It did not address the needs of racialized students whose schooling suffered because of systemic racism. Nor did it offer assistance to those children who lived with the impediments of poverty. Bill 82 did not provide funding unless a student fit the physiological or psychological model of disability. Interestingly, the population of special education classes would be heavily weighted toward boys.[7] Girls who may have been coping with learning disabilities remained largely invisible, untested, and without the additional resources they needed.[8]

For the everyday classroom teacher, the special education legislation legitimized the medical-psychological discourse. The widespread acceptance of the veracity of psychology elevated external standards above the educational judgment of teachers. As special education strategies spread, all classroom teachers were required to reconfigure their lessons for those students who were identified by formal psychological testing. Specialists prescribed strategies that were approved at formal meetings of parents and administrators, a process known as the Identification, Placement, and Review Committee (IPRC). Bill 82 began the practice of testing for academic skill levels without reference to a curriculum. It legitimized modern forms of standardized testing.

The elementary teachers did not challenge the coercive pressure of Bill 82. They hesitated to contest the expertise of psychologists by claiming the legitimacy of their experience on the front line of education. Moreover, special education secured jobs. Stephenson was able to move her special education agenda forward without any resistance from teachers.

Stephenson's legacy would dovetail nicely with neo-liberal sentiments. Bill 82 defined a special education program as "an educational program that is based on and modified by the results of continuous assessment and evaluation and that includes a plan containing specific objectives."[9] Coming from the last minister of education in the Conservative party's uninterrupted four-decade reign, the pedagogical shift contained in the heart of Bill 82 laid the groundwork for the dictums of accountability and high-stakes testing that would later create such turmoil for educators.[10]

Initially, the policy initiatives developed to institutionalize Bill 82 had suggested that teachers would have responsibility for "administration of oral medication . . . lifting and positioning, assistance with mobility, feeding and toileting, and general maintenance exercises . . . speech remediation, correction and habilitation programs."[11] Although teachers had been performing many of these non-teaching tasks in a number of boards, institutionalizing this practice in policy threatened to increase its prevalence.

In a survey conducted by the FWTAO during the 1984–85 school year, teachers reported giving oral medication, lifting physically disabled students, expressing bladders, toileting, feeding, putting braces on and taking them off, emptying urine bottles, administering fluoride rinse, and providing head-lice checks.[12] The unions responded to the survey by negotiating limits to teachers' responsibility for medical procedures.[13] The trustees hired educational assistants to perform what had formerly been teachers' work.

## Protocols for Resistance

The leadership of the FWTAO and the OPSMTF had developed a sense that they were "virtually legislated to negotiate jointly."[14] In the fall of 1981, a work group of the executives of the two unions met to formalize the collective bargaining protocols that had been put in place during the Lambton, Brant, and Peel strike actions. The work group would "attempt to reach consensus on joint policy to present to the Joint Executive."[15] Now that they had found joint bargaining to be successful, they needed to establish a permanent agreement as to how they would advance through escalating job actions and ratification votes. Finally in 1986, the OPSTF reported, "The Task Force which was established with FWTAO to review the joint policy and procedures has completed its task."[16]

Before bringing in the 1982 wage controls, the Davis Conservatives changed certain of the collective bargaining procedures by introducing the Municipality of Metropolitan Toronto Amendment Act, Bill 127. It integrated the seven metropolitan area boards into the largest single negotiating unit in Ontario.[17] Bill 127 rolled the six boards of education—East York, Etobicoke, North York, Scarborough, City of Toronto, and York—into the already existing Metropolitan School Board.[18] It placed additional restrictions on teachers in the metropolitan area that were not applied to the rest of the province, including a cap on increases in the education tax. The effect was to restrict improvements in salary and staffing.[19] Because the seven locals of each union were forced to negotiate as one bargaining unit, the unions cautioned that strikes that previously would have been limited to one board would now include all of the affected teachers in the metropolitan region, closing an inordinate number of schools.

The unions complained and encouraged their members to write letters, but with wage controls in place, the teachers stayed in their classrooms.[20] Ontario had found labour's Achilles heel; the labour codes that established the rules of engagement between labour and the state could be unilaterally revised through legislation.[21] The ability of the state to legislate labour relations gave it a formidable advantage over the unions.

## Funding for Catholic Schools

Back in 1964, Premier Robarts had come up with a compromise to accommodate parents who sent their children to the Roman Catholic separate school system and the rest of the province's voters, who were largely Protestant. He provided funding for the separate system up to Grade 10, but not for Grades 11 to 13. That had worked to appease Catholic parents without alienating Protestant voters. Twenty years later, Catholic parents were demanding that their children complete their secondary education in the school where they started it rather than moving to the public system for their final three years.

Davis was set to retire as premier in 1984. Before leaving, he surprised even his education minister by agreeing to full funding for the Roman Catholic separate system.[22] The idea had been around for some time, but Davis's timing was awkward. The boards had been coping for over a decade with declining enrolment and the job losses that went with it. Expanding the Roman Catholic school system threatened to rob the public system of students and exacerbate the employment situation.

Granting full funding to the separate system cost the Conservatives non-Catholic votes in the 1985 provincial election. They lost their majority for the first time in forty-two years. That gave the Liberals an opportunity. Liberal leader David Peterson negotiated an agreement with Bob Rae, leader of the Ontario New Democratic Party (NDP), to defeat the Conservative government in a non-confidence vote. He was then able to form the government. Peterson would become the first elected Liberal premier since Mitchell Hepburn won the 1937 election. It would be the Liberals who would advance Bill 30, the amendment to the Education Act, providing the funding for Catholic students to complete their education in their own schools.[23]

The OPSTF and the FWTAO apprehended risks to their members in the full funding of the separate system.[24] A new element had entered the public discourse; the principle of parental choice was gaining popularity. "Choice" was a central tenet of the new right, one that was being used as an argument by those in support of public funding of private schools.[25] In both B.C. and Alberta, private schools had become a threat to the public system when governments started to fund them.[26]

*The Report of the Commission on Private Schools in Ontario* came out in 1985.[27] Davis had appointed Bernard Shapiro, director of OISE, as the sole commissioner. Shapiro did his best to calm the reactivity of public education supporters. Shapiro's report resounded with wording such as "philosophic diversity," "multicultural," and "secular pluralism." He concluded his report with a thinly veiled pitch for public funding of private schools.

The issue of two publicly funded school systems did not go away, but the transition to an additional three grades in the separate system was not as desperate a situation as the unions had feared. Teachers in the public system who were threatened with losing their job were permitted to change to the separate system.[28] Despite Shapiro's support for private options, other private schools did not gain access to the public purse. Parents who chose to send their children to a private system were free to do so, but their taxes continued to support universal public education.

## Uncoupling Gender from Work

Four years after Stephenson's affirmative action program was announced, some boards of education still remained reluctant to implement it.[29] In December 1984, Minister Stephenson launched the Affirmative Action Incentive Fund.[30] The FWTAO Affirmative Action Committee reported to the annual general meeting, "With the announcement by the education minister ... FWTAO's priority of targeting for an affirmative action policy and programme in every school board by 1985 was given endorsement and support." Under pressure from the FWTAO locals, the number of boards using the affirmative action incentive funding went "from 10 percent of public boards in 1985 to 60 percent in June of 1986."[31]

The 1985 Liberal/NDP coalition lasted two years. Then Peterson called a second election and won it with a significant majority.[32] The Liberals were cautious about everything in their handling of the education portfolio, given that it had been the cause of the Conservatives' defeat. Having taken two years to develop it, Minister of Education Chris Ward finally tabled Bill 69, an amendment to the Education Act. It required school boards to include mandatory affirmative action programs in their hiring and promotion policies for September 1990.[33] The minister was quoted as saying, "From now on, employment equity will be the rule, not the exception."[34]

Employment equity had arrived after decades of effort. It was the first of two wars that needed to be won if women were to achieve equality with their male peers. The second would be over pay equity.

Equal pay for work of equal value had been one of the recommendations of the Royal Commission on the Status of Women in 1970.[35] The concept was then enshrined in the Human Rights Act in 1977: "It is a discriminatory practice for an employer to establish or maintain differences in wages between male and female employees employed in the same establishment who are performing work of equal value."[36] But that clause applied only to the federally regulated workers who worked in the federal public sector. The provinces had to write their own legislation to cover workers in the provincial public sector. Nine years later, Bill 154, An Act to Provide for Pay Equity in the Broader Public Sector and in the Private Sector, was finally introduced in the Ontario legislature. It was passed in early 1987, a decade after the Human Rights Act took effect.[37]

The salary grids that equity programs were challenging were not going to be reformulated without resistance from trustees. The OPSTA warned that pay equity legislation would "significantly increase the costs to school boards . . . boost the salaries of lower-paid women teachers with little seniority" and result in "higher taxes for homeowners."[38] The FWTAO brief was eloquent in its response:

> The fact is that pay equity will cost money in exactly the amount by which women are currently subsidizing the economy. The fact is that someone is paying a heavy price now: the women who work in their thousands at undervalued jobs. No injustice can be

permanently tolerated in a civilized society on the sole grounds that its correction would cost money.[39]

The OTF policy of "equal opportunity and equal pay" proposed in 1946 had finally been passed in 1950 (over the objections of the OPSMTF). But the FWTAO had never been willing to put its members on picket lines without the men.[40] Legislation was a more palatable solution.[41]

It would be the state that would impose, not only the requirement for pay equity, but a collective bargaining process for determining "work of equal value." As feminist historian Rosemary Warskett points out, pay equity legislation does not achieve equal wages in and of itself.

> Although pay equity and employment equity legislation have often led to questions regarding the construction of the wage hierarchy, they do not challenge the concept of hierarchy itself. . . . Occasionally the successful application of pay equity has resulted in changes in the gender order that in turn threaten and shake up the hierarchy itself. This is not only threatening to management but to those unionists wishing to maintain the status quo or protect their relatively privileged place in the workplace.[42]

This was precisely the effect any discussion of pay equity had on the OPSMTF.

The means of achieving pay equity started with the project to repatriate the Constitution undertaken by Pierre Trudeau. Pressure from the National Action Committee on the Status of Women moved the prime minister to include "sex" in the Canadian Charter of Rights and Freedoms.[43] Then Section 15, the Equality Rights section, was suspended by the federal government for a three-year period to give employers time to prepare for the cost of equal rights in the workplace.[44]

The Davis government, like other provincial governments across Canada, used the three-year grace period to make provisions for 17 April 1985, when the equality rights provision would come into effect. Education Minister Stephenson provided additional funding to boards of education to ensure that they included the cost of pay equity in their budgets.[45] It would be up to the unions to police their employers' compliance.

Ontario's *Green Paper on Pay Equity* was released in the fall of 1985 as the reins of government were being handed to the Liberals.[46] It had been written to provide guidelines to address pay equity. The green paper stated that the wage gap between men and women working full-time stood at 38 per cent, meaning women earned 62 cents for every dollar men earned.[47]

Two years later, the Peterson government passed the Ontario Pay Equity Act, a major step in recognizing an inequity women teachers had been organizing against for a century.[48] Among other things, the act required the unions to negotiate equity terms individually with each of their boards, something the teachers had been avoiding. The trustees were prepared to use these negotiations as an opportunity to trade away other items for pay equity.[49] To alleviate the threat of massive labour unrest, the legislation created a Pay Equity Commission that was charged with resolving conflicts and avoiding situations where teachers resorted to strikes or trustees opted to lock teachers out. The Pay Equity Commission then established the Pay Equity Hearings Tribunal to decide individual cases.[50]

The FWTAO brought Shelly Acheson, the human rights director of the Ontario Federation of Labour, into their offices to lead workshops to train their collective bargaining teams in how to negotiate pay equity.[51] The Women's Bureau of the Ontario Ministry of Labour also provided materials that women could use to develop their bargaining positions. It was a unique collaboration of labour and the state, brought together by a white-collar, all-women union.

The FWTAO, in its brief to the committee studying the Pay Equity Act, noted the list of exceptions, particularly those that applied to the 75 per cent of women who worked in non-unionized jobs and/or in small businesses.[52] The state appeared to be willing to provide equality only to those who were able to demand it.[53]

There were those within the men's union who were nervous that their more generous pay scale was going to be applied to all teachers.[54] Some administrators feared that their qualifications and responsibility were being devalued.[55] Nonetheless, the OPSTF preferred a joint task force to work on the implementation of the legislation.[56]

As the elementary teachers' unions began the process of comparing jobs, they found an interesting anomaly. When they examined the data on secondary teachers, discrepancies were found that could not be accounted for by a simple dollar difference between the elementary and the secondary pay grids. Because many elementary teachers did not have university degrees, low-paid non-degreed categories had been included in every elementary salary grid. When making comparisons between themselves and the secondary teachers through the pay equity lens, the elementary teachers discovered that no secondary salary grid in the province had a non-degreed category. On the face of it, that made sense if all secondary teachers were required to have university degrees. But during the investigations of job categories, it was learned that 9 per cent of secondary teachers did not have degrees.[57] Those without degrees were generally the teachers who taught in the trades and service courses. They had entered teaching with credit for their work experience. Once hired, they were placed in a degreed category based on a system of workplace equivalents. That meant they could reach the top secondary salary level without ever having obtained a university degree. The elementary salary grids did not permit similar advancement because they all contained the non-degreed categories.

The vast majority of the secondary teachers without degrees were men. The difference in salary between the non-degreed teachers in secondary schools and the non-degreed teachers in the elementary system could only be explained as a consequence of gender. It was exactly that kind of structural inequity posing as gender neutrality that the pay equity legislation was intended to address.

A second unexpected demographic anomaly emerged during the investigation that would turn the members of the OPSTF around. When the qualifications of all the teachers in the provinces were reviewed, it was revealed that while 37.2 per cent of women teachers did not have degrees, 12.4 per cent of men teachers also did not have degrees and consequently stood to benefit from the pay equity program.[58] Suddenly, the OPSTF and the FWTAO could agree on pay equity. The issue did not pit men elementary teachers against women elementary teachers; the correlation was between the different pay scales of the elementary and the secondary teachers.

The solution was to remove non-degreed categories on the elementary salary grid. Eliminating the non-degreed categories did not provide the elementary non-degreed teachers with the same salary as their non-degreed secondary peers, but it did provide the unions with a means of forcing trustees to redesign the salary grid to make it more equitable. The FWTAO reported that the average increases for teachers affected by the pay equity plans would be from $3,000 to $13,000 per year.[59]

### Cuts and Strikes

Provincial wage and price controls ended in 1984. But by then the rhetoric of the marketplace had taken hold and corporate interests were not about to concede anything. Politicians had become enthralled with the politics of retrenchment and were turning their backs on the role of the state to provide universal social services.

Although Canada had returned to normal levels of inflation by 1984, Ontario's Conservative government continued to reduce its funding for education.[60] In response, teacher militancy, freed from the constraints of wage controls, resurfaced. In April 1985, the Catholic teachers and the French-language teachers in their amalgamated boards in Toronto went on strike for five days to achieve a cap on class sizes and a 9 per cent increase in wages over two years.[61] The Toronto strike would be followed by a flurry of strikes by locals of the OSSTF, OECTA, and AEFO.

In early 1987, the economic news in Ontario was decidedly positive. The value of the Canadian dollar was rising, while the inflation rate had dropped and remained stable for some time. The Peterson government had made education a priority, creating a political climate that was conducive to improving conditions in the classroom. The environment was right for elementary teachers to find their voice again.

Joan Westcott had cut her labour teeth as the FWTAO president during the Lambton, Peel, and Brant strikes. She had a new position as FWTAO's executive director.[62] The OPSTF's new chief administrator, secretary-treasurer Dave Lennox, had yet to prove himself on the labour front. He declared his colours with his first newsletter article in his new role, listing those locals that had recently taken strike votes.[63] Westcott and Lennox both understood the need for a convincing demonstration of union strength while political conditions were favourable.

The change in the administrative leadership of the unions, in conjunction with a rebounding economy, spawned a new spirit of rank-and-file militancy. Locals appeared to be vying to be the first to go on strike. In Lanark County, a settlement was reached in February 1987 after members voted for provincial assistance, the first step in preparing for a strike.[64] They achieved 180 minutes of preparation time per week for all teachers. In April, Peel Region elementary teachers voted to accept a tentative agreement reached with the assistance of an ERC mediator rather than going on strike.[65] The elementary teachers of Metropolitan Toronto also took their proposal for preparation time to an ERC fact finder and waited. Dryden District's teachers narrowly averted a strike and won the second-highest salary scale for elementary teachers in Ontario.[66] In Prescott-Russell, Lincoln County, Bruce County, Dufferin County, Renfrew, and Canadian Forces Base Petawawa, teachers took strike votes and then achieved their agreements.[67]

Nearing the end of the 1986–87 school year, no elementary local had gone on strike since the Brant County dispute in 1979. Despite numerous strike votes, the teachers had not yet had to enforce their demands with a picket line. The litmus test for teachers finally came from the largest board in Ontario, the Metropolitan Toronto School Board.

In the spring of 1987, Toronto teachers were still finding their way through the joint negotiations that Bill 127 had forced on their collective bargaining. At the same time, they were staring at declining enrolment and the possibility of job losses as a result of Davis's extension of full funding to the Roman Catholic separate school system. Tensions were running high when the elementary teachers had presented their proposal to the ERC fact finder on 6 October 1986.[68]

Eight months later, the 1986–87 school year was about to end, and the Toronto elementary teachers were still without a collective agreement.[69] In early June, the membership rejected the board's final offer by 81 per cent.[70] That put them in a position to strike for September. Their issue was preparation time, the lack of which was a persistent reminder that not only were elementary teachers paid less than secondary teachers, but they were in their classrooms during the hours that secondary teachers were preparing lessons and marking students' work.[71]

The Toronto teachers' Rationale to the Factfinder had said, "40.3 percent of the elementary collective agreements contained some provision relating to preparation time."[72] It also revealed that while over 60 per cent of Toronto teachers between Junior Kindergarten and Grade 6 received no preparation time at all, over 50 per cent of the Grade 7 and 8 teachers in the Metropolitan region received in excess of 30 minutes per day.[73] There was a distinct divide between those who taught younger students and those who taught the more senior students, a distinction that could also be drawn along gender lines. The unions framed preparation time as a fairness and universality issue; every teacher deserved the same amount of time to mark papers and prepare lessons. They emphasized that many secondary teachers in the province were guaranteed 80 minutes of preparation time per day, while Toronto's trustees were offering elementary teachers a mere 40 minutes per week. This offer was regarded as little better than no preparation time at all in the lower grades, while the Grade 7 and 8 teachers considered it a threat to what they already had. The unions would not back down from their demand of 180 minutes per week.

On 18 June 1987, the 9,600 elementary teachers within the boundaries of the legislatively established Metropolitan Toronto School Board rejected the trustees' final offer and voted 80 per cent in favour of strike action.[74] During the summer, trustees and the unions held further meetings, but the preparation time issue remained unresolved. By the time teachers returned to their classrooms in September, both sides were making immediate preparations for a strike.[75]

The Metropolitan Toronto strike lasted four weeks.[76] To his credit, with a majority government secured and the strike taking place early in his mandate, Peterson stayed out of the dispute. The teachers settled for a guarantee that all teachers would receive a minimum of 120 minutes of preparation time per week by the end of the third year of the collective agreement and a salary increase of 5 per cent each year. Those were significant gains, but many of the teachers who had walked the picket lines for eighteen days, particularly those in the intermediate grades who had seen no increase in their preparation time, felt the settlement was not enough.

Although teachers in Toronto were disappointed, the strike brought preparation time to the forefront.[77] Negotiators became key players in the locals. The January 1988 edition of the *FWTAO Newsletter* raised the profile of the local collective bargaining representatives by including a picture of each of them, indicating a heightened interest in contract negotiations.[78]

As the 1989–90 school year began, the London locals took a strike vote demanding that every teacher receive 150 minutes a week (30 minutes per day) preparation time and a cap on class size reducing the maximum number of students in each grade by one.[79] On 31 October 1989, they settled without strike action. Other strike votes were taken in the Lakehead and Sault Ste. Marie locals.[80] The elementary teachers were starting late, but their newfound militancy was producing improvements in their working conditions.

By 1991, elementary teachers in fifty-two boards would have preparation time of 150 minutes a week on average.[81] Only four boards would remain without language on preparation time.

The provincial government's contribution to local funding for education had been reduced from 61 per cent in 1975 to 46 per cent in 1987. That resulted in 15 per cent of education costs being downloaded onto the municipal tax base, leaving trustees to find ways of balancing their budgets while dealing with teacher negotiations.[82]

For years Ottawa's elementary teachers had acceded to their trustees' demands. As a result, they had fallen from being among the highest-paid teachers in the province to being among the lowest-paid.[83] During the 1989–90 negotiations their mood changed. For the first time, the Ottawa elementary teachers were prepared to set up picket lines. The route by which they arrived at that decision was one of the more unusual moments in teachers' collective bargaining.

In the fall of 1989, the board hired a professional negotiator to represent their interests at the bargaining table. His presence as a "hired hand" widened the gap between the teachers and trustees.[84] By the spring of 1990, negotiations had stalled. The trustees were unwilling to move on the key issue of salaries. The teachers agreed to meet with an arbitrator to settle their outstanding issues.

In a bizarre twist of collective bargaining logic, the trustees looked back at the teachers' record of compliance and then presented the arbitrator with what amounted to a formal challenge directed at the teachers. They said that if the teachers were serious about the unresolved issues still on the table, then the recourse open to them was to go on strike. They further accused the teachers of trying to make gains without risking the personal losses they would incur in a strike, in essence, calling them labour cowards. The arbitrator found against the teachers. Their options were to capitulate or to strike.

The issues being contested were more than a test of wills over salaries.[85] The FWTAO and the OPSTF teachers were nervous about the effect of the 1986 legislation that had given francophone Ontarians control of French education in the province.[86] Ottawa had a large number of francophone civil servants, and anglophone teachers were threatened by the expansion of the French-language system taking students out of the English system. By 1988 there were enough French teachers in the area that four new bargaining units of the AEFO had been created.[87]

The strained relationship between the board and its 1,300 elementary teachers erupted into a full withdrawal of services on 19 April 1990.[88] Daring teachers to strike turned out to be a dangerous strategy for a board. After the schools had been closed for twenty-six days, the trustees agreed to the teachers' demands. The teachers voted 94.8 per cent to ratify their new agreement.[89]

The trustees were consistent in their tactics. At the same time as they were alienating the elementary teachers, the trustees were also sowing dissatisfaction among their secondary teachers. The OSSTF local had been working to rule during the elementary teachers' strike, giving Ottawa the distinction of being the first board in Ontario where both the elementary and the secondary panels were involved in workplace sanctions concurrently. As the elementary teachers' strike was coming to an end in May 1990, the secondary teachers' work-to-rule escalated into a full withdrawal of services, despite the end of the school year being only a month away. That strike continued over the summer and into the first days of September 1990.

The trustees were determined. In a time of neo-liberal ascendancy, they repeatedly challenged the teachers. In turn, the teachers shifted from disgruntled compliance to organized resistance, what Alan Sears has called an "infrastructure of dissent." He was referring to the language, theory, and tactics of resistance as they evolve at a grassroots level.[90] The Ottawa area teachers had become politicized by their first strike. The infrastructure they developed at that time, intellectual as well as material, supported subsequent campaigns.

The success of strike votes prompted the elementary teachers to take a look at what was going on in the rest of the country. Both the FWTAO and the OPSTF invited the British Columbia Teachers' Federation (BCTF) president, Elsie McMurphy, to speak at their 1987 annual general meetings.[91] Her speeches explained how the long-serving B.C. Social Credit government, arguably the most right-wing government in the country, had repeatedly tried to undermine her union.[92] The FWTAO members responded to McMurphy's speech with promises of letters and some financial aid, one of the few times that Ontario elementary teachers publicly supported another union's militancy.[93]

## Early Retirement

In the late 1980s, the numbers of students entering school rebound-ed.[94] Teachers welcomed the end of declining enrolment with relief. The unions had some space to consider other issues. A higher birth rate, the result of baby boom parents having more children (known as the "echo generation"), was one aspect in turning the tide.[95] The other was retirements. Teachers who had been hired in the late 1940s and early 1950s were reaching retirement age. Suddenly teachers were being hired again.

Then the Peterson government helped to create a teacher shortage. Teachers' pension funds were showing a higher rate of return than was needed for payout requirements. The teachers successfully argued for using the surplus to enhance the plan. An agreement between the government and the teachers' unions granted early retirement "windows" for those teachers near the end of their careers.[96] Between 1985 and 1989, senior teachers who were close to their retirement date would be permitted to retire early without the penalty that would normally be incurred. The penal-ty-free early retirement window was also part of an effort to absorb some of the teacher surpluses still obvious in 1985, an effect it was remarkably successful in achieving. In 1970, some 853 teachers from all five affiliates retired.[97] In 1980, that number rose to 1,119 retirements. In 1986, the second year of the window, 2,660 teachers retired. In 1989, as the plan was about to end, 4,191 teachers took their pensions. Trustees were happy to see the retirements. They were more than willing to hire new teachers for half of what they were paying experienced ones. However, more teachers made the move to retirement than either the union or the Liberal govern-ment had anticipated.

The sudden spike in retirements focused attention on the teachers' pension plan. All five affiliates had advocated for con-trol of their pensions. They had been offered some hope in 1987 when the Liberal government commissioned Malcolm Rowan to lead a task force to examine public sector pensions. Two of that task force's recommendations had been significant for teachers.[98] The first was that pension funds should be invested in the market. Second, that plan members should participate in decision making regarding investments and plan benefits. Although Rowan's main concern was future costs to the province, those two recommendations echoed the unions' position.

The teachers wanted to take advantage of investment strategies in a bull market that could increase their benefits. The pension plan they were paying into did not include a satisfactory mechanism for negotiating enhancements, even in years when there was a surplus. Peterson appeared willing. In the fall of 1988, government and OTF representatives began discussions to develop an equal partnership.[99]

Despite its initial readiness to sit down with the teachers, the Peterson government backtracked in January 1989. The Liberal caucus rejected giving up this readily available source of revenue. In June, legislation to amend the Teachers' Superannuation Act received first reading. The amendments retained state control of the teachers' pension.[100] As well, any surplus generated by the fund would pay what the state owed the teachers rather than being reinvested in the fund to improve benefits.[101] Finally, despite the surpluses, the contribution rate would increase. Teachers responded with rallies and a letter-writing campaign, but they were not willing to defend their pension plan with widespread labour disruptions.[102]

## Equal Value in the Classroom

In 1988, Ontario's economy was the strongest it had been since the 1960s. Inflation was down and the GDP was stable. Although the NDP had had to pressure the Liberals during the coalition to introduce the Pay Equity Act, once it was in place Peterson declared pay equity a priority and he was prepared to support it. Chris Ward was the minister of education and a supporter of equity programs. He had been involved in moving the Pay Equity Act through the legislature.[103]

Once the OPSTF agreed to collaborate with the FWTAO on pay equity, the two unions could set about creating the instrument they would need to identify work of equal value. At the end of 1988, they set up a joint task force to develop the literally named Teacher Job Description / Job Content comparator.[104] The comparator was a tool intended to facilitate the process of removing the non-degreed categories from elementary pay grids across the province. It compared the work of female-dominated job categories within a board with the work of male-dominated job categories in the same board. This controversial project cut across the grain of fetishization of formal qualifications.

The unions found there was no pattern determining which teachers had degrees and which did not, although the pervasive factor was gender. The distribution of teachers who had degrees also varied between boards. Of the sixty-three elementary teachers in the Prince Edward County board, all had basic university degrees.[105] The process for placing those teachers on the salary grid would go unchanged by the Pay Equity Act. Immediately to the north of them, the Hastings County board employed 593 elementary teachers, of which 35 per cent, or over 200, did not have a basic degree. Despite the influx of additional provincial money to cover costs, the long-term effect of increasing the salaries of a significant percentage of teachers was a concern for trustees in boards like Hastings County.

For the FWTAO, pay equity had been a major victory. It recognized pay differences as a systemic problem across employment sectors, not just in education.[106] Threadbare arguments that declared that the differences in salaries were a result of qualifications, experience, and position did not account for broad disparities between men and women. The OPSTF continued to work with the FWTAO, agreeing to the women's union taking the lead in pay equity negotiations with trustees.[107]

Certain boards resisted pay equity. The most influential case became known as the Wentworth/Perth decision, the result of which set the standard for future judgments across the province.[108] The Wentworth and Perth trustees refused to accept the pay equity schedule designed by the unions and took the issue to the Pay Equity Hearings Tribunal for a ruling.[109]

The tribunal decided in favour of the teachers and declared one pay equity plan for all elementary teachers.[110] The trustees pushed back immediately, serving notice that they would seek a judicial review. By this time, the economy had begun to weaken. In July 1990, Peterson suddenly abandoned his support for pay equity and sought to intervene in the judicial review on the side of the Wentworth/Perth trustees.[111]

The Liberal caucus had become nervous about the cost of implementing the Wentworth/Perth decision, estimated at $60 million. On 13 July 1990, Minister of Education Sean Conway issued a memorandum backtracking on pay equity: "Under the pay equity legislation, school boards are required to continue to nego-tiate pay equity plans with teachers and they may do so within the existing salary grid system."[112] Teachers with degrees would have to accept lower salary increases if they wanted pay equity for non-degreed teachers.

On 6 September 1990, for the first time in its history, the NDP was elected to form the government of Ontario. When the new gov-ernment took office, Premier Rae withdrew the government's inter-vention in the pay equity appeal, saying that it did not make sense for the government to intervene in its own tribunal.[113] With gov-ernment intervention removed, the teachers won the appeal.[114] In April 1991, with the new premier on side, the elementary teachers' unions and the boards throughout the province began to negotiate pay equity plans based on the Pay Equity Hearings Tribunal decision in Wentworth/Perth.[115]

While the moment when men would carry picket signs demanding equal pay for women had not yet arrived, the pay equity legislation was the entry point for the first feminist issue to enter teachers' collective bargaining. It was a breakthrough for what political science writer Jill Vickers has called negotiating "as if women mattered."[116]

The tribunal's decision was significant for teachers. Over 28 per cent of full-time elementary teachers were without degrees. The difference between men and women elementary teachers was pronounced; 85 per cent of teachers without a degree were women.[117] While only 12.4 per cent of men teachers did not have a degree, 37.2 per cent of women teachers did not.[118] The Ontario Pay Equity Act represented one of the most concrete efforts undertaken by any jurisdiction in Canada to narrow the wage gap between men and women. And unlike the legislation in other provinces, the Ontario act covered private industry as well as the public service.

## Paltry Pregnancy Leaves

The FWTAO established pregnancy leave provisions as its second priority for collective bargaining in 1987–88.[119] Conditions for pregnant teachers had changed considerably from the days when women were required to resign after becoming pregnant.[120] Legislation had been amended in 1971 to permit women who were near term or had given birth to receive unemployment insurance benefits for fifteen weeks or to receive a paid maternity leave from their employer for the same period.[121] For unionized workers, the legislation permitted supplemental unemployment benefit (SUB) plans from employers to top up what women received from their unemployment insurance benefits. Because it was a legislated benefit, the OPSTF was willing to support pregnancy leave in collective bargaining.

During the 1980s, all unions, including the teachers, were making efforts to negotiate SUB plans. It was understood that women who left their jobs to bear children still needed their incomes to support their families. Yet as late as 1990, the FWTAO would still be advising women, "No teacher should ever resign under pressure because of pregnancy . . ."[122] That pressure was coming from the boards.

The federal pregnancy leave benefit was subject to the unemployment insurance rules. This mean-spirited approach linked women's right to give birth with unemployment and limited their benefits accordingly. Locking pregnancy leave into the unemployment insurance plan absolved the state of having to tax for it, since the funding came from the premiums workers and their employers paid. It also placed a cap on women's entitlements. The seventeen-week time frame for post-partum women to convalesce was arbitrarily selected by the largely male architects of the plan.

In unionized workplaces, the two-tiered pregnancy leave regime created an uneven result, as a consequence of unions having to negotiate SUB plans.[123] The cost to the employer of a top-up benefit was directly proportional to the percentage of women in the workplace. Teaching was a disproportionately female sector, so trustees tended to resist enriching SUB plans. The women's union never successfully defeated the trustees' argument that, in the age of "the pill," women had a choice in the decision to become pregnant. Trustees did not feel obligated to explain who would have the babies if women did not. During the development of pregnancy leave benefits and SUB plans, collective responsibility was unable to prevail against the rhetoric of personal choice.

A modicum of progress was made by the teachers' unions. Of five settlements reported in the fall of 1990, two had negotiated

SUB plans covering the two-week waiting period before unemployment insurance benefits commenced.[124] By the end of the school year, fifty-one boards were paying some supplement for the two-week waiting period, usually the unemployment insurance rate of $408 per week.[125] Only five locals were able to achieve a top-up to a percentage of salary for the entire leave period of seventeen weeks. Enriching SUB plans never became the highest priority for the teachers' unions, although some locals did achieve improvements for the fifteen weeks following the two-week waiting period. They ranged from top-ups to 60 per cent of salary in Frontenac up to 95 per cent of salary in Nipissing.[126]

During the 1987–88 round of negotiations, some male teachers expressed a fear that women would use the pregnancy leave provisions to continue to accumulate seniority while not working. They suggested breaking away and pursuing their own negotiations.[127] The OPSTF executive calmed the fears of its anxious members by assuring them that the women's union was not seeking exceptional circumstances under which women teachers were able to accrue seniority. In point of fact, accumulation of seniority while not in the workplace was key to pregnancy leave.[128] Viewed through a masculinist lens, the workplace and raising children were separate and disconnected spheres. For a woman with a family, a tight connection existed between the workplace, the material support it provided, and the unavoidable requirements in bearing children. Hers was the same body in the classroom and in the delivery room. Despite elementary education being a highly feminized sector, no strike vote was ever taken in support of improving pregnancy and parental leaves.

The history of the struggle for reasonable pregnancy leave benefits demonstrates a paradox of women's status in the social order, one that is both material and biological. Biological difference cannot be addressed by juxtaposing rights and needs in every instance.[129] Rights, in the instance of the workplace, have been historically structured for a homogeneous male and for that reason never included the right of a woman to bear children. Men could claim a wage that would support a family to meet their needs, but a woman could not claim a wage that would meet her needs while creating that family.

## A Place for Women in the OPSTF

The battle between the FWTAO and the OPSTF over amalgamation sapped the strength of both unions. The men's long-running campaign for one union generated deep suspicion among women teachers. The conflict was constant, or to put it bluntly, the men continuously applied pressure to all echelons of the FWTAO, from making overtures to the rank and file to join the OPSTF as voluntary members, to gender-baiting its leadership. Their advances were successful with some locals, but for the most part their campaigns aroused deep animosities that promoted divisiveness and mistrust between the two organizations. The men never convinced a majority of the women of the FWTAO of the benefit of one organization.

On 22 June 1982, Supplementary Letters of Patent, issued by the Ontario government, had been received by the Ontario Public School Men Teachers Federation approving its request to change its name to the Ontario Public School Teachers Federation.[130] The FWTAO had immediately mounted a legal challenge.[131] It argued that the name change misrepresented the men's union.[132] The court dismissed the challenge.[133] The renaming further opened the door for the OPSTF to stake its claim to representing women in education.

The name change was indicative of other adaptations within the men's union. With FWTAO members becoming voluntary OPSTF members, the men had to modify their policies. Mary Hill won a second election in 1985.[134] That same year, the men's union abandoned its opposition to affirmative action programs.[135] By this time, almost fourteen hundred members of the FWTAO were voluntary members of the OPSTF.[136]

In its search for women members, the OPSTF initiated a campaign to organize occasional teachers.[137] They would not be voluntary members; they would be fully entitled members of the OPSTF, with the legal protections that went with union membership.

Historically, neither of the two elementary teachers' unions had shown any interest in organizing other workers. The Ontario Public Service Employees Union (OPSEU) was the first union to organize occasional teachers under the Ontario Labour Relations Act.[138] Occasional teachers had been without representation since 1975, when Bill 100 had taken them out of the teachers' unions. Both the OPSTF and the FWTAO had tried to organize them as teachers, but had little success convincing the Ministry of Education to make changes to the legislation to grant occasional teachers union membership within the OTF guidelines.

The OSSTF found a way to break through that legal impasse by revising the OSSTF constitution to align with the Ontario Labour Relations Act.[139] The AEFO, OECTA, and OPSTF followed the OSSTF model and made the necessary modification to their constitutions. On 11 March 1986, the Ontario Labour Relations Board released its decision, making the OPSTF a trade union within the Labour Relations Act.[140] The men had come to believe that bringing women into the union's membership, in whatever form, was worth the financial costs of organizing drives. Organizing the occasional teachers would give the OPSTF a familiarity with labour relations under the Labour Relations Act regime, an experience that would become useful in the 1990s.

The FWTAO chose not to organize occasional teachers. That left it holding a narrow position in the education sector with a membership comprised almost entirely of classroom teachers. By not taking up the cause of the occasional teachers, the FWTAO undermined its claims of concern for all women workers and shut itself off from a new source of members.

In December 1986, the Kent County occasional teachers ratified the first contract negotiated by the OPSTF. The newly elected occasional teacher president, Lilias Kerr, and her vice-president, Shirley Brown, had been presented to the annual general meeting the previous summer as negotiations for their contract were still underway.[141] The inclusion of the occasional teacher locals furthered the efforts of the OPSTF to represent itself as an organization sensitive to the needs of both men and women.

The OPSTF continued to rewrite its policies to adjust to its newest members. Under the leadership of Mary Hill, the men's union added an affirmative action section to the "Rights and Responsibilities" portion of the union directives.[142] The policy appeared under the terms of reference of the OPSTF Status of Women Committee. This committee was "to monitor regularly the professional status of women in education and to advise the Executive and Assembly on the need for appropriate action with respect to any developing trends . . . to develop a model for affirmative action consistent with OPSTF policy."[143] The best that could be said for these directives was that they were ambiguous. As policies, they had to be acceptable to the men in the OPSTF, who still greatly outnumbered the women. They also had to appeal to the aspirations of the women that the OPSTF was seeking to attract. Ambiguity was a strategy that furthered both agendas.

By the summer of 1987, the OPSTF had ten occasional teachers' collective agreements negotiated, bringing 2,500 new members into the union at a time when it was losing teacher members at a rate of 1 per cent per year.[144] By 1989, the number of new members had doubled, with 5,000 occasional teacher members entering the fold.[145] It was a significant increase to a membership of 23,000, even more remarkable since the school system had come through two decades of declining enrolment. By the early 1990s, the OPSTF would be able to declare that 50 per cent of its membership was female, although only a third of those newly affiliated would be voluntary members from the FWTAO.[146]

## The Charter Challenge

In the final battle between the two unions, the OPSTF made the first move. It chose a charge over well-worn ground, the margins of which had been redrawn by the Canadian Charter of Rights and Freedoms. The OPSTF's offensive had no chance of succeeding, but it would set events in motion.

Section 15 of the Charter came into effect on 17 April 1985. It read:

15. (1) Every individual is equal before and under the law and has the right to the equal protection and equal benefit of the law without discrimination and, in particular, without discrimination based on race, national or ethnic origin, colour, religion, sex, age or mental or physical disability.

Note the inclusion of sex in the list. It goes on to say:

(2) Subsection (1) does not preclude any law, program or activity that has as its object the amelioration of conditions of disadvantaged individuals or groups including those that are disadvantaged because of race, national or ethnic origin, colour, religion, sex, age or mental or physical disability.[147]

On 18 April, Margaret Tomen applied to the OTF for membership in the men's union.[148] Tomen was a principal with the Windsor board, the same board for which the OPSTF's chief executive officer, Dave Lennox, had worked. She was also a voluntary member of the men's union. The OPSTF covertly financed her case against itself.

Predictably, the OTF denied Tomen's request. She then took the case to the Ontario Divisional Court. In court, Tomen accused the men's union of violating the Charter by discriminating against her on the grounds of sex. She demanded that the OTF be required to change its Bylaw 1, which established union membership for teachers and prevented her from joining the men's union as she believed the Charter permitted. The FWTAO was not named in the challenge. The OPSTF was hoping to contain the case to a contest between Tomen and themselves, which they intended to lose. The ruse did not work; the court agreed to hear arguments from the FWTAO.

By establishing a scenario where the men's union was accused of discriminating against women, Tomen appropriated the language that had been fought for by the National Action Committee on the Status of Women. Men not permitting women to join their organization was the kind of limitation that the Charter was intended to address. On the face of it, Tomen's appeal was to force the men's union to open its doors to women. But more precisely, her intentions aligned with the goals of the OPSTF, to eliminate the women-only structure of the FWTAO. It was an attack on the women's union couched in the language of gender equity.

Margaret Wilson, the secretary-treasurer of the OTF at this point in her career, was called as a witness. She stated in her affidavit:

In essence, there is not any advantage to be gained by a member of FWTAO becoming a member of OPSTF, with the exception that there is an advantage to the OPSTF. The advantage is that OPSTF would receive the fee referable to the female teacher, which would have been paid to FWTAO.[149]

She was careful not to express an opinion on amalgamation.

The FWTAO filed a motion to quash the proceedings, claiming that the Divisional Court had no jurisdiction over the OTF bylaws.

The three judges agreed, and the court dismissed Tomen's application. The women's union had won in the judicial system.[150]

In December 1986, Tomen appealed her case to the Supreme Court of Ontario before Justice Ewaschuk.[151] This time the OPSTF was not the only respondent; the FWTAO and the OTF were named. Again, Tomen requested that she be permitted to switch her affiliation to the men's union. On 16 September 1987, Justice Ewaschuk presented the second decision on the issue of union membership for elementary teachers, much to the jubilation of the FWTAO.[152] He ruled that it was an internal matter between the affiliates and not subject to the Charter. He indicated that if teachers wanted to change Bylaw 1, they could vote to do so within their own organization, the OTF. His ruling included the observation that "the *Charter* was designed to protect individuals from government's tyranny. The *Charter* was not designed to permit individuals to tyrannize other private individuals or groups in the name of individual rights."[153] The OPSTF appealed the decision immediately, but that appeal too would lose in the Supreme Court.[154]

Justice Ewaschuk's ruling created some controversy, coming as it did during the heyday of second-wave feminism in Canada. Newspaper editorials came out on both sides. In Elliot Lake, the ruling was lauded by the *Tabloyd* as "a decision of inestimable benefit to the women of Ontario."[155] In North Bay, the *Nugget* compared the situation of women teachers being confined to their own union to that of the Ayatollah's rule in Iran.[156] The *Ottawa Citizen*'s editorial comments portrayed the FWTAO as an anachronistic organization, its leaders forcing women to remain within its ranks out of a concern for "protecting their turf and personal power."[157]

The second decision should have brought an end to the entire matter of amalgamation. Once the court had made its ruling, the judicial system had a precedent-setting reference to the Charter on teachers' union membership. Such precedents generally determined the future course of decisions in the Canadian judicial system. Justice Ewaschuk had ruled that the fledgling human rights legislation did not apply.

The OPSTF investment of time and resources in the fight for amalgamation had been going on for so long that it had become a defining purpose of the organization. When the judicial system closed off the direct route to the Charter, the men immediately sought another channel.

The OPSTF put together a transfer-of-membership form for six FWTAO members who indicated their desire to become members of the men's union.[158] The six women presented the completed forms to the OTF board of governors. As expected, they were all denied. Each of them then appealed to the OTF executive for reconsideration. At the same time, one of them, Linda Logan-Smith, filed a complaint with the Ontario Human Rights Commission. Logan-Smith was the president of the Elementary Teachers' Association—York Region, an amalgamated local with a large membership. Under the added weight of her human rights complaint, OTF governors agreed to grant Logan-Smith the opportunity to appeal her case before them. That decision would be pivotal to the course of events for the FWTAO.

The OSSTF and the OPSTF used the OTF refusal of the six women's requests for a transfer of membership as a springboard to mount a petition-signing campaign with their members. The OSSTF was hoping a win for the OPSTF case would permit them to raid the secondary teachers of the AEFO and the OECTA. The two unions collected thirty thousand signatures on a philosophical statement of human rights requesting that women teachers have a choice of affiliation.[159]

Logan-Smith appeared before the OTF board of governors on 9 April 1988 to request that the denial of her right to become a member of the OPSTF be overturned. But the appeal was never the focus of the exercise. By permitting Logan-Smith to appear before them in person, the OTF governors provided a venue for a dramatic public relations coup by the OPSTF.

The thirty thousand individual petitions were presented to Minister of Citizenship Gerry Phillips and Human Rights Commissioner Raj Anand at the OTF hearing for the Logan-Smith appeal.[160] The presentation was a well-staged press conference complete with a group of two hundred teachers rallying to support Logan-Smith in her efforts to become an OPSTF member.[161] As the OPSTF and OSSTF organizers had hoped, the stacks of signatures captured the minister's attention.

The women's union, the Catholic teachers' union, and the French teachers' union voted against Logan-Smith's appeal.[162] While the appeal lost, the petition campaign was a success. In June 1988, Minister Phillips appointed a single-person Ontario Human Rights Board of Inquiry.[163] Dr. Daniel Baum was selected to hear the cases of Tomen and Logan-Smith. The first day of the hearing was 14 October 1988.[164]

## Reconfiguring the Education Dollar

In the late 1980s in Ontario, cost-cutting, smaller government, and tax reduction became hegemonic. Despite having the benefit of a solid performance from the economy during its time in office, the Peterson government had to respond to voters' anxiety.

The Liberal government required a platform from which to launch a revised vision of education.[165] George Radwanski, an editor with the *Toronto Star*, was appointed to study the dropout rate among high school students.[166] His report, released in 1987, made a number of recommendations. They included destreaming of high school programs, establishing early childhood education, and introducing standardized testing of students.[167] In a partial response to the report, Minister of Education Chris Ward revealed that he was considering some sort of province-wide "minimum standards" for

Grades 3, 6, and 8.[168] The unions pushed back against standardized tests, arguing they would ghettoize schools, as testing was simplistic and culturally biased in its approach.[169] For the moment, the idea was set aside.

Of more immediate concern to the public school unions was the enabling legislation for full funding of the separate schools. Davis's promise had come to fruition. The problem for the Peterson government was how to provide the additional funding for the separate boards without alienating the majority of voters in the province who were public board supporters.

Davis himself provided the solution. Before retiring, he had established the Macdonald Commission to examine education financing. The commission's report came out after the 1985 election with recommendations that included pooling commercial and industrial education taxes and redistributing them among all boards across the province, both separate and public.[170] The Liberals accepted the commission's advice as the means of achieving a politically palatable distribution of education funds. Although the public teachers' unions were able to show that forty-eight public boards would lose revenue as a result of the Macdonald Commission's recommendations, pooling had the appearance of fairness and equalizing payments meant no tax increase.[171] It also had the advantage of pitting the public and the separate teachers' unions against each other, undermining any organized resistance from the OTF table. The Macdonald Commission's proposals allowed Peterson to move forward with the education funding that had been promised to Roman Catholic parents.

While reining in spending and lowering taxes were key planks in the expanding neo-liberal agenda of the late 1980s, they advanced unevenly over the political terrains where they took root. In Ontario, the mood had not been entirely turned against social responsibility. The Peterson government may have been seeking ways to keep education funding in check, but it also made concrete improvements in the provision of early childhood education that provided some relief for working families who were paying thousands of dollars per year in child-care expenses. Nor were Kindergarten and Junior Kindergarten programs supported by the neo-liberal vision of education. Quite the opposite, any expansion of existing Kindergarten classes was an extension of social policy that was not in character with right-wing demands for the relocation of social programs to the private sector. The extension of Kindergarten to include a younger cohort indicated that, while Peterson understood the austerity mood of the times, he was not committed to the politics of retrenchment.

By 1990, all political actors in Ontario had to respond to the political shift to the right, yet neo-liberal forces did not occupy all the ground. Even as the federal government cut taxes and paid for them by reducing transfer payments, some provincial governments continued to address their constituents' demands by reallocating their own resources. Although well established by the end of the 1980s, neo-liberalism was not seamless and had not achieved mastery. The forces of labour and the left still held some sway and were able to bring their constituents out to the polls. As the province headed into the 1990s, the forces of the right were still vulnerable.

## CHAPTER 5

# Social Democracy in a Neo-liberal Era

O n 6 September 1990, Bob Rae became the first NDP premier of Ontario. With Prime Minister Brian Mulroney in his sixth year in Ottawa, the NDP had been able to cobble together a coalition of labour and social activists to capture the imagination of those who opposed the federal turn to neo-liberalism. Rae was given the opportunity to mount a counterattack on the new right. The OPSTF president, Bill Martin, optimistically predicted a shopping list of improvements under the NDP: increased education funding, improved labour laws, state-funded child care, and a resolution of the dispute over control of the teachers' pension.[1] With an NDP government in Queen's Park, the teachers' unions also hoped to resolve pay equity.[2]

Neo-liberalism had advanced during the 1980s.[3] Two reports had been published by the Premier's Council that indicated a more entrepreneurial spirit in the classroom. *Competing in the New Global Economy* was published in 1988 and *People and Skills in the New Global Economy* came out two years later.[4] In 1990 the Conference Board of Canada pushed further into the schools by establishing the National Business and Education Centre, directly linking business interests and education policy.[5] When the NDP came to power, it did not critique the turn to the right that education was taking.

Rather, Ontario's socialist party began to bring education into line with advancing globalism.

Marion Boyd became the first NDP minister of education in Ontario.[6] During her one-year term, she moved on some of the recommendations of the Radwanski Report and continued to develop equity programs for women. A year later, Rae made Boyd minister of community and social services and appointed Tony Silipo minister of education.

Silipo was a lawyer and former chair of the Toronto District School Board.[7] His sights were on reforming the school system in the light of the Radwanski Report. He began by announcing destreaming in the secondary schools.[8] The practice of requiring students to choose academic or applied courses, often with the advisement of guidance counsellors, had come under heavy criticism as limiting the opportunities of students from working-class and visible minority families.[9] Streaming needed to be eliminated, but Silipo's top-down style would be a problem.

The new minister's second initiative was to implement Radwanski's recommendation that, wherever possible, special education students be integrated into regular classrooms. While students who were having difficulty in school did need additional resources, the research had not shown segregation to be an advantage in any but the most extreme circumstances.

In addition to those changes, Silipo began to develop a standard curriculum for the province.[10] It would come with a common set of assessment tools, a project the Liberals had considered when they were in power. Silipo also announced that the NDP would introduce the Junior Kindergarten programs that had been initiated under the Liberals.

A year after taking office, Silipo announced his new design for education. Although similar changes to what he was proposing had been discussed for decades, the education portfolio suffered from ministerial impatience and Silipo's unwillingness to build consensus in a diverse constituency. Teacher resistance to the broad sweep of changes soon became politically unpalatable.[11]

Rae moved Silipo out of education and made Dave Cooke the new minister of education. The third education minister in as many years, Cooke was given the job of slowing things down. In early 1993, he appointed Monique Bégin and Gerald Caplan to form the Royal Commission on Learning and began a full review of the education system, the first since the Hall-Dennis Report had been released in 1968.[12]

It was not only changes in the curriculum that had been creating conflict in the education system. The NDP victory had arrived during a period of particularly rancorous negotiations. In southwest Ontario, Lambton County trustees had entered the 1990 round of negotiations with a new approach, concession bargaining.[13] They used the 1990–91 recession to demand that teachers surrender their retirement gratuity. In addition, they refused to provide teachers with preparation time.[14]

The OSSTF local was also in negotiations. One month after the election, the 450 secondary teachers withdrew their services.[15] Four school days later, the 680 elementary teachers followed. The Lambton County Board of Education had the distinction of being the first Ontario board to have all of their teachers on strike at the same time, besting Ottawa's record. The OSSTF strike lasted ten workdays and resulted in a settlement that left their retirement gratuity intact with no concessions demanded in return. The elementary teachers would have a much harder fight.

The trustees first asked Lambton elementary teachers to agree to limiting payment of the retirement gratuity to those teachers who had reached the age of sixty-five before retiring. In 1971, teachers had negotiated a "90 factor" for retirement, meaning that once their age plus their years of teaching equalled ninety, they could retire with no penalty.[16] Only a few teachers taught to age sixty-five. The teachers refused the offer.

The trustees then proposed to grandfather the retirement gratuity to existing staff if the elementary teachers accepted a minimal pay increase. That would create a rift between senior teachers and any new hires. The teachers again refused.

The trustees' final offer was to leave the gratuity intact if the teachers would take a 0.75 per cent reduction in their salaries.[17] They insisted that the retirement gratuity was a high-cost item for which they needed a concession from the teachers. The teachers were not interested in concessions. Furthermore, the secondary teachers had kept their gratuity and their preparation time.

The preparation time the trustees offered was 110 minutes, less than three 40-minute periods per week. The wage package was also less than that of the secondary teachers. The response was to strike. Lambton elementary teachers were on the picket line from 15 October to 23 November 1990.[18] The strike ended with the Lambton trustees agreeing to meet all of the teachers' demands.[19]

Two weeks before the Lambton County strike began, the FWTAO executive, in a conference call, had increased strike pay to thirty-five dollars per day from day one, and a provision was made to pay child-care expenses for strike-related activities.[20] Strengthening their infrastructure had built member confidence, while the experience of a strike opened discursive space for open resistance. The elementary teachers had come to accept militancy as an instrument of choice in labour relations.

### OPSTF Organizing Drives

Elected with a strong mandate from the unions, the NDP made substantial improvements to labour legislation. New protections for workers included mandatory just cause for dismissal, consolidation of bargaining units, and a ban on replacement workers.[21] In the early days of the NDP government, the OPSTF prepared to take advantage of these more progressive pieces of legislation.

The men's union had advanced its program of expansion in stages. In 1984, it had followed OPSEU and the OSSTF in successfully organizing occasional teachers.[22] By 1990, its strategic campaign to organize other education workers had grown into a larger unionization project. The OPSTF began "expanding non-statutory membership in the Federation to include any person engaged in *any* educational capacity in a school or school board," embracing those who were not affiliated with the OTF.[23] Not all such organizing efforts would prove successful, however; unionizing private school teachers never did gain traction.[24]

The organizing of First Nation schools under the Canadian Labour Relations Board (CLRB) had begun in the fall of 1988.[25] The OPSTF organizer met with teachers at Lakeview School at M'Chigeeng First Nation (West Bay) in preparation for the unionization drive. For models, the OPSTF had agreements with First Nation school boards and the teachers' unions in Manitoba and Quebec.[26]

The OPSTF plan was finalized in December with the understanding that the federal teachers would become a "branch" of an already existing "district" or local.[27] While that would provide nearby resources to the new organizations, it did not acknowledge the unique circumstances under which teachers worked in the federal band schools. Two years later the OPSTF annual general meeting finally approved an independent branch structure for organizing First Nation schools.

The organizing drives for occasional teachers and other support workers in the elementary schools had not been going entirely smoothly. While support personnel in some boards promptly joined the OPSTF, other unions—the OSSTF, the Canadian Union of Public Employees (CUPE), and OPSEU—were all vying for new members from the non-teaching sector within schools.[28] In July 1990, the OPSTF hired Harold Vigoda, a teacher from Toronto, to be the full-time occasional teacher organizer.[29] At the end of the year, the OPSTF won its bid to capture professional support personnel and educational assistants working in the public elementary schools.[30] Vigoda then became involved in organizing efforts on First Nations.

Although the OPSTF had received a request from Asubpeeschoseewagong First Nation (Grassy Narrows) teachers, the test case for First Nation schools had come from southwestern Ontario.[31] The union successfully applied for certification through the CLRB to represent the federally employed teachers at Walpole Island First Nation elementary school, near Windsor.[32] It was granted on 23 November 1990. In April 1991, the *OPSTF News* welcomed the twenty-four new members of Walpole Island Elementary School as part of the "OPSTF family."[33] That would have been the moment to highlight an Indigenous woman activist, but Cathy Hampshire, the new Walpole Island local president, was not mentioned in the newsletter.

Walpole Island's teachers would turn out to represent the beginning of a complicated membership drive that immersed the union in the conflict between the Canadian state, with its long history of colonialism, residential schools, and institutionalized racism, and the Band Councils.[34] Indigenous communities were fighting for control over the education of their children and wanted to remedy what historians Bernard Schissel and Terry Wotherspoon have called the "equity disparity" in Canadian federal education policy. Federal per-pupil funding was well below that received by provincial public schools.[35]

Beyond urbanized Southern Ontario, the OPSTF organizers found the relationship between Band Councils and outside agencies was far more adversarial. Viewed by First Nation leaders as outsiders bringing non-Indigenous labour relations into Indigenous communities, the OPSTF met increasing resistance.

At that time, the union had not publicly acknowledged the legacy of the residential schools. While the B.C. Teachers' Federation had begun that conversation with Indigenous leaders in June 1988 and brought the issue into discussions with the B.C. education community, Ontario teachers' unions lagged.[36] Even an interview with George Erasmus, the National Chief of the Assembly of First Nations, in the April 1991 *OPSTF News*, did not mention the residential school system.[37]

In July 1991, the OPSTF received a letter from a teacher who worked for the M'Chigeeng First Nation band school on Manitoulin Island, requesting that the union organize the teaching staff there.[38] That year, the men's union also received requests from the teachers employed by the Mundo Peetabeck Education Authority in Fort Albany, the Kashechewan First Nation on the Albany River, and the teachers at Sagamok Anishnawbek near Espanola.[39]

As the OPSTF began its campaign for representation, problems arose with the mandate of band Education Authorities.[40] Education had become a shared responsibility between the federal state and the Band Council, with each First Nation having its own Education Authority. A clear delineation of responsibilities and power had not been included in the policy changes when they were written. As a result, the Education Authority was not entirely separate from the Band Council, resulting in some confusion as to who the employer was.[41] As well, some Education Authorities had more than one reserve within their jurisdiction, with multiple chiefs and councils claiming authority. In his report to the provincial executive, Vigoda noted:

> The chief of the [M'Chigeeng First Nation] Indian band does not recognize the authority of the CLRB. The Band believes that they are a First Nation and did not reply to the CLRB hearings with respect to our application. . . . To this date the Chief [of Mundo Peetabeck] has not responded . . . there is "absolute turmoil" with "no light at the end of the tunnel," with respect to the native school in North Shore District [Sagamok Anishnawbek].[42]

Most of the Education Authorities took a similar position, not recognizing the authority of the CLRB.

With the Band Councils refusing to negotiate, the OPSTF reluctantly began to withdraw its applications as the bargaining agent.[43] The organizing campaign collapsed in the fall of 1992, leaving Walpole Island the only First Nation school to have representation from the OPSTF. Further requests from teachers in First Nation schools were addressed with regrets, informing teachers that organizing while their Band Council refused to recognize labour law would be next to impossible. When the time came for the Walpole Island teachers to negotiate a collective agreement, that Band Council adopted the same position as the other First Nations. Unable to get a first contract, the relationship between the OPSTF and Walpole Island teachers was severed.[44]

The failure of the OPSTF to organize the First Nation schools was in part the result of the failure of the Meech Lake and Charlottetown accords. First Nation leaders were insisting on a greater degree of self-government. That is not to say that Band Councils did not harbour the same anti-union sentiments inherent in employee-employer power relations elsewhere. The number of teachers working in the federal system willing to write to, and meet with, representatives of the OPSTF indicated a level of conflict between the Education Authorities and their teachers that was pervasive across the province. That said, the conflict between the Band Councils and the OPSTF suffered from a lack of Indigenous organizers among the union staff. To have any hope of success, the union needed to seek out the support of Indigenous activists who would not be seen as representatives of white-Canadian culture. Without local activists' involvement, the union was without any means of accessing community support.

The OPSTF president, Gene Lewis, in his letter of 27 October 1992 to the principal of St. Ann's School in Fort Albany notifying him of the withdrawal of the application to the CLRB, stated:

> I believe that prior to this decision being made you had a conversation with Executive Assistant, Harold Vigoda. I understand that the two of you concluded that at this point in time the OPSTF application would be viewed as being insensitive to the Indian struggle for autonomy and would be misinterpreted by the community that you and your teachers serve.[45]

The letter, to some degree, admitted the inability of the OPSTF to ally the union with First Nation political and social goals.

Although the attempt to organize teachers in the federal schools on reserves was a failure, the sum total of the OPSTF's organizing efforts had an effect on how members viewed their union. Pursuing the organization of educational assistants, occasional teachers, diagnostic specialists, and teachers working in federal schools on First Nations forced the OPSTF to engage with interests beyond those of the male classroom teacher and the school administrator and to include women's needs in their deliberations.[46]

## Achieving Pay Equity

The NDP was serious about pay equity for women. The process of comparing job classes was supposed to have been completed by the beginning of 1990, but the Wentworth/Perth appeal had held up that process. When the NDP abandoned the appeal, the requirements of the act could be reinstated.

The first pay equity plan was negotiated with the North Shore Board of Education in the fall of 1990.[47] In late February 1991, the FWTAO negotiated a "blueprint equity plan" with the Ontario Public School Boards' Association (OPSBA) covering 3,800 women in forty boards.[48] As predicted, the plan provided "salary increases from $3000 to $13,000 for pre-degree teachers."[49]

The legislation had not addressed all of the inequities that produced the wage gap between women and men. Some women's job classes had no equivalent male job classes. In July 1993, the NDP amended the act to permit a proportional value comparison.[50] Women working in the public sector in female job classes would be compared to male job classes in the same organization.

The proportional value comparison process ensured that pay equity would become entrenched in the education system and be enforced through collective bargaining. The deadlines written into the legislation forced the trustees to participate. In 1992, an additional $190 million was allocated to the Ministry of Education to facilitate pay equity adjustments.[51] Another $118.8 million would be made available in 1993. Both the FWTAO and the OPSTF tracked the number of boards that accessed the funding and applied pressure to those that did not apply for it.[52]

The FWTAO took the lead in developing the comparison system and the strategy that would be used for negotiations.[53] The OPSTF willingly aligned its efforts with the women's union once it became apparent that its members would benefit. In 1992, the men's union completed negotiations with OPSBA on a co-ordinated pay equity plan on behalf of its occasional teachers.[54] By March 1995, thirty-six boards would have signed on to the "OPSBA Plan" and three were pending.[55]

By the beginning of the 1992–93 school year, the FWTAO had all but succeeded in achieving one of its founding objectives, equal pay for equal work; only five of seventy-seven boards of education had not signed.[56] Pay equity legislation had taken seventy-four years of lobbying and organizing to achieve. It required a sympathetic social democratic government intent on reforming labour laws to enshrine pay equity in provincial legislation.

While pay equity was being negotiated, the FWTAO continued its lobbying campaign for affirmative action in promotions. The 1989 amendments to the Education Act, Bill 69, had required boards to hire more women administrators, with the very limited goal of reaching 50 per cent by the year 2000.[57] Yet a year after the legislation was enacted, as many as twenty boards of education had not begun to implement equity policies.[58] Three years after, only 30 per cent of principal and vice-principal positions were held by women. In 1993, the NDP government introduced Bill 79, the Employment Equity Act.[59] Bill 79 would bring affirmative action to an even wider range of Ontario workplaces than the Liberals' plan.

Business interests, in particular, hated affirmative action. They condemned the act at every opportunity. The press mounted a three-pronged attack against the legislation. Commentators accused affirmative action of being reverse discrimination against able-bodied white men, ignoring the reality that able-bodied white men had benefited from preferential treatment in public education since the passage of the Common School Act of 1846. While claiming affirmative action set quotas and punished employers that did not meet them, critics of affirmative action disregarded previous opportunities employers had had to voluntarily integrate women into the workplace. Supporters of the status quo demanded that "merit," not biology, determine hiring and promotions, overlooking the male-based assumptions that formulated the characteristics of merit.[60]

The Employment Equity Act was far-reaching in its effect. By entrenching affirmative action in legislation, it established the discursive terrain for gender equity in the workplace. It defined inclusive language, identified forms of bias, gave a precise meaning of harassment, and recognized the harm of stereotypical portrayals. The act brought the language of the Ontario Human Rights Code onto the shop floor, the office, the hospital ward, and the classroom in a rigorous fashion that addressed human rights from a woman-centred standpoint.[61]

The FWTAO was one of a number of unions that educated its members by publishing booklets, providing workshops, and training its members to understand the issues of bias and discrimination.[62] It expanded its own programs and materials by including the Ministry of Citizenship's Commissioner of Employment Equity displays and videos in its workshops.[63]

The women's union had the experience to sidestep some of the traps of affirmative action. Protecting the jobs of women with less seniority was one of those. The staff were given training in the "seniority principle debate." The booklet cautioned:

> Employer groups have identified seniority as a potential major barrier to employment equity. . . . Employer groups generally call for an endorsement of the merit principle in the preamble to the Bill and in appropriate sections.

It went on:

> On the other hand, unions strongly defend the seniority principle. For example, one union identifies the issue as not who is the most qualified. Rather, it is whether the person with the seniority has the ability and skill, with training and accommodation if necessary, to perform the required job.[64]

By 1995, other unions associated with the education sector were backing the efforts of the FWTAO to advance affirmative action, but like the teachers, they stopped short of militancy.[65] On the eve of the proclamation of Bill 79, women teachers joined the other members of the Women's Coalition for Employment Equity on the front steps of Queen's Park.[66] To the degree that unionized women achieved access to affirmative action programs, the decades-long campaign was successful.

The OSSTF's adoption of affirmative action provides an interesting comparison to the FWTAO's stand. In 1992, almost 60 per cent of its members were male and the OSSTF was actively advocating for affirmative action.[67] Under president Margaret Wilson, the women of the OSSTF had finally been able to convince their male peers to move forward on gender equity.[68] However, the women of the OSSTF were not able to convince a majority of their male peers to throw their weight behind demands for more women in positions of authority until the legislation demanding that promotion policies be changed was on the horizon. The FWTAO, on the other hand, had taken an equity position on promotions at its inaugural meeting in 1918. The late response of the OSSTF to affirmative action offers support for the FWTAO's assertion that a women's union was the best means to achieve improvements in women's lives.

In 1995, Mike Harris's newly elected Conservative government repealed the Employment Equity Act and the memoranda attached to it. The minister of education, John Snobelen, a man who mistook ministerial brinkmanship for a theory of leadership, dismantled the affirmative action programs. The FWTAO rushed to train its chief negotiators and employment equity contacts to embed equity language in their collective agreements.[69] Having initially achieved workplace equity entitlements through legislation, women teachers then enshrined it through their labour practices.

## Teacher Control of Pensions

With the 1990 election of the NDP government, the talks to make changes to the teachers' pension plan, which had been shelved by the Liberals, were reopened. The buy-back problem for teachers who had been involved in legal strikes was easily resolved. In June 1991, the government confirmed that workers were entitled to take part in a strike without risking their pensions.[70]

Control of the pension plan by the unions was a more difficult problem to solve. Employee-managed pension funds were not the norm.[71] Unlike Quebec, Ontario had not constructed one large pension plan for public service workers; it had smaller, individual plans attached to each group.[72] The teachers' pension was invested entirely in Government of Ontario debentures, which provided a very limited return. Teachers had become impatient when successive governments had used the accumulated capital in the pension fund for various initiatives, but then did not improve the plan.

Negotiations with the NDP for a revised pension plan began in the spring of 1991 and were completed by August of that year.[73] The new agreement for the composition of the renamed Ontario Teachers' Pension Plan Board included four government representatives and four OTF representatives, with a ninth person appointed as a neutral chair by agreement of the members of the board, a distinction that required the unions to endorse the choice.[74] The teachers had finally gained control over their pensions. In the future, their own management of their pension funds would tie teachers' retirement fortunes to the marketplace and would see their pension plan become one of the largest investors in North America.

As neo-liberalism's grip deepened over the next decade, the new premier's decision would prove to be critical to teachers' ability to protect their pensions in a time when workers in the private sector were losing theirs. Importantly, gaining control of their pension plan would prevent it from becoming a bargaining chip in the battles with Premier Harris after his election in 1995.[75]

## CHAPTER 6
# The Social Contract

Almost immediately after being elected, the NDP government was faced with the beginnings of the 1990 recession.[1] Although the economic downturn did not run as deep as others had, it lasted significantly longer than most.[2] In that moment, the representatives of social democracy squandered the opportunity to break from the policy direction that Ontario had been pursuing for the previous fifteen years.[3]

With the economy not recovering as hoped and Ontario's credit rating under siege, the NDP government announced transfer payment increases to boards of education on 21 January 1992. They were 1 per cent, 2 per cent, and 2 per cent over the next three years, well below the rate of inflation.[4] The OPSTF briefing notes in preparation for a meeting with the minister of education warned, "This is playing havoc with negotiations and negatively affecting teacher morale."[5]

As 1992 wore on, the economy did not show signs of recovering. Rae became focused on alleviating the deficit.[6] He seemed to believe that his labour credentials would hold him in good stead as he worked out the details of what he called a "social contract."

The Social Contract was framed as achieving labour peace while reducing expenditures in the public service. It ignored the destructiveness of this solution.[7] In attempting to build support for his Social Contract, Rae blunted union militancy, undermined the labour movement, and demoralized its activists. It was not a "social contract"; rather, workers were being asked to pay what amounted to a wage tax, so that the private sector would not see their taxes rise.[8]

The Social Contract demanded $2 billion in cuts to the public purse.[9] The education sector had to reduce its spending by $520 million. The teachers were forced to take twelve unpaid leave days, amounting to a 6 per cent pay cut. Negotiated salary increases were deferred for three years. The minister of education announced that the mandatory implementation of Junior Kindergarten was delayed.[10]

Twelve private sector unions argued for supporting the NDP in recognition of the thousands of jobs that Rae had saved at Algoma Steel and de Havilland Aircraft.[11] They pointed out that Rae had enacted anti-scab legislation, made it easier to form unions, funded thousands of child-care spaces across the province, and moved forward on pay equity. The public sector unions argued that the cuts to their wages were going to pay for those programs.

On 14 June 1993, Rae tabled Bill 48, the Social Contract Act. Passed by the NDP majority with barely a handful of dissenting social democratic votes, the act forced the entire public sector to accept pay cuts in the form of layoff days.[12] It also restricted collective bargaining. Despite the historical bond between labour and the NDP, Rae had abandoned his constituency.

## The East Parry Sound Strike

Seven months before the Social Contract came into force, the ERC fact finder, E.S. Lavender, had issued his report on the East Parry Sound County negotiations. Although he'd lectured both sides for failing to come to an early resolution, his recommendations had come down on the board's side:

> The years of incremental improvements to all three areas
> of wages, fringe benefits and working conditions are over.
> Teachers in East Parry Sound are urged to lift their heads
> above their local situation and recognize the realities in the
> Province.[13]

The report had given the East Parry Sound County trustees the backing they needed to seize the teachers' retirement gratuity.

The other issue in East Parry Sound had been staffing allocations. The trustees had attempted to remove any language that restricted their ability to determine the number of teachers on their payroll. When the FWTAO and the OPSTF went looking for comparisons in other locals, they discovered that staffing provisions were absent in all but a few collective agreements.[14] Negotiations went nowhere over the winter. Then in June, the Social Contract arrived. Job protection would become critical as the unions struggled with its impact.[15]

Each board of education was given a dollar figure that was their "Expenditure Reduction Target." The teachers' pension board made a donation of $325 million from the surplus in the pension fund to lower those targets, but teachers would still lose some working days.[16] The trustees and the unions were legislated to enter into collective bargaining to negotiate how they would achieve the Expenditure Reduction Target. The East Parry Sound County board would become the test case.

The East Parry Sound teachers had been divided on becoming the front line for establishing staffing clauses for the rest of the province. As the negotiating team prepared to put the board's final offer to a ratification vote, the provincial and local negotiators were unable to reach a consensus. In the confusion, the teachers rejected the offer by an extremely narrow margin.

Paula Knopf, chair of the ERC inquiry called after the dispute was settled, reported:

> No one on the Teachers' committee spoke against the tentative agreement, but the chief negotiators chose not to speak in its favour. They chose not to speak at all. Only the Branch Affiliate Presidents spoke in favour of acceptance. . . . We also note that Gene Lewis, President of OPSTF, addressed the teachers and recommended against acceptance. . . . The motion to accept was lost by only seven votes.[17]

Despite the slim margin, the negotiating team made the decision to go ahead with a strike. With eight other boards preparing to follow the East Parry Sound County example, the unions were desperate.[18] Fifty per cent plus seven was an extremely weak position from which to launch a strike, but regardless, the board's offer had been rejected. With uncharacteristic boldness, the teachers walked out on 6 October 1993.

The trustees prepared to invoke the "60 day provision."[19] The clause, titled "Working Conditions may not be altered," read:

> 10(3) Where notice has been given of desire to negotiate to make or renew an agreement, the terms and conditions of the agreement . . . shall not be altered until either, (a) an agreement or a new agreement comes into force or the agreement is renewed, as the case may be; or (b) . . . sixty days have elapsed after the Commission has made public the report of the fact finder . . . whichever first occurs.[20]

A year after the fact finder's report was made public, the trustees presented a revised collective agreement to the teachers that stripped monetary clauses and seized the teachers' retirement gratuity.[21]

Up until the East Parry Sound negotiations, the 60-day provision had received little attention. The background to its inclusion in Bill 100 is instructive. It is an example of how the state and employers arrange conditions against workers. In late 1974, after two and a half years of talks, Minister of Education Wells had given the final version of Bill 100 to the teachers' unions to review before it went before the legislature. The language on working conditions stopped at 10(3)(a) above.[22] However, the trustees had been pressuring the minister for a "management rights" clause.[23] After the teachers had approved the final draft, Wells inserted 10(3)(b), the 60-day provision. Because the clause received no debate, the teachers missed the change in the final reading of the bill. In the middle of the East Parry Sound labour dispute, Wells was quoted as saying that the clause had been included "'as a very, very last resort,' . . . no one thought then about it being used for cutbacks."[24] His recollection of events was disingenuous at best. Wells's reprisal for the province-wide strike of 18 December was neglecting to inform the teachers of that small change in Bill 100.

During the first week of the strike, the board hired "lay assistants" as replacement workers to keep the schools open. Replacement workers had not been used since the Lakefield strike in 1963. When the unions objected to the lay assistants, they were informed that the NDP's recent amendments to the Labour Relations Act banning the use of replacement workers did not apply to Bill 100.

Knopf summed up the consequences in her report:

> The placement of the ad [for lay assistants] in the newspaper on the first day of the strike effectively sent a message that the Board was preparing itself for a long strike, not for a speedy negotiated resolution.[25]

The unions addressed the issue of replacement workers with a letter to the premier and copied it to the opposition parties.

> The East Parry Sound Board has hired replacement workers to go into the schools, across the picket lines of elementary public

school teachers on legal strike. . . . We think it is outrageous that a public employer has taken such action, and we trust you will immediately act to prohibit the East Parry Sound Board of Education from employing strike breakers.[26]

Despite this lacuna in his replacement-worker legislation, Rae did not insert himself into the dispute.

The mood of the strike turned more hostile as it dragged on.[27] The trustees agreed to an open debate at Burk's Falls, but, four days before it was scheduled, announced they would not be attending.[28] After that they withdrew completely from public view and refused to meet with the teachers until their terms were met.

The strike had been underway for a month when the trustees furthered their fortress image by hiring security guards to protect the board of education offices. The picketing teachers at the board office had been following standard strike protocol by holding those who wanted to enter the building at the picket line for two minutes and then letting them through. They had been doing this for weeks without incident. When the security guards arrived, they immediately began to clear the way into the board offices by pushing aside the picketers. A conflict erupted between the guards and the teachers. A witness to the encounter, John Stopper, recounted the dispute in a letter to Norm Mason, Director of Education:

Mr. Smith . . . asked the guard, "Can you push people and not be charged with assault?" The guard's response was, "Yes." Mr. Smith then questioned him further, "What would happen if I touch you?" His response was "I'll lay you out on the fucking sidewalk."[29]

On 10 November 1993, the East Parry Sound County secondary teachers went on strike.[30] By this time, the elementary teachers had been out for twenty-five teaching days.

While the unions were focused on East Parry Sound, labour battles deriving from the Social Contract spread to other boards. On 8 November 1993, the Windsor elementary teachers went on strike. The FWTAO and the OPSTF again raised their strike pay to thirty-five dollars per day.[31]

With tensions mounting in East Parry Sound, the two local presidents requested arbitration.[32] The Rae government named two arbitrators to settle the strike, but both sides had to agree to arbitration. The trustees remained intractable.

The trustees then asked the teachers to join them in requesting a jeopardy hearing from the ERC.[33] If the two sides went together, so went their logic, they could pressure the ERC to ask for back-to-work legislation. When the trustees would not agree to settle any of the major issues beforehand, the unions refused to go to the hearing.[34]

The trustees eventually found an ally in the Conservative party.[35] At a public meeting organized and chaired by Ernie Eves, member of provincial parliament for Parry Sound, the trustees proposed to pay teachers their salaries if they returned to work and downgraded their strike to a board-directed work-to-rule. The trustees presented a list of duties that teachers would resume. It was a cataloguing of their normal workday. The teachers refused the offer.

On 17 November the East Parry Sound County strike had become the longest elementary teacher strike in the history of the province.[36] For Rae, the strike was a test case for his Social Contract. His government had instructed trustees to work out the details of cost-cutting with their teachers, and that was what they were doing.

The ERC finally did act. It presented Minister of Education Cooke with a jeopardy advisement, acknowledging that students were at risk of losing their year.[37] With that, the minister legislated the teachers back to work on 29 November 1993. The strike had lasted thirty-eight days. Cooke appointed an arbitration board to decide the terms of the collective agreement.

On 2 March 1994, the arbitration board approved the old collective agreement.[38] The teachers had preserved their retirement gratuity and the other benefits the trustees had tried to claw back, but the arbitrators did not address staffing, the issue that had been at the heart of the strike.

Knopf's report to the ERC was released in July 1994. She estimated that the board had saved $1.8 million by not having to pay staff during the strike.[39] She ruled that in future the board would be required to open its financial records to the union during collective bargaining. Allowing both sides to see where education funding was being spent would raise the level of trust at the negotiating table and enforce the trustees' accountability. That ruling would become common practice for negotiations throughout the province.

## The Windsor Strike

The Social Contract intensified conflicts that arose during contract negotiations. Windsor experienced a strike that almost did not happen, indeed, did not have to happen. The ERC fact finder's report had been released on 9 July 1993 and negotiations had continued over the summer.[40] The teachers grudgingly agreed to the conditions of the Social Contract, a 5 per cent reduction in salary taken as unpaid days, and a 4.75 per cent reduction in the number of teachers employed by the board, the equivalent of 33.5 teaching positions. Implementation was left to be decided in the new school year. By all indications, negotiations were over and a settlement had been reached.

Despite the concessions offered by the teachers, the trustees refused to ratify the new agreement. They waited until sixty days after the fact finder's report was released and invoked the 60-day clause in mid-October.[41] They announced that they would be reducing salaries by 2.5 per cent, retroactive to January. Another 2.5 per cent reduction would come into effect after the Christmas holiday. The salary cuts required the average teacher to immediately repay $1,520 of past wages and to expect a second reduction of $1,500 over 1994.[42]

Furthermore, no new teachers would be hired to replace those who were retiring or who had resigned, and forty-two teachers would be laid off. The remaining teachers would have to absorb the surplus students into their classes. Preparation time was reduced, and further restrictions were placed on the use of supply teachers for absences. The trustees appeared to be goading the teachers into a strike they had wanted to avoid.

The teachers prepared for a strike vote, but just before it took place, the chair of the board, Jane Sparrow, released a statement to the media. She attacked the unions for using Windsor's "schools and students in another local battle in their provincial war to exempt teachers from the financial realities of the 1990's."[43] She accused the teachers of seeking immunity from the effects of the "harsh economic climate." Then the board hired occasional teachers and security guards.[44]

The unions reported that the board was spending $9,600 per day on occasional teachers and another $2,400 per day on private security, while rolling back teachers' wages.[45] When Cooke was made aware of the situation, he sent a letter to every board of education stating that the Ministry of Education would not cost-share the salaries of the replacement workers while teachers were on strike.[46] The minister of labour, Bob Mackenzie, also promised to change the legislation restricting the use of strikebreakers to apply to the education sector.

Like the East Parry Sound County board, the Windsor trustees were using the Social Contract, paired with the 60-day clause, to circumvent the bargaining process. However, Windsor was not a rural board; it represented an industrial city where many families had a history of union membership. They understood the teachers' fight.[47] Some of the most vocal parents took their support for the teachers to the first board meeting held after the strike started and shouted down the trustees' explanations for prolonging the strike.[48]

After nearly three weeks on the picket lines, fifty teachers then made the short drive to Essex, where Rae was holding meetings.[49] The two local presidents were granted a brief face-to-face with the premier during the lunch break. They brought the additional demands that the trustees were making beyond the Social Contract to his attention.[50] They also complained about the use of replacement workers. Rae promised to look into the two issues. The meeting was a coup for the teachers.

By the Christmas break, the talks between the trustees and the teachers had completely broken down. Windsor's trustees would not agree to arbitration. The two provincial presidents, the FWTAO's Barbara Sargent and the OPSTF's Gene Lewis, sent a letter to teachers across the province asking them to make a twenty-dollar donation to alleviate some of the hardship being experienced by the teachers in East Parry Sound and Windsor during the Christmas holidays.[51]

With no resolution in sight for January, Cooke made an effort to end the strike through mediation.[52] The unions agreed to his conditions.[53] Their six-week strike ended in time for the new year.[54] The final agreement was accepted late in June by 57 per cent of the teachers and 54 per cent of the trustees. It was a very weak approval rating from both sides, an indication of smouldering animosities.[55] The teachers kept their old collective agreement and the wage scale that went with it, but like the East Parry Sound County teachers, they were unable to establish staffing provisions.

The two strikes persuaded trustees in other boards to abandon plans to downgrade teachers' collective agreements. The teachers had pushed concession bargaining off the table.

Cooke would not agree to remove the 60-day provision in Bill 100, despite pleas from the unions.[56] However, by the end of 1994, boards had exhausted what use they could make of it and the 60-day provision would disappear as a collective bargaining tactic.

Ontario's first NDP government would become a case study in the contradictions of governing as a reformist, social democratic party in the era of neo-liberal capitalism. The teachers had expected Rae to involve them in the development of teacher-friendly policies; instead, the NDP made deep changes to the education system that soon alienated teachers and dissolved their support for the party.[57] Former OPSMTF president Ron Poste's newsletter summed up teachers' disappointment with "How Do You Like Socialism—So Far?"[58] The NDP had not offered the alternative it had promised.

## The Baum Decision

As minister of citizenship in the Peterson cabinet, Gerry Phillips had made a good political choice in appointing Daniel Baum to settle a disagreement between two unions regarding a question of human rights. Baum was a professor in the Osgoode Hall Law Faculty, a labour arbitrator and a human rights adjudicator.[59]

As in past instances in this fight, the FWTAO was not named to the case. The inquiry was asked to examine the actions of the OPSTF and the OTF, not those of the FWTAO. The FWTAO attempted to stay the proceedings in the Divisional Court.[60] However, the Human Rights Commission was not the court system; it was a new entity with an untried judicial role. This time the Divisional Court ruled against the FWTAO and decided that the Human Rights Commission did indeed have the authority to investigate Tomen's case, allowing her to leave the FWTAO and become a member of the OPSTF.[61] The OPSTF's staging of the petition presentation alongside Logan-Smith's appeal to the OTF had worked.

The final battle over a women-only union would involve all five affiliates of the OTF. The FWTAO was limited to intervenor status in the proceedings, along with the three other OTF affiliates. The OSSTF was granted intervenor status in support of its efforts to bring all secondary teachers under its flag. The OECTA and the AEFO were granted intervenor status to defend their membership rolls against the OSSTF. Along with its five affiliates, the OTF itself appeared before the Board of Inquiry. In an effort to appear more inviting than rapacious, the OPSTF suspended other elements of its amalgamation campaign until Baum rendered a judgment.

Although the FWTAO was appealing the Ontario Court ruling to the Supreme Court of Canada, the Board of Inquiry under the Ontario Human Rights Code (Baum Inquiry) proceeded. The Supreme Court's decision denying the FWTAO leave to appeal arrived on 27 June 1991.[62] By then, the Baum Inquiry was in its ninetieth day of hearings.

On 31 March 1994, nearly six years after he was appointed, Baum delivered the long-awaited decision.[63] He ruled in favour of Tomen and Logan-Smith. The nine-year battle was coming to a close for these two women. The eighty-year battle between the two elementary teachers' unions was about to be concluded.

Judy Darcy, the president of CUPE, declared, "The simplistic view of equality which apparently underlies this decision has no place in Ontario in 1994."[64] Activist and author Judy Rebick was even more pointed: "Dr. Daniel Baum's decision is a serious setback for the women's movement. The right of women to organize to promote equality has long been recognized in human rights decisions."[65] The FWTAO appealed the ruling under Section 13 of the Charter, claiming that the FWTAO was "a special program designed to relieve hardship or economic disadvantage."[66]

Ultimately, only the FWTAO would pay the price of losing members. Baum did not grant the OSSTF access to the secondary teachers of OECTA or the AEFO. The elementary teachers were the only unions divided by sex, a prohibited ground addressed in his decision.

Karen Schucher, one of the lawyers who worked on the FWTAO case, makes a compelling argument that the Baum decision was seriously flawed.[67] She suggests that Baum failed to comprehend the balance in the Charter between individual rights and group protections. Schucher is critical of Baum's refusal to credit the expertise of feminist witnesses. She quotes Justice Rosalie Abella, then a member of the Ontario Court of Appeal, whose dissenting view stated that Baum did not properly consider the evidentiary record presented by the FWTAO and the expert witnesses it called. Abella wrote:

> There was overwhelming evidence to explain the historic need for a separate affiliate for women elementary school teachers; evidence of the crucial role it played in ameliorating disadvantages experienced by women teachers in the workforce; and evidence that compulsory membership—and dues—are both an integral part of the labour relations matrix. . . . This evidence, with respect, was not properly considered.[68]

With little understanding of a feminist perspective, Baum had dismissed each of the FWTAO witnesses. About Linda Briskin, professor of social and political thought at York University, he said, "Even if I should accept the conclusions reached by Professor Briskin, I would have difficulty applying them to elementary schools."[69] He underscored the compulsory nature of individual membership in the FWTAO and repeatedly returned to freedom of choice.[70] He refused to acknowledge the validity of evidence that analyzed the lived experience of women through concrete examples and he openly questioned the research abilities of many of the witnesses. One was the Australian feminist researcher, Dale Spender. "I have difficulty giving any considerable weight to Dr. Spender's testimony for a number of reasons," he wrote.[71]

Baum went so far as to question the academic integrity of Dorothy E. Smith, chair of the Department of Sociology at OISE: "The statistics that Dr. Smith has used to support the conclusions reached concerning the comparison between FWTAO and OSSTF are questionable."[72] Baum's disregard for particular forms of academic research demonstrated the problems the judicial system has often had in addressing key aspects of women's experience.

The FWTAO immediately appealed.[73] That ruling was released in June 1995. It also went against the women's union. Almost eighty years of women's unionism in Ontario's education system was brought to an end by human rights legislation intended to advance women's equality. It was a bitter pill for the members of the FWTAO to swallow. It was made more difficult by the knowledge that the victory Justice Ewaschuk had handed them had been thrown away. The gesture of giving Linda Logan-Smith a second hearing at the OTF table had been turned against them. Bitter indeed in the hearts of the FWTAO women who believed in the importance of a women-only union.[74]

Although the FWTAO and the OPSTF had always fought alongside each other in their labour relations with their mutual employer, that alliance had never been enough to unite them under one flag. The men were never able to adopt a position that was attractive to any but a minority of the members of the FWTAO, while the majority of women teachers had remained loyal to their unique union. In the end, the women elementary teachers decided for amalgamation, although it was a choice that most felt was forced upon them.

## CHAPTER 7

# Mike Harris and the "Common Sense" Counterrevolution

The new-right reform of education relied on the construction of a valorized, seamless, and fixed "taxpayer" as a universal referent. This remaking of citizens into taxpayers permitted neo-liberal apologists to claim that the most pressing issue in education was maximum return on the investment of public dollars.[1] Accountability and transparency called for institutionalizing management strategies that would scrutinize the economy of education. The more indeterminate advantages of education—providing children with the capacity to participate as citizens, offering an understanding of the world that reached beyond their neighbourhoods, and developing in students a critical sensibility that offered them opportunities to transform both themselves and their world—were being shelved.

A distinctly neo-liberal vision of education was advanced with the release, in January 1995, of the report of the NDP's Royal Commission on Learning, entitled *For the Love of Learning*. Among its 167 recommendations was "the formation of an Ontario College of Teachers, as a professional self-governing body responsible for setting professional teaching standards . . . governing renewal of teacher certification every five years."[2] It also proposed time limits on principals' appointments, additional oversight powers for boards of education, and the dismissal of teachers who did not master computer technology.[3] Teachers were shocked.

Upsetting teachers even more, the NDP's Common Curriculum was finally released in February.[4] It required an extensive rethinking of pedagogy and promised a new design for report cards.[5] Changing teachers' working conditions at any time was guaranteed to create dissatisfaction, and these revisions were far-reaching.[6] The FWTAO's Joan Westcott commented, "The future picture of education in this province has been on a rollercoaster. We haven't been able to clarify the comments made by the Minister on one initiative before he announced the next one."[7] What remained of support for the NDP among teachers evaporated.[8]

With NDP education policy reshaping the face of education, elementary teachers sat on their hands during the election that put Harris in power. Harris pledged a 20 per cent reduction in the education budget.[9] This was comparable to a promised $500 million cut to welfare benefits. Still, the two elementary teachers' unions refused to become politically engaged during the election. The OPSTF reissued its Directive P. It read: "Federation shall be non-partisan and without affiliation with any political party . . ."[10] While it purported a neutral professionalism, Directive P killed teacher support for the NDP among OPSTF members.

The election of the Mike Harris Conservative government on 26 June 1995 would be the apogee of neo-liberalism in Ontario in the twentieth century. Little would be left untouched by the Conservatives' election platform, the "Common Sense Revolution." About education it falsely stated, "Ontario spends $14 billion a year on primary and secondary education—more per-pupil than any other province—and still gets a failing grade."[11] In fact, Ontario was fifth in per-pupil expenditure, 2.4 per cent above the Canadian average.[12] Harris vowed to reform the education system "based on the principles of providing excellence . . . accountability to parents and . . . reduc[ing] the burden on taxpayers."

Education would come under fire, not solely for its cost, but also because it occupied a contradictory position in the neo-liberal state. While business interests decried the form it had taken under the welfare state, education remained the foremost disciplining mechanism for training workers and for developing a citizenry that would embrace the vision of the new right.

With neo-liberalism ascending, a transformation was needed in how teachers encouraged students to think about the entitlements of citizenship. Although the "gig economy" would not emerge for another decade, by 1995, the employment landscape had become polarized between "good jobs," those with decent wages and benefits in unionized workplaces, and "bad jobs," those with low pay, few (if any) benefits, and no union protections. The ability of citizens to claim state supports was being reduced, with a commensurate increase in social precarity.[13] Harris's reforms lent credibility to the often-criticized theory by economists Samuel Bowles and Herbert Gintis of a "correspondence principle," that public education demonstrates a correspondence between the structures of the workplace and the structures of the school.[14] Seizing control of education and disciplining teachers to accept a more market-centric system were essential elements in advancing neo-liberalism.

When Rae required all boards of education in the province to negotiate the conditions of the Social Contract simultaneously, the teachers' unions had expanded their internal structures, increased provincial staff, and improved communications with their locals and with other unions. Rob Fairley, the former president of the Toronto Hydro workers, was brought in to speak to the teachers' negotiation teams. His was a language that the teachers had not heard before:

> Don't wait until the heavy artillery hits you—get ready now. . . .
> Trade unionists are ill prepared to deal with the attack because
> our analysis became vague, and our organizations were shaped

during a period of relative labour peace. The consciousness of our membership has been shaped during the same period. . . . It is urgent that we get our bearings, figure out how to get grounded again, and *source* some power.[15]

Fairley's comments reflected the unvarnished truth of a labour movement on the defensive.

Harris came to power as the right seized the political discourse. Corporate and political elites had developed and funded organizations whose sole purpose was to develop populist, neo-liberal rhetoric as support for right-wing parties.[16] Using dubious research methods, the ultra-conservative Canadian Taxpayers Federation and the Fraser Institute focused on undermining workers' protections and denigrating social supports.[17] The Ontario wing of the Taxpayers Federation openly attacked teachers and their unions, distorted facts, and played on popular misconceptions of teachers' work.[18]

By late 1995, Harris had drastically cut funding for education and slashed the social programs that many of the families of school-aged children depended on. This would not be a labour battle; fighting the Harris Conservatives would require a political battle. And a one-day walkout, such as teachers had undertaken in 1973, would not be sufficient.

## Restructuring, Retrenchment, and Standardized Testing

Harris moved his agenda forward early in his mandate. He promised to increase teaching time, reduce preparation time, and raise the pupil/teacher ratio.[19] He would replace teachers in non-teaching roles with lower-paid workers and cut in half the number of sick days that were available to teachers.[20] Furthermore, Ontario's unique Grade 13, having been established in 1921 as preparation for university, would be eliminated.[21]

While much has been written about the conflicts between the teachers and the Harris government, the momentum for state-union antagonism in the educational sector had been building for some time. A year before Harris was elected, the Ontario Public School Boards' Association, the Ontario Separate School Trustees' Association, the Association française des conseils scolaires de l'Ontario, and the Association franco-ontarienne des conseils d'écoles catholiques had convinced the Ministry of Education to fund a study in support of retrenchment, or the notion of reducing expenses in any way possible. The authors developed a working paper entitled "Restructuring: New Realities, New Beginnings."[22] The document declared retrenchment to be a "hallmark of modern life" despite a lack of evidence that such cost-cutting measures could produce the promised results. The ground had been prepared even before Harris arrived.

The apparatuses for the neo-liberal reforms Harris promised had taken time to develop. One of the most important of these was the design of measurement tools for processes that previously had been considered non-quantifiable. Standardized tests that could be centrally administered and scored were widely used in the United States. They were a cornerstone of education policy in the Common Sense Revolution: "With a core curriculum set province-wide, and standardized testing at all levels, we know we can spend more efficiently, while improving the quality of education we offer to students."[23]

Critics of the U.S. testing regimes pointed out that most of the results could be predicted by simply considering income levels in the catchment area of the school being tested.[24] Schools in areas where parents were in the upper income brackets consistently scored higher than schools where parents had lower incomes. Often called "high-stakes," the tests narrowed the education project to efforts to score well. Standardized testing gave the state the power to control the education agenda from the micro to the macro. In almost all locations where this type of testing was introduced, funding levels were tied in some fashion to test scores. In some American jurisdictions, higher-scoring schools received more funding. In other districts, lower-scoring schools received additional funding for dictated remedies. Publishing test results and attaching funding to scores were the social shaming and economic carrots and sticks that gave the tests their teeth. Standardized testing became the discipline mechanism used by the neo-liberal state to enforce the restructuring of education.

In Ontario, all three political parties had been involved in the development of the testing regime. Province-wide testing had first been suggested by the Liberals when they were in opposition. The NDP legislated the tests into the education system when they came to power. Finally, the Harris Conservatives became the first government to administer the tests in the schools, making standardized, province-wide testing the practice in Ontario. The Harris government then created the Education Quality and Accountability Office (EQAO) and charged it with managing the testing regime and publishing the results.[25]

The OTF did not mount any militant opposition to the testing regime when it was put in place. Neither did the elementary teachers' unions, whose members would be most affected by EQAO testing. In the fall of 1996, the five OTF affiliates announced that a Federation Co-operative consisting of the FWTAO, OECTA, OPSTF, and OSSTF had been awarded the contract for training their members to mark the tests.[26] Despite the complaints of frontline teachers, the unions capitulated to the Conservative government and encouraged their members to participate. The teachers did not apprehend how the testing regime would reconfigure the classroom.

## The Legislative Juggernaut

While the state carried the mantle of elected authority, teachers maintained their credibility with the parents of their students. The wedge that the Harris government tried to drive between parents and teachers would be played out on the streets with picket lines and marches, press releases and legislation, but the demonizing of teachers did not penetrate into local classrooms.[27]

It did not take long for the legislative juggernaut to drop. In the fall of 1995, the Conservatives moved to repeal the NDP's legislation on labour protections, employment equity, and those laws that supported affirmative action policies.[28] Bill 7, An Act to Restore Balance and Stability to Labour Relations and to Promote Economic Prosperity, undermined workers' rights and weakened their organizations.[29] Among other things, the bill reduced the ability of workers to form unions, made it more difficult to achieve a first contract, and permitted the use of replacement workers during strikes.

Bill 8, An Act to Repeal Job Quotas and to Restore Merit-Based Employment Practices in Ontario, repealed the NDP's Employment Equity Act.[30] It removed equity provisions from the Human Rights Code, the Police Services Act, and the Education Act. It denied women any legal recourse for equity issues in their workplaces.[31] The funding that had been dedicated to equalizing women's pay scales went to pay for tax cuts.[32]

Gender equity in education took on a new urgency. The FWTAO Employment Equity Committee reported to the annual general meeting, "FWTAO was aware of this plan and altered the employment equity workshop plans for the year dramatically."[33] The employment equity contacts for the locals were to be included in the provincial collective bargaining training sessions. Employment equity became a bargaining priority.

The FWTAO sent letters of protest to the minister of citizenship, culture, and recreation and to the minister of education. The locals were instructed to organize a "Flood the Fax" day. They reported six thousand faxes sent to the ministers' offices. The FWTAO managed to get on the agenda of the Standing Committee on Bill 8 to present its objections.

With half of its membership now women, the OPSTF aligned with the FWTAO. It agreed to contribute one dollar per member to the OTF and went into partnership with the OSSTF for a media campaign called "Cuts to Public Education Hurt."[34] When Harris slashed social assistance by 21.6 per cent, the FWTAO gained intervenor standing in the court battle opposing the cuts.[35] The government's plan to reduce funding for the Junior Kindergarten programs mostly affected FWTAO members. With very few exceptions, Kindergarten teachers were women.[36] In November, the FWTAO sent a letter to the NDP caucus enlisting their support in saving the Junior Kindergarten program, with a reminder that although the new premier had promised not to touch classroom funding, that promise was quickly forgotten once he was elected.[37]

A week later, Ernie Eves, minister of finance, announced that transfer payments to the boards of education would be cut by $400 million, about 9 per cent. When added to the other cuts in the new school year, the total amounted to nearly $800 million.[38] At the same time, Minister of Education Snobelen issued a memorandum declaring the amalgamation of school boards and major cuts to Junior Kindergarten. He confirmed that EQAO testing was being implemented and the College of Teachers was being established. The memorandum also required arbitrators in the education sector to consider the province's ability to pay. The teachers' unions needed to find allies.

Bill 7 had caught the Ontario Federation of Labour's attention, but the federation's leadership, the presidents of affiliated private and public sector unions, were cautious about mass action in the aftermath of the strong mandate Harris had won. It was not until their own rank and file began to call for mobilization that the labour leaders began to develop the Days of Action, a campaign of city-by-city general strikes.[39] The first was planned for London on 11 December 1995. A second was tentatively planned for Hamilton sometime in February 1996, but only if the London action was successful.

The Days of Action provided a forum for teachers to overcome their aversion to large-scale mobilizations.[40] Although the teachers' unions were not involved in organizing the London Days of Action, many teachers did march there with the other unions.[41]

In the December 1995 issue of the *OPSTF News*, chief executive officer Dave Lennox called for solidarity at the local level:

> The new government has instituted a "slash and burn" regime . . .
> I believe it will be a critical time to show our solidarity. This may
> occur at the provincial level, but more likely, it will occur within
> each school board.[42]

The FWTAO president, Sheryl Hoshizaki, related her personal experiences in meeting with women teachers across the province in the December issue of the *FWTAO Newsletter*.[43]

> While I spoke with teachers who felt underappreciated and
> overworked, I also heard many teacher stories that were based
> on love, compassion and worry about the disappearing oppor-
> tunities facing the children in their classes. . . . Our campaign
> demonstrated that as women teachers we are not simply a spe-
> cial interest group, but professionals who serve children and help
> build the future of Ontario.[44]

Harris imitated the blitzkrieg tactics that had proven successful at the national level for Margaret Thatcher and Ronald Reagan.[45]

In addition to other pieces of legislation tabled in the first session of the new parliament, the government brought forward the omnibus Savings and Restructuring Act: Bill 26. It was a massive assault on workers.[46] The bill amended labour relations legislation by declaring all public services essential and established the "ability to pay" requirement for arbitrators in all sectors. The Common Sense Revolution, and the ruthlessness with which it was enacted, combined a free-market economic agenda that appealed to business interests with an ultra-right social policy that appealed to social conservatives. It would prove to be a potent mix.

The Conservatives were exploiting any opportunity for divisiveness in the teachers' ranks, and if there was one issue that divided the two panels more than any other, it was preparation time. In early January 1996, the OSSTF received a leaked document that outlined the government's plans for finding "efficiencies" in education.[47] It included a 10 per cent reduction in supervision costs by putting a cap on teacher preparation time. The cap reduced secondary teachers to one forty-minute period per day and elementary teachers to twenty minutes per day. For some elementary teachers, the twenty minutes would be no change at all. For others, it would cut their preparation time in half.

Still, the teachers were not opposed to everything in the governments' plan. The leaked document also recommended lowering the retirement age by two and a half years to bring in lower-paid, "younger teachers who are more likely to be receptive to change, and to smooth the transition to a smaller work force."[48] That was an improvement to the pension plan that the unions had been seeking for some time.

While the secondary teachers had their strike issue in the proposed reduction of preparation time, elementary teachers found theirs in the threat to end retirement gratuities.[49] The government confirmed that it intended to reduce the number of sick days available to teachers and to end the practice of accumulating them.[50] With the leak now public, the unions began to prepare for the worst.

## Hamilton Days of Action: Joining Labour

The Roman Catholic teachers of the OECTA organized a demonstration at Queen's Park for 13 January 1996. The forty thousand people who marched from Toronto's city hall to the legislative building included parents, students, and teachers from all five unions.[51] At the end of January, the Ontario Teachers' Federation affiliates came together to approve a co-ordinated strategy for the rest of the year. The announcement of an OTF Action Plan came out in a new format called the *Communiqué*.[52] The first edition carried the signatures of all five of the union presidents and the OTF president. It launched the organizational structure for the unified efforts of the teachers' unions against the Harris government.

The OTF president had never wielded any power in the affiliates. The role of president was taken on by each of the affiliates in turn. It called for chairing meetings, communication with the Ministry of Education, and liaising with the pension board. The unusual decision of the unions to unite under the OTF granted the umbrella organization an unprecedented level of authority.

The OTF Action Plan committed the teachers to the Hamilton Days of Action and established work groups to develop and co-ordinate the strategy of the campaign. On 19 February, the OPSTF's new bulletin, the *Shock Absorber*, informed members that the local presidents of all five OTF affiliates, more than six hundred teachers and education workers, had met in Toronto to be "briefed on the initial stages of a province-wide action plan to fight the cuts."[53] The unions were introducing a new level of political engagement.

The OTF Action Plan was replicated in the locals. It included a "school based meeting of school staff" using the OTF/Affiliate guide.[54] The local political action committees, made up of representatives from all five unions, were to meet to make decisions on mobilizing.

The list of grievances against the Harris government had grown by the end of January. The unions pinpointed ten government initiatives attacking education.[55] At the same time as teachers were being threatened with increases in their workload, Harris intensified surveillance of them. Parents were to have an increased role through a new entity called School Councils, which would have decision-making authority. The College of Teachers would wield absolute power over certification and disciplining of teachers. And the EQAO was ready to start its first round of testing, politicizing the student assessment process. Minister of Education Snobelen had been quoted as saying that he wanted to "manufacture a crisis in education."[56] Such a crisis was inherent in the sheer number of changes teachers were facing.

Snobelen liked to quote the Conservative election claim that Ontario was spending more for its schooling than any other province. The figures showing Ontario was fifth in the country were pointed out to the education minister; nonetheless, he continued to misrepresent the cost of education in Ontario. Exaggerated claims of bloated funding for an inadequate system fuelled notions of bureaucratic waste in the schools and fed the Conservative base.

In February 1996, the elementary teachers contributed funding for the two-day Hamilton Days of Action.[57] The unions also set aside funds to defend teachers who took a day off work to protest on the Friday. The leaders of all five unions confirmed that they would be present and for the first time acknowledged the possibility of a province-wide strike.[58]

The locals chose to bring their buses to Hamilton on the Saturday.[59] The 24 February 1996 march in Hamilton was one of the largest political protests in the province's history. Over one hundred thousand people gathered on a cold, windy afternoon to retrace the steps of those who had fought for the nine-hour workday in 1872.[60] The symbolism was apt; the current government was making an effort to return to the age of unfettered capitalism against which workers had first organized.

The chosen parade route through Hamilton included surrounding the Sheraton Hotel where the Conservative party was holding its policy conference. When the marchers arrived, they were met with concrete barricades behind which police, dressed in riot gear, stood several ranks deep. It was a sight the teachers had never experienced, but they were not the only ones who wavered.[61] Despite the mass of marchers who filled the streets, the Ontario Federation of Labour organizers complied with the police request to cancel their planned march around the hotel. "Concerns over safety," was the reason given.[62] A committed crowd of a hundred thousand marching against the practices of the neo-liberal state dispersed because the leadership chose to retreat at the request of the authorities. The Hamilton Days of Protest were, as Athabasca University's Paul Kellogg has suggested, a lost opportunity for what could have been a meaningful and effective confrontation of neo-liberal political actors.[63]

Further Days of Action, held in cities across the province, galvanized labour organizations and other groups that were feeling the heavy hand of neo-liberalism. For the teachers, photographs of flags and picket signs representing all five unions appeared in their newsletters, inspiring more teachers to turn out as the campaign advanced.

The members of OPSEU went on strike the Monday following the Hamilton march. The executive of the men's elementary teachers' union called "for strong, visible OPSTF support of the OPSEU strike."[64] David Rapaport, former president of OPSEU Local 503 in Toronto and author of *No Justice, No Peace*, noted that elementary teacher activists were among the teachers who walked the OPSEU picket lines to support Ontario public service workers' resistance to the Harris regime.[65] The teachers were beginning to understand that the issues were the same for all the public service unions.[66] When the April *OPSTF News* acknowledged an OPSTF member had been injured by the Ontario Provincial Police while on an OPSEU picket line, it was the first time the elementary teachers had recognized one of their own supporting another labour organization.

Harris had appointed the Ontario School Board Reduction Task Force, which released its findings in January 1996. Known as the Sweeney Report, it recommended amalgamating boards and cutting administrative positions.[67] In March, the general legislative grants for the 1996–97 school year were released, showing cuts of nearly half a billion dollars to the basic per-pupil grant.[68]

Remarkably, when the NDP's Social Contract came to an end in April 1996, the Conservative government did not interfere with the restoration of the teachers' grid increments.[69] Negotiations between trustees and the unions to move young teachers to their rightful place on the grid began immediately. By September 1996, 80.5 per cent of teachers had their grid position restored with all or a portion of their increment increases included in their new collective agreements.[70]

Some boards resisted grid restoration. In Renfrew County, the trustees insisted that the teachers assume 40 per cent of the cost of their benefits package premiums and receive no salary increase in exchange. The teachers voted for work-to-rule. They began their withdrawal of non-essential services on 27 November 1996.[71] After two weeks, the trustees agreed to mediation and to fully restore teachers' grid placements. The Renfrew County dispute would be the last time the elementary teachers would engage in any form of withdrawing their services as two unions.

### The College of Teachers: Management by Stress

The Ontario College of Teachers Act, introduced in mid-December 1995, gave the teachers a minority of the representatives on the college governing council. Its most contentious issue was the requirement for constant retraining at teachers' expense.[72] That requirement imposed financial and scheduling demands, forced people in isolated communities to travel to larger urban centres, and placed additional hardship on women teachers who bore the brunt of family care.

The former president of the OSSTF, Margaret Wilson, who had led her union during the province-wide strike in 1973, was appointed the College of Teachers' first registrar. The college was a non-grievable route to the disciplining of teachers that required another layer of specialized service from the unions. To front-line teachers, the process was opaque, punitive, and absolute. Teachers were already under constant scrutiny from trustees, principals, and members of the community, and a residual patina of bourgeois morality still clung to them.[73] Creating another level of investigative processes parallel to that of the justice system was fundamentally disturbing and a return to a more repressive age.

On 6 March 1996, Snobelen released his "tool kit" of cost-cutting measures to be implemented by boards of education.[74] Management by stress figured prominently. The trustees in a number of boards responded to the proposed funding reductions by immediately issuing layoff notices to their youngest teachers.[75] By May, many of those teachers who had been given layoff notices would see them rescinded, but in the meantime the trustees' vacillations created panic. In some boards, trustees approached the unions with a request for a reduction in wages as a means of saving the youngest teachers' jobs.[76]

The trustees' actions further radicalized teachers. Elementary teachers turned out to the Days of Action marches in substantial numbers across the province.[77] In doing so, they became comfortable with attending rallies, chanting slogans, and marching holding picket signs—the on-the-ground experiences of becoming politicized.

### Divide and Conquer: Principals, Preparation Time, and the Paroian Report

In August 1996, the two unions had just finished their annual general meetings when Snobelen announced he was considering taking over board/teacher negotiations and ending teachers' right to strike.[78] He had appointed Leon Paroian, a well-known lawyer and Conservative supporter, to examine teachers' collective bargaining.[79]

Paroian's report would come out on schedule, on 1 November 1996. Entitled *Review of the School Boards' / Teachers' Collective Negotiations Process in Ontario, 1996,* it included recommendations that extracurricular duties be mandated, working conditions be non-negotiable, principals and vice-principals be removed from the union, and teachers' strikes be either banned or severely restricted.[80] The report went on to suggest bringing an end to the Education Relations Commission, the body that oversaw negotiations in the education sector; repealing Bill 100, the legislation that had defined collective bargaining between teachers and trustees for a quarter century; and placing teachers under the Labour Relations Act, which, among other things, would threaten the very existence of teachers' unions as unique entities.

The new FWTAO president, Margaret Gee, called upon her members to be heroic:

> The Royal Commission on Learning (1994) referred to teachers as heroes and certainly this statement needs to be remembered. With recent government cutbacks affecting classrooms so drastically, it takes the courage of heroes to face the many daily challenges that every classroom teacher experiences in trying to do more with less support and less resources. . . . Education is under attack.[81]

While Paroian had been holding hearings, the labour unions were planning the Toronto Metro Days of Action.[82] Bill Martin, the OPSTF representative on the OTF, urged his members:

> I encourage all of you to become more politically active. . . . Friday, October 25th and Saturday, October 26, 1996 will be our next opportunity to voice our displeasure on the direction that this government is taking education. . . . It is imperative that the educational sector in this province is well represented.[83]

Tens of thousands of teachers showed up on 26 October to march with other workers and community activists from Nathan Phillips Square to Queen's Park.[84] That demonstration of union solidarity and political militancy was historic for its size and for the fact that the teachers were at the heart of it. Afterwards, FWTAO executive director Westcott assured her members that the Days of Action were having an effect:

> The turnout of teachers to the October 26 march and rally as part of the Metro Days of Action in Toronto did have an impact. One only has to note the Premier's comments that day and the few days after to identify that.[85]

Although the trustees generally supported the government's hard turn to the right, approval was not seamless. At a Thunder Bay Board of Education meeting, trustees from across Northern Ontario criticized the Conservative government's intention to amalgamate their boards into enormous entities.[86] The OPSBA information clearing house included a list of trustee meetings against the funding cuts that were held in East York, Windsor, and Wellington County.[87]

The Ontario Public Supervisory Officials' Association, led by the directors of education, were also critical of the Harris government. Their position paper, "Our Future Together," accused the government of "the perpetuation of simplistic myths . . . and the clearly inaccurate analysis being advanced by the Ministry of Education and Training to prove that the school system is 'broken.'"[88] By the end of 1996, teachers, senior administrators, and the trustees were fighting the Harris government.

It was strategic to constructing neo-liberal hegemony to attack teachers and undermine their credibility both as professional educators and as unionized workers. The myriad of reports, studies, think tanks, and attack ads indicated a sophisticated understanding of the process of formulating public opinion. In its efforts to manage the discourse on education, the Conservative government was able to find support within the education elite. It commissioned a study from the University of Toronto's OISE. The *Study on Costs: Ontario Public Elementary/Secondary Education Costs as Compared to Other Provinces* reported positively on the Conservatives' education policy.[89] Critics pointed out that the study challenged the figures of Statistics Canada, used faulty methodology to inflate numbers, and ignored comparisons that would have contradicted its conclusions.[90] But regardless of its weaknesses, the study gave "teacher bashing" credibility.[91]

The Conservative vision disconnected education from actual, living students with their multiplicity of human needs. Eliminating the student as person, and framing education in the abstract as a mechanical process, allowed political actors to ideologically reform education. The Harris government's efforts to undermine the teachers' unions were necessary to blunt the effect the unions might have on slowing education reform and retrenchment. The teachers were protecting their livelihood and their working conditions and they had a cause, the moral obligation to protect their students against an identifiable threat in the person of Mike Harris.

## CHAPTER 8

# Fighting Back

Harris was in his second year as premier in the spring of 1997, as the York Region elementary teachers were preparing to go on strike. There were two issues. The trustees were attempting to decrease teachers' preparation time from the 200 minutes in the collective agreement to 120 minutes. They were also proposing to reduce the number of teachers they employed, a reaction to the cuts in the provincial budget. The board chair defended the reductions by suggesting that "the teachers should be directing their comments to Education Minister John Snobelen."[1] He did not suggest the trustees do the same.

In April 1996, the board had broken the collective agreement by instructing principals to reschedule half of the teachers' preparation time to the mornings before classes began or to the afternoons after classes were dismissed. The trustees claimed that the preparation time was still there, but it had been "reallocated." The ERC fact finder, Richard Jackson, saw it for the provocation that it was. "It is . . . open to interpretation that [the board of education's] approach shows contempt for both the process and its teachers. . . . In effect there has been no real bargaining and the Board must bear the largest share of responsibility for this fact."[2]

The teachers rejected the board's demand for concessions and voted 83 per cent to strike.[3] Joan Heeler, the FWTAO local president, was emphatic in her defence of the strike as a professional responsibility:

> I want to make the issue perfectly clear to everyone. The issue here is not money—it's concern for York Region students period. York Region elementary teachers will give up their daily salaries and take a strike if that's what is needed to restore the preparation time that is essential for a sound educational program.[4]

With negotiations breaking down, the ERC mediator convinced the trustees to return to the bargaining table. At 8 a.m. on 24 March 1997, after having bargained all night, the two sides reached a tentative agreement, an hour before the strike was set to begin. Although the teachers did not walk out, nor commence a work-to-rule, York Region was to be the final labour dispute engaged in by the OPSTF and the FWTAO under Bill 100.

## Finding Allies

Harris had chosen to prolong the media war against the teachers. In doing so, he gave the unions time to organize their response and to shape it to the actions of the government. While the minister of education and the premier persisted in discrediting teachers and their concerns, the unions continued to politicize their members and expand their campaign.

After much debate, the Conservative caucus had settled on amalgamating the boards rather than following through on earlier rumours that they would abolish them altogether.[5] Snobelen introduced Bill 104, The Fewer School Boards Act, in late autumn of 1996, reducing the 129 boards across the province to 72.[6]

The teachers' unions reacted by escalating their campaigns. In December 1996, OPSTF Secretary-Treasurer Lennox appealed to his members' professionalism as a gateway to political activism:

> This time we will be called upon to stand up and be counted as never before. It will be each member's problem, not just a far away provincial concern. We will be tested and may be asked to undertake political action that we distain. We simply must meet this challenge with our full resolve. To do less would undermine our beliefs and our very existence as professionals.[7]

Lennox was acknowledging the ideological contradictions of professionalism. Teachers viewed teaching as requiring special skills that elevated them above other workers. Yet, it was their strikes for salaries and working conditions that had only recently gained them a decent standard of living. In this moment, Lennox was calling upon his members to defend their professional status, using the tactics of labour, in a political protest.

OPSTF president Jeff Holmes suggested that coalition building needed to become the primary focus. "We must work with parents, student groups, seniors, other unions and anyone else concerned about the future of our schools. None of us can do it alone. It's only by standing together that we have a chance of success."[8] New allies included the Canadian Federation of Students and People for Education, an organization led by Annie Kidder.

As the elementary teachers moved closer to a major clash with the Conservatives, they began to reach out to other labour organizations to inform their own activism. At least one member of the OPSTF staff attended a workshop on law for political activists put on in 1996 by the Labour Council of Metro Toronto and York Region.[9] With thousands of teachers attending the Days of Action rallies, the unions needed to educate all of their members on the legal boundaries of protest.

In the fall of 1996, the FWTAO had begun a publicity campaign called the Future of Education. It included an hour-long television show that local cable channels picked up.[10] As the 1996–97 school year began, the FWTAO initiated a second campaign, You Can Make a Difference:

> Contact with your local [member of provincial parliament] is also important to ensure that he/she knows the impact of the government cuts on your school. . . . Teachers are not alone in our fight to maintain the good education system that has been built through hard work over many years. Parents particularly are on side.[11]

Teachers became engaged in the process of deconstructing the claims of neo-liberal inevitability that much of the media and most right-wing political figures were making.[12]

The FWTAO used its experience of building feminist alliances to strengthen its solidarity with the Ontario Coalition for Better Child Care and the Ontario Education Alliance. As well, it provided a full-time staff worker at the Ontario Federation of Labour's office and reassigned six other staff to work on the campaign.

The government seemed intent on provoking the teachers' unions into some kind of confrontation. After Snobelen announced that he would remove the ability of school boards to raise money through taxation, rumours began to circulate that the government was preparing to act on the recommendations of the Paroian Report. It would repeal Bill 100 and remove the right of teachers to strike.[13]

The OPSTF became concerned with potential threats from other unions.[14] With the final ruling on the Baum decision having come down in the spring of 1995, the two unions were in the process of amalgamating. If they were put under the Ontario Labour Relations Act, they would need to have each member sign a membership card. Without the protection of Bill 100, raids from other unions, decertification, or the loss of statutory membership were all possibilities.[15] The FWTAO and the OPSTF hastily developed a card-signing campaign for membership in the new union they were forming, the Elementary Teachers' Federation of Ontario.[16]

By March 1997, they were making preparations for a province-wide walkout in the event that the Conservative government removed their right to strike.[17] Locals were told to form joint committees with the other teachers' unions, collect signatures on petitions, develop radio campaigns, and organize rallies.[18]

Persistent rumours continued to circulate that Snobelen would take principals and vice-principals out of the unions.[19] The OPSTF, the union with the largest percentage of its membership in administration, approved an Action Plan to Retain the Right to Strike, preparing the way for a province-wide strike that could proceed without the agreement of the other OTF affiliates.[20]

Near the end of the school year, the FWTAO released a booklet to every elementary school entitled "A System in Peril: Education Bargaining in Ontario," which outlined the effects of the proposed changes. It gave teachers a discursive platform with which to refute the government's claims. About the right to strike, it was emphatic: "Without the right to strike, teachers would have little clout in bargaining. It is the ability to go out on strike that gives employees a more equal balance of power; as you know, this is rarely exercised."[21] The booklet closed with the refrain, "Teachers' Working Conditions are Children's Learning Conditions."

In the spring of 1997, Labour Minister Elizabeth Witmer announced she would limit collective bargaining in the public sector. Bill 136, The Public Sector Labour Relations Transition Act, would apply to OPSTF members who were not classroom teachers.[22] An OPSTF memorandum advised teacher locals that they could expect similar restrictions to follow. Such comparisons helped to build a sense of common injury between teachers and the other education workers. An OPSTF press release in response to Bill 136 stated:

> A delegation from the Ontario Public School Teachers' Federation (OPSTF) is at the Ontario Federation of Labour's Emergency Convention today. The presence of the delegation clearly shows solidarity with the labour movement in its struggle against the undemocratic and anti labour Harris Tories.[23]

Attendance at an Ontario Federation of Labour meeting was something new for the elementary teachers. While their motivation may have been to push back against the threat Harris posed to education, through that campaign, they began to participate more fully in the strategies of the broader labour movement.

The unions' success in politicizing teachers was evident at the August 1997 annual general meetings. The FWTAO delegates unanimously passed motions supporting a province-wide strike if the government removed principals and vice-principals from the union, attacked teachers' pensions, or undermined bargaining rights.[24] Approval was also given for collaboration with labour councils and support of the ongoing political action program. The OPSTF delegates passed similar motions.[25]

In the face of a strong and united labour front, the government modified its stance on Bill 136. The changes to public sector bargaining were amended in September 1997, with public sector workers retaining the right to free collective bargaining.[26] The amendments preserved most of the previous labour relations conditions for public sector unions, with the notable exception of pay equity, leaving the unions to negotiate it into their collective agreements.[27] Pressure from labour groups had somewhat blunted the Common Sense Revolution.

### Bill 160

On 22 September 1997, the Harris government tabled Bill 160, the Education Quality Improvement Act, a document that targeted boards of education, teachers, and their unions with a range of legislative changes. As promised, it removed the ability of school boards to levy taxes, eroding the authority of trustees. It placed teachers under the Ontario Labour Relations Act. The minister of education was given the power to override collective agreements and the cabinet could unilaterally prevent or end a strike.[28] Trustees were given new powers to modify how seniority would be determined and to replace certain categories of teachers with non-teachers. The school year was extended; staffing and class size language was swept aside. Trustees were given the ability to reduce teachers' preparation time. Bill 160 also removed the school boards' obligation to deduct union dues, threatening union security. The teachers had little choice but to launch their campaign.

The campaign plan was modelled on the OTF Action Plan from the Hamilton Days of Action.[29] In an unusual move, the affiliates recognized the president of the OTF—Eileen Lennon, in 1997—as the spokesperson for all five of the unions.

This decision would become problematic. Lennon had been the president of the OECTA from 1988 to 1990, but she was unknown to teachers in the other unions. Their loyalties were to their own leaders. The reverse was also true; the loyalties of the presidents were to the best interests of their own members. The selection of Lennon as spokesperson for all the teachers left gaps between the public voice of teachers and the objectives of the individual unions. Although the intention was to establish a single voice during the strike, Lennon's conversation would be with the press, not with teachers on the picket lines.

Lennon's presence would also provide a screen for the leaders of the unions, allowing them to speak directly to their own members while shielding them from having to consider their commitment to the whole body of striking teachers. Captives of their history, the unions could remain distanced from each other even as they prepared to engage in a battle with a common foe.

The unions announced their intention to commence information picketing with a rally of twenty-four thousand teachers in Toronto's Maple Leaf Gardens on 6 October 1997.[30] The crowd overflowed onto Carlton Street, forcing its closure. Lennon made particular note of the fact that the government had listened to the OFL and modified Bill 136. She offered teachers the hope that they would see the same success in their current battle. The Maple Leaf Gardens rally finished up with a march to Queen's Park.

These preparatory events focused teachers' attention on the effects of the government's proposed cuts. The FWTAO noted that information picketing would "foster solidarity among our teachers," as well as educate the rank and file to the niceties involved in walking a picket line, "to conduct ourselves, within the limits of the law, reflecting our concerns for the health and safety of all."[31] Local presidents were directed to activate committees to organize, support, inform, and supervise picketers. The locals began making picket signs and setting up rosters for picket duties. They were charged with contacting the media and becoming practised in delivering the union's message. Synchronizing media communications would be particularly important when five unions were involved.[32]

The escalation of the teachers' campaign had an immediate effect. The much-despised Snobelen was moved out of education to become the minister of natural resources, and Dave Johnson became the minister of education. Lennon declared that teachers were "cautiously optimistic."[33]

A week after Johnson was appointed to education, the teachers and the government were again at an impasse. Finance Minister Ernie Eves denied that the cuts were intended to remove a billion dollars from the education budget.[34] Eves's denial undercut the attempts of Johnson and the teachers to reach an agreement. The talks between the teachers and the new minister of education collapsed.[35] The photograph on the front page of the Tuesday edition of the *Toronto Star* showed a grim FWTAO president, Maret

Sädem-Thompson, and OTF president Lennon facing reporters.[36] On Thursday, Premier Harris gave a televised address to the province in which he decried "the inexcusable slide in the quality of our schools" and attacked teachers as a "special interest group."[37] His inflammatory rhetoric set the stage for what was to come.

The strike began the following Monday, 27 October 1997. The media would label it "one of the largest strikes in Canadian history."[38] The five teachers' unions comprised a membership of 150,000 teachers and education workers.[39] Communications continued to be released under the signatures of Lennon and the five union presidents.[40] The key issues for teachers remained the billion dollars in cuts to the education budget, the loss of ten thousand teaching jobs as a consequence, increases in the size of classes, and the right of teachers to collective bargaining. Copies of the letters of support that arrived from teachers' organizations across the country were circulated among picketers.[41]

The unions' press releases highlighted the shift of authority from "local communities to Cabinet" and the effect of Bill 160 on the political economy of schooling.[42] Fewer teachers meant more students in classrooms, less time for teachers to spend with individual students, and, overall, more work for teachers. A smaller education budget meant fewer secretarial and custodial staff, leaving teachers responsible for completing essential paperwork and for aspects of cleaning in their classrooms. Bill 160 also gave the trustees permission to replace certified teachers with non-teachers in non-classroom settings, threatening special education teachers, librarians, and others in specialized positions.

Although the goal of the strike was to bring an end to Bill 160, the teachers' demands were actually quite tame. The unions presented their "Five-Point Plan to Resolve the Impasse Regarding Bill 160" to Johnson during the first days of the strike.[43] The plan asked for the minister to return to the negotiations table to discuss the transition to amalgamated boards and any extension of the school year. It proposed that the issue of differentiated staffing be presented to the College of Teachers for study and that funding issues be forwarded to the courts to determine their constitutionality. Lastly, the teachers demanded that the regulation of working conditions and the removal of the right to strike be dropped from Bill 160. This final point was the only non-negotiable demand. The Five-Point Plan offered the government breathing room, but Harris refused to be moved off his agenda. Three days into the strike, he applied for a court injunction against the teachers.[44]

Some teacher activists had hoped that their province-wide strike would trigger a general strike of all the unions in the province. The OFL did encourage other unions to support the teachers but did not go beyond that.[45] The reasons were many. While teachers had been a major presence at the labour marches on Saturdays, they had not closed the schools on Fridays in the cities where Days of Action took place. Without a history of labour solidarity, the teachers could not expect other unions to risk their members by participating in sympathy strikes. More to the point, the OFL had never led a province-wide general strike.[46] The relatively ineffectual Days of Action, with their rolling strikes, were as militant as the OFL had ever been. The unions were still recovering from the divisions created by the NDP's Social Contract, making a co-ordinated attack against the Harris government uncertain.[47]

Moreover, the teachers' unions never asked the OFL to mount a general strike. When the president of CUPE Ontario, Sid Ryan, called for a general strike, the OTF response was, "Individual unions will make their own decisions."[48] Canadian labour historian Douglas Nesbitt summarized the reticence of the OFL leadership:

These Days of Action were disarticulated from a more focused strike target, namely Bill 136 and Bill 160. The opportunities and momentum for unions to join in common strike action were many during September and October but each was passed up as the challenge to each offending bill and the Days of Action were treated as separate campaigns.[49]

The opportunity for a general strike was available, but the OFL leadership would not reach out and grasp it.

On Monday of the second week of the teachers' strike, the court handed the teachers a win.[50] Justice James Macpherson dismissed the Harris government's request for an injunction, despite the strike being illegal.[51] It was a setback for the Conservative government. As Harris discovered, the decisions of the courts are not always predictable, and judges do have some autonomy.[52]

The court decision vindicated the teachers. On the second Tuesday of the strike, they were in their strongest position, with public support building.[53] Still, they were unable to convince the government to return to the table even after they offered concessions.[54]

Teachers made history with their strike, but it was not enough. On Wednesday, 5 November 1997, at the height of their success, the leaders of the AEFO, FWTAO, and OPSTF announced they would be looking for ways to end the strike.[55] Despite chants of "We won't back down," three of the unions were doing just that.[56] From then on, the government could sit and wait. On Thursday, twenty-two thousand parents and students joined teachers for a rally in front of the legislature. Another rally with OFL affiliates was planned for Saturday at Queen's Park, billed as a gesture of appreciation from the other unions.[57]

The OPSTF had sent a survey limited to its local presidents asking if the unions should continue the protest "in, or out of the classrooms?"[58] If the FWTAO did the same, it did not reach all their local presidents.[59] At the end of the second week of the walk-out, the ever-present television cameras recorded the collapse of teachers' resistance with only three of the five union presidents standing before the cameras: Diane Chénier of the AEFO, Maret

Sädem-Thompson of the FWTAO, and Phyllis Benedict of the OPSTF.[60] Under a pall of inter-union squabbling, the elementary and French teachers' unions opted to return to work.[61] Despite the support of labour unions and parents, the united front that had been the teachers' strength disintegrated. Lennon was no longer a presence.

The decision to return to work left a widespread sense of betrayal within the ranks of all five unions. The pronouncement had been made without a vote of the membership, the normal protocol in a labour dispute. Only a co-ordinated groundswell from the rank and file could have prolonged the strike, and no mechanism had been put in place for that level of feedback.

The three unions had not contacted the local presidents or the provincial staff in the field in advance of their back-to-work broadcast. That misstep left the locals in disarray.[62] To add to the confusion, the OSSTF and the OECTA had not agreed to participate. The rank and file were outraged.[63] The teachers in the Toronto locals demanded a vote of the full membership before returning to work. OSSTF president Earl Manners warned the *Toronto Star*, "The political protest will continue far into the future, although the form it may take will obviously have to change."[64]

Teacher anger was palpable. Local FWTAO president Barb Gunning reported having to speak to a mixed group of teachers who seemed to hold the FWTAO singularly responsible for the premature return to work.[65] That was an unjustified attack on the women teachers of the FWTAO, who had been as solid in their support of the strike as any of the other unions. However, the face of the striking teachers had been OTF president Eileen Lennon, and the responsibility for ending the strike rested with the three presidents who were women. The teachers, particularly male teachers, were reacting to a situation no one was openly acknowledging. Women did control that strike. This was an example of what Briskin has noted in her study of nurses' unions; with the majority of strikes in Canada coming from the largely feminized public sector, labour militancy was becoming feminized.[66]

Briskin also makes the connection between neo-liberal austerity measures, anti-strike legislation, and attacks on women workers. The eventual two billion dollars in cuts to education, the attempt to remove teachers' right to strike, Harris's refusal to negotiate as he had with the private sector unions, and the vilification of teachers in the media were indicative of a more entrenched demand for compliance from Harris—a demand that education workers, who were predominantly women, fall into line. As feminist writer Rebecca Coulter points out, this was particularly evident when one of the first pieces of legislation of the new Conservative government had axed the employment equity legislation.[67]

The political reasons for returning to work were easier to explain. The opportunity to make amendments to Bill 160 ended on the evening of 5 November 1997.[68] In the legislature, the Liberal opposition delayed passage of the bill by one day. The purpose of the strike had been to defeat the bill. When the government would not negotiate or permit the teachers to offer solutions, negotiations ceased. Harris was not going to meet with the teachers and Bill 160 would go ahead unchanged. The unions' legal advisers suggested that a return to work would build the goodwill of the public at a time when no other gains appeared attainable. The AEFO, FWTAO, and OPSTF took their lawyers' advice and folded their tents.

Despite its failures, the extent of the protest exceeded anything seen before in Ontario's education sector.[69] Arriving on the heels of the OPSEU strike and the OFL Days of Action, the teachers' strike formed a critical component of resistance to the neo-liberal state. Most importantly, teachers were successful in retaining the right to strike. The government tinkered with the preparation time of secondary teachers, but preparation time remained in teachers' collective agreements, as did other working conditions. Despite massive cuts to the education budget, Harris had been forced to compromise on Bill 160.

Once the teachers went back to work, any power they had to force negotiations evaporated. They took the battle to the courts with a constitutional challenge to that portion of Bill 160 that removed the ability of boards to raise revenue through taxes on private property, an argument that law professor Harry Glasbeek points out characterized them as the protectors of property rights, thus breaking their solidarity with the grassroots organizations.[70] Despite a short-term win for the teachers in the lower court, the Ontario Court of Appeal decided in favour of the government. Because it concerned the ability of the trustees to tax, the legal arguments ended up pitting the public school teachers against the Roman Catholic separate school teachers. That further broke teacher solidarity.

On 31 March 1998, the provision in Bill 160 removing principals and vice-principals from their union was enacted.[71] The move was viewed as punishment for those school administrators who had joined the teachers on the picket lines.[72] Hiving off these members of the unions demonstrated how little the Conservatives feared the teachers in the aftermath of the strike. The unions could have requested the resignations of all of their principals and vice-principals in protest and left the schools without administrators; instead, they appealed the legislation in the courts.[73] They lost.

Principals and vice-principals were given three months to make their decision: return to classroom duties or stay in their administrative positions.[74] Most, but not all, stayed in their jobs and formed their own professional organization, the Elementary Principals' and Vice-Principals' Association of Ontario.[75] This organization and others that emerged would be absorbed into the Ontario Principals' Council.[76]

Once under the Ontario Labour Relations Act, the teachers' locals and the provincial bodies became the same creature. In the future, collective agreements would have to be provincially vetted clause by clause before the negotiating teams could agree to them. That required a higher level of expertise than was available in most locals. Under the new regime, provincial union staff seated at the table during local negotiations would become critical to a more bureaucratic bargaining process.

The defeat of the teachers was an ideological victory for the Harris government. The Common Sense Revolution was both ideological and economic in its intent and it succeeded at both. The teachers did not rise up again to check its progress. The Conservative government reduced spending on education by two billion dollars, as much in this one sector as the NDP government had cut over the entire Social Contract.[77] Ontario entered the second decade of the twenty-first century as one of the lowest-spending provinces for education in Canada, significantly below neighbouring jurisdictions in the United States.[78]

Ironically, by removing principals and vice-principals from the unions, Harris eliminated a voice of moderation. The absence of school administrators at the provincial table permitted the unions to make a stronger connection with labour. In 1995, the FWTAO and the OPSTF had tentatively joined the labour movement to march in the Days of Action. In 1998, united under the ETFO, they immediately joined the OFL. After three years of battling the Harris government, they were ready to enter the house of labour.

The defeat of the 1997 Ontario teachers' strike was one indicator of the weakened condition of organized labour at the end of the twentieth century. Even with over one hundred thousand teachers on picket lines across the province, the unions were unable to turn the Conservative caucus from its neo-liberal agenda.[79] Organized labour had come to a point where a radically rightwing provincial government could defeat their best efforts in a mere two weeks.

For nearly fifty years, the relationship between unions and their employers had been governed by statute and by arbitrators' decisions.[80] Union leadership rose or fell on their ability to negotiate within these authorized frameworks. The legal status of workplace strikes had become as important as the content of the dispute. However, political strikes occupied a legal grey zone. Leaders were not familiar with how to manage their members during such protests, were unsure of the outcome, and were nervous about leading them.

Following the collapse of the strike, the internecine battles between the five teachers' unions provided ample opportunity for finger pointing and blame. A small consolation they could take from their defeat: they were among the few workers' organizations that took the fight against neo-liberal policy to the steps of the legislature. Polls taken during the strike indicated a migration of public support from the government to the striking teachers.[81] If nothing else, future governments, not so intent on punishing public service workers, would need to take a more conciliatory approach to teachers' concerns now that a major disruption to the education system was a realistic threat. Public policy, political strikes, and public sector labour relations had become intertwined. However, such considerations were of little comfort at the losing end of the strike.

The Harris government continued to seek ways of reducing funding to education. Replacing senior teachers in the higher salary categories with beginning teachers was one way. The unions wanted to make the "85 factor" retirement window permanent, but a change of that magnitude required the approval of the state.[82] With the state owing the pension fund for its part of the unfunded liability, Harris indicated he was willing to lower the retirement age in exchange for forgiving that debt.[83] The teachers accepted the deal. In May 1998, the unions revealed that ten thousand teachers would be eligible for early retirement.[84] Many of them would take the early option. The teachers now had control of their own pension and had negotiated the enhancements they had been seeking. It was one victory in a period when the teachers would see few.

## The Decision to Amalgamate

For the elementary teachers, the 1997 strike came at a critical time in their internal politics. Harris's teacher-bashing rhetoric offered them an especially visceral rationale for building union strength. He was a common enemy at a time when the animosities between men and women teachers had to be put aside. FWTAO president Margaret Gee acknowledged that reality in her December 1996 article titled "Teachers as Agents of Change." In it she said:

> At the same time that the government is imposing rapid change upon us, we are also moving towards a large organizational change. . . . With times as they are, it is important that we find some stability for teachers and reduce the high stress level of our members. Solidarity on school staffs can help to offset the decline of individual teacher morale as we go through these challenging times together.[85]

After eighty years, the women's union and the men's union were poised to form one amalgamated organization.

On 1 July 1998, eight months after the collapse of the two-week strike, the FWTAO and the OPSTF ceased to represent the elementary teachers of Ontario. In their place stood the ETFO. At seventy thousand members, it was the largest teachers' union in Canada; 80 per cent of its members were women.[86] In the shadow of the most militant display of teacher resistance in the history of the province, Ontario's public elementary teachers moved to end the partitioning of their membership by gender. Under the leadership of Phyllis Benedict, the first ETFO president, women and men teachers stood side by side on the floor of the ETFO annual general meeting debating the issues that had separated them for decades. Across the province, similar conversations were being held in the new ETFO locals.

Had they been determined to have their own union, women teachers could have continued with the FWTAO. With a membership at the time of 40,100, the FWTAO was three times the size of the OPSTF's 13,400 members and nearly 6,000 members more than the next largest teachers' union, the OSSTF.[87] The reasons for not doing that were complex. By the late 1990s, feminism had lost its appeal for many younger women. They were able to enter a workforce that gave them a broader range of choices than had been available to their mothers. New teachers took for granted gains— such as pregnancy leaves, access to promotions, and pay equity— that had been fought for by the previous generation of feminists. Many women felt that feminism had achieved its goals. Because of positive changes in society's view of women's abilities, the FWTAO could not depend on its commitment to improving women's work lives as sufficiently attractive to a younger generation. Feminism itself was suffering the effects of a backlash, fuelled by neo-liberal efforts to suppress wages for both men and women.

Almost four thousand women teachers had become voluntary members of the men's union by 1997; they would transfer their allegiance to the OPSTF.[88] The FWTAO could expect a majority of the women who had voted to amalgamate their locals would also leave. Those locals included the sizable Hamilton, York, and Carleton associations. The voice of women teachers was divided. Those who supported amalgamated locals or who were voluntary members regarded the Baum decision as a victory for teacher unionism and for women's freedom of association. The FWTAO leaders were aware that the exodus of disaffected members would risk the union's financial security. The FWTAO had to choose between remaining a smaller, independent organization or having a significant presence in an amalgamated union over which women had some control. When the decision was presented in an all-member vote, 88 per cent agreed to forming one union.[89] Ironically, that number was only marginally lower than the 92.5 per cent agreement in the OPSTF survey on amalgamation.[90]

When the elementary teachers met as one organization in the first ETFO annual general meeting in August 1998, it was with a constitution already prepared.[91] The two organizations had been negotiating the details of that document since 1994.[92] The new constitution provided designated positions for women and maintained 6 per cent of members' dues for women-only programs, ensuring women's interests would be protected.[93] It also included an enlarged defence fund, sending a clear signal to the membership, the trustees, and the state that the new union would not be passive. While the elementary teachers' unions of the past had often appeared to be more preoccupied with their differences than they had been with achieving gains through collective bargaining, the new union held the potential of a more focused militancy.

## CHAPTER 9

# Finding a Voice

## Gendered Unions

Gender, as it operated for eighty years in Ontario's two elementary teachers' unions, was a social process where individuals were treated differently based on their sexual identity in a situation where everything else was equal.[1] It was a foundational social process that established power relations, organized hierarchies of authority, and determined the legitimacy of one's experience. It was intrinsic to the formation of two separate elementary teachers' unions in Ontario. Gender intersected with class in shaping the political economy of the classroom and in institutionalizing labour relations.

The example of the Ontario elementary teachers demonstrates how the aspirations of workers can take different forms. The FWTAO and the OPSTF/OPSMTF sat together during labour negotiations, but beyond collective bargaining and the occasional political campaign, they retained their independence from one another. The uniquely gendered form of unionism that the elementary teachers assumed was the result of women having formed the first teachers' union. Because first-wave feminism was the historical context for the establishment of the FWTAO, feminism remained integral to the women's union.

In the FWTAO, women were able to construct a professional identity that challenged the hegemony of patriarchy and disrupted a paternalistic vision of how education was to be structured. It not only acknowledged women's ability to meet family responsibilities and manage the rigours of the classroom, but it also championed the capacity of women to fulfill the responsibilities of administration.

While the existence of the FWTAO was important to women teachers as the only OTF affiliate that advocated entirely for women, it did not make feminist objectives part of its collective bargaining strategy until they were supported by legislation. The FWTAO fought for its members both as teachers and as women, but for the most part, it did so on separate terrains. While it was a women-only union, it was also in harness with the OPSTF. Negotiating as one body undermined feminist aspirations when the compromises that were an outcome of having competing organizations seated on the same side of the table would not permit those aspirations space.[2] Simply put, the men would not align themselves with equity campaigns until they benefited OPSTF members, and the women's union had no desire to go it alone. While an amalgamated union was one means of resolving this impasse, the solution of separate negotiations remained untried.

Women were not viewed as equals in collective bargaining.[3] As Warskett points out:

> One of the important criticisms levelled at the union leadership by feminists at the time was that they had no interest in unionizing women. When there were attempts, the industrial male worker was adopted as the exemplar.... In turn, union organizers charged that women had no commitment to the workplace, were fearful of militant action, unwilling to confront management and hence reluctant to undertake strike action.[4]

This mischaracterization of women unionists was reflected in the blame laid at the feet of women after the 1997 strike.

Professionalism had always been more important to women teachers, who had limited opportunities in the workforce, than it was for the men, who had other options. For women, respectability preceded community status. Even into the mid-twentieth century, a woman could lose her teaching job if she was seen in a local bar. In education, respectability was a precondition of employability for a woman, a standard that was much more loosely applied to men, who could frequent bars and even more prurient enterprises.[5]

Women teachers had to align with what feminist labour historian Joan Sangster calls "women's fidelity to the rules of respectability."[6] Although the rules changed over time and in various locations, women were expected to know and embody what stood for respectability by local community standards. Professionalism in elementary teaching also included an ethos of care and moral guidance that aligned with respectable femininity, making it more difficult for women to separate themselves from their professional identity. Their behaviour had to be congruent with their position as professionals.

That differed from professionalism as discussed in the OPSTF. There "professional" was often used to berate peers for not sharing the same vision of professional conduct, one derived from a range of contested behaviours.

Professionalism distanced the elementary teachers from the larger labour movement, removing them from discourses of labour, but it was also a factor in keeping the two unions conjoined. With few exceptions, they would only associate with each other. The exclusive relationship between the FWTAO and the OPSTF was unusual within labour organizations.

The issues they held in common were the issues of "sameness." There were no improvements to salary, benefits, or working conditions to which women teachers would disagree. The issues of "difference" remained outside of collective bargaining by virtue of the OPSTF's ideological position that the women would be getting an "extra" benefit not available to the men. For the men's union, the long-held labour testament that "justice for one is justice for all" did not reach across the gender divide.

At the heart of the battle over amalgamation was the very real challenge the FWTAO presented to male supremacy. Men held entitlement to positions of "authority over," understood as the inherent superiority of men's thoughts, viewpoints, abilities, and decision-making capability as compared to women's. The widespread acceptance of male superiority entrenched the secondary status of women, minimizing their unique ideas, their particular perspectives, their personal aptitudes, and their ability to make right decisions. As Warskett states, the extension of male norms to women does nothing to challenge the masculinist hierarchy itself.[7] The often-stated belief that when 50 per cent of school principals were women, equity would be achieved in no way reflected the face of the workplace, where 70 to 80 per cent of the elementary teaching population in any board was women.[8] The 50 per cent goal sustained the assumption that principalships were the rightful property of men and women were being granted an equal share of those available.

The OPSTF paternalistic vision of amalgamation assumed that the men would not give anything up. The women of the FWTAO, on the other hand, were clear that an amalgamated union meant fundamental changes. In every other teachers' union in the country, men occupied a disproportionate number of seats on the executive, even when women were in a majority. As Sangster writes, male superiority was "woven into the fabric of daily life and social practices."[9] While the activists in the FWTAO may have been aware of the ideological underpinnings supporting the prevalence of men in elected positions, women in the other teachers' unions appeared to uncritically continue the practice.

The OPSTF fight for amalgamation was vicious. As an organization, it could have heard the women of the FWTAO express their preference and then supported its sister union. That is not beyond imagining. But this is not simply a story of two unions with differences of opinion. The men of the OPSTF held a heated animosity for the FWTAO. Entitlement is not enough to explain the magnitude of the men's hostility.

Sangster has identified a gendered form of paternalism that is inherent in the power relations of patriarchy.[10] Paternalism is an ideological process that establishes a hierarchy of credibility, the granting of believability of one world view over another. By including gendered paternalism as an organizing principle of the workplace and a means of enforcing patriarchy and male dominance, we can explain to some degree the reactivity of the men of the OPSTF to the very presence of an independent women's union.

Gendered paternalism legitimized patriarchy. When the FWTAO demanded an alternative organizing of the school system, access to promotions, and equal pay, it confronted the paternalistic structure of institutionalized patriarchal authority. Women were challenging social structures of male supremacy and paternalistic deference. They were overruling masculinity itself, exploding the myth of male superiority.

Paternalism buffered men from having to accept the viewpoints of women. The men of the OPSTF never did view the FWTAO as the equal of their own organization. Their inability to perceive male privilege was rooted in a paternalistic discourse that supported their masculine explanatory viewpoint.

While gendered paternalism had been weakened by the feminist movement, the school system had been organized under its direction. Had the elementary teachers been one union, they would have had these ideological battles within the union itself, as did the members of other unions, with women winning whatever successes they could. But because there were two unions, the fight was a public one between these two organizations. The majority of women teachers continued to value the protected space of the FWTAO for developing their politics. It was a place where they could voice their grievances and articulate a common response to the intractability of the men with whom they shared their workplace.

While the FWTAO was a safe place for women to be heard, the moratorium on discussing amalgamation blocked opportunities for debating changes to the way the union represented women teachers. It opened the FWTAO, an organization committed to providing a voice for women, to accusations of muzzling members who articulated unpopular views. The moratorium was intended to deny supporters of amalgamation a platform, but it also froze the discourse in 1977 terms. Members were prevented from examining the contradictions of a woman-only union. Such exchanges on the floor of the annual general meeting could have generated adaptive arguments for a women-only union and given voice to alternative strategies with which the FWTAO could have approached the amalgamation of 1998. As feminism waned in the public imagination, the moratorium denied younger members, who were questioning the tensions inherent in having two elementary teachers' unions, the opportunity to engage with the language of feminism in their own house.

By the time the Baum decision came into effect in 1995, the political landscape had shifted to the right. The OFL's call for collective action against Harris closed the gap between teachers' professionalism and their unionism. At the same time, the FWTAO and the OPSTF closed ranks over Harris's attacks on affirmative action and pay equity, fusing feminism with class warfare. The Baum decision was a defeat for the women's union, but the formation of the ETFO was not a direct outcome of a resolution to that human rights case. The FWTAO was not forced to end its women-only status. The loss of a unique voice for women was part of a more general dampening of feminism in the 1990s.

By 1997, the right of women to equal treatment had become widely accepted. The FWTAO had achieved access to promotions and pay equity, the most visible reasons for a women-only teachers' union. As they went into negotiations with the OPSTF over amalgamation, the women teachers were certain of their own strength as a union. With a guarantee of 6 per cent of the budget for women's programs and designated seats for women at the executive table, the FWTAO was able to ensure its voice would be carried forward, at least in the short term.[11] When faced with an uncertain future as an independent organization, the members of the FWTAO chose amalgamation, trusting that their larger numbers would make their voices heard in the new organization.[12] In the new union, they would outnumber men three to one.

The strike and the amalgamation were independent events, but the two weeks on the picket lines eased the historically antagonistic relations between the two unions. Maret Sädem-Thompson, the last FWTAO president, after listing some of the moments when the FWTAO and the OPSTF acted together against the Conservative government, proclaimed:

> In solidarity there is strength. The unions, our federations, make us strong. Recognizing this strength in unity, the delegates of the FWTAO and OPSTF annual meetings met jointly at the first meeting of the Elementary Teachers' Federation of Ontario (ETFO) on August 15, 1997, to collectively tell this government that elementary teachers and education workers believe in the power of united action.[13]

The ending of the strike, with the FWTAO president and the OPSTF president standing together in front of the television cameras, had aligned the elementary teachers, if only in defeat.

## The Construction of Resistance

From the beginning, public education was contradictory. Schooling was an advantage to workers in that it provided them with the necessary skills to negotiate the barriers of capitalist society. Yet, with very few exceptions, it disadvantaged them by sorting and fixing them in their class position. The process of citizenship training preserved the authority of the state, but the skills students learned also enabled them to participate in the political life of the nation and to engage in acts of resistance.

Because education is a project of moral performance, whenever the economic system required a different set of behaviours in the workplace, the school system was modified to develop these desired habits in students. Each time the education system shifted, teachers were forced to adjust in a dialectic between state pressure, institutional submission by trustees, and organized resistance from teachers.

In Western democracies, the mid-twentieth century brought with it an expansion of the rights of citizens under the rubric of social citizenship.[14] Social citizenship was an effort to mitigate the meanest features of capitalism. Publicly funded social programs provided a minimum level of security for citizens regardless of their income level. Social citizenship fuelled the construction of the welfare state by offering an enhanced vision of the responsibility of the state and the entitlements of citizenship.

As neo-liberalism gained traction in the mid-1980s, this expanded view of citizenship began to be reversed. Social citizenship represented an obstacle to the omnisufficiency of the marketplace and the economic elites' insistence on their own entitlement. Ideologically, neo-liberalism demonized any program that improved the general welfare of citizens. Teachers resisted neo-liberalism not only because it attacked their material well-being and demeaned their work, but also because it undermined the broad entitlements of a liberal education and diminished their students' life chances.

As a political project, neo-liberalism had distinctive characteristics that affected the education system.[15] Foremost among them, market and trade freedom masked as individual, personal freedom. Students needed to be trained to accept, as inevitable and unalterable, an entrepreneurial world of precarity.

Despite the new right's cultish endorsement of the market as the primary means of governing the economy and its workings, the elementary teachers in Ontario were able to make significant improvements to their working conditions.[16] The willingness of locals to support strike votes and the use of mediation proved effective. As historian E.P. Thompson understood, workers' organizations develop while they are in motion.[17] By participating in the one-day strike of 1973, the elementary teachers had awakened to the strength of unionism.[18] While they continued to view themselves as professionals and did not identify with the labour movement, once they began to use the tactics of labour to pursue the benefits achieved by other workers, notably the secondary teachers, Ontario elementary teachers became conscious of their collective strength. They were then able to push back against trustees' demands and bring that conversation to the picket line.

The 1995 election of Mike Harris brought a stark dismantling of the welfare state. Alan Sears identifies this period as the construction of the "post-liberal" education system. Although schools were institutions beset with problems, the teachers in them believed that they were offering their students opportunities to improve their quality of life. The neo-liberal vision of education highlighted retrenchment and academic reform, narrowing the scope of opportunities for students. The shift to the right destabilized teachers' professional identity and the social responsibilities that they believed they carried. To the elementary teachers, the post-liberal education project undermined their professionalism by making them complicit in denying their students the entitlements of secure employment and robust social programs. At the same time, the new regime threatened their own job security. All that prevented a return to the circumstances of the past was their unions and their commitment to them.[19]

By tabling Bill 160, the Education Quality Improvement Act, the Conservative caucus threw down the gauntlet in 1997. This is a critical point. The Harris government challenged the teachers by threatening to eliminate those things in their work lives that teachers had fought to achieve, including preparation time, caps on class size, the right to strike, and the obligation of the board of education to collect union dues. The teachers' unions had to counter or be rendered irrelevant.

By this time the leadership had the confidence of having led a number of contentious strikes. They had developed an ideology of resistance that invigorated activists and provided a lens through which teachers saw resistance as effective. Importantly, the Days of Action provided experience in coalition building that was essential to support a political strike. The Harris government became the common enemy that unified them.

The teachers' unions were not simply reacting to a billion dollars being cut from the education budget. On an individual level, they were also resisting the redesigning of the purpose of education that was represented by the College of Teachers, EQAO testing, and the ascendancy of measurable literacy and numeracy to the exclusion of other subjects. Teachers viewed training students in the imperatives of good citizenship as integral to their personal relationship with their students. The psychological/social basis of teaching was to offer students a future, one that hopefully emerged from students' own interests. Paring down education to a standardized and measurable form closed off alternatives that teachers had traditionally been able to offer. Harris's restructuring agenda destabilized the foundation from which teachers approached their students.

The outrage teachers exhibited in 1997 was further enflamed by a violation of what E.P. Thompson has identified in another context as the "moral economy." The moral economy of the classroom balanced students' needs and abilities, the curriculum, teachers' professional judgment, and sufficient resources. Teaching included a concern for students, however imperfectly it may be presented. The Harris Conservatives' neo-liberal intrusions replaced an economy of learning with the economics of productivity.

While the focus and purpose of the unions were the interests of their members, the unions also had to align with individual teachers' sense of connectedness to those with whom they spent their days. This contradiction is addressed through the unions' acknowledgement of "professionalism" as a sense of responsibility for someone other than oneself. Like the 1973 strike, the two-week 1997 strike was a moral commitment from the teachers, not only to protect themselves as a collective, but also to defend their students.

Despite its anticlimax, the 1997 strike was the most expansive political campaign in the history of the OTF affiliates.[20] The marches and rallies across the province shifted popular support to the teachers' camp, particularly among parents of school-aged children. While their representatives often appeared awkward on local news reports, teachers' credibility remained secure. Even Harris's constant vilification of the unions was unable to discredit the teachers themselves.

The collapse of the strike was an ideological victory for the Conservative government. Harris was successful in reducing the education budget in order to pay for his tax cuts. For their part, the teachers' unions could claim to have won on the key issue of retaining collective bargaining.

The removal of principals and vice-principals was not a huge loss to the union. While school administrators had held many of the leadership positions, they had been a small minority of the membership. Ironically, by legislating them out of the union, Harris eliminated a middle-management filter that had muted the voice of the rank and file. Demands for improved working conditions would become stronger in the future.

The unions learned from their missteps in 1997. Never again did the OTF become the voice of striking teachers. Once the Liberal government legislated provincial bargaining for teachers in 2014, each provincial organization became the negotiating body for all of its locals. By the time Doug Ford's government came to power in 2018, all teachers' collective agreements had been set to expire in the same year, allowing teachers to legally march together to protest Conservative funding cuts, with each president speaking for their own membership. Political activism and collective bargaining were linked, providing a much stronger platform for teachers' resistance and providing the unions with a more focused campaign.

Equity, as a principle of social justice, would remain a key feature of the ETFO, a direct connection to the roots of feminism that had animated the women's union.[21] The ETFO has placed the issues of women's work lives, including childbearing and family responsibilities, on the negotiating table.[22] The elementary teachers' equity campaigns have been expanded to support a full range of sexual orientation and gender identities and to combat racism. When the amalgamation was finalized, the FWTAO had recognized sexual orientation as a prohibited ground of discrimination in 1990 and was developing programs to eradicate racism and homophobia. The FWTAO Guidebook stated, "A member of FWTAO who thinks she has been discriminated against on the basis of race, ancestry, place of origin, citizenship, creed, sex, sexual orientation . . . should first call the FWTAO office in Toronto." By 1998 a program called Untying the Knots of Prejudice, which included homophobia, had brought together a focus group to develop strategies within the schools.[23] Although such programs were being developed in some locals before 1998, particularly in Toronto, no province-wide campaigns appear to have been instituted in either of the elementary unions.[24]

Viewed through a feminist lens, the amalgamation of the two elementary teachers' unions brought about the end of a unique organization that had spoken entirely with the voice of women. While women teachers' experiences and interests were never homogeneous, the ending of the all-women union, with its expertise and resources speaking for women by women, was a loss for Canadian women.[25] Although the ETFO has maintained and broadened the feminist/equity roots of the FWTAO, its membership is 75 per cent women, but not its leadership.

Examined through a class lens, it is evident that the amalgamation created a more powerful union in the ETFO. The years of suspicion and mistrust that had undermined the strength of both the FWTAO and the OPSTF came to an end. The elementary teachers could pursue their objectives as one body with one voice. In the summer of 2000, delegates to the annual general meeting voted to affiliate with the Canadian Labour Congress and the Ontario Federation of Labour.[26] Ontario elementary teachers formally joined the labour movement.

Bringing the two organizations together strengthened the elementary teachers' bargaining position. In 2005, under president Emily Noble and general secretary Gene Lewis, the ETFO negotiated two hundred minutes of preparation time, one forty-minute period per day for every full-time teacher in the province.[27] It was a dramatic show of strength from the young union. Importantly, the elementary teachers' salaries and benefits came to equal those of the secondary teachers of the OSSTF, although their working conditions still lagged.

More recently, the 2019–20 battle with the Ford Conservative government has demonstrated how politicized elementary teachers have become. When I talked with ETFO members on the picket lines, the feeling was that the dispute would not be resolved quickly, yet there was no sense of dread. The decision to engage in a revolving pattern of strikes ensured every teacher of an income while still attacking the political actors making the decisions. It was also apparent that teachers believed the public was on their side— and there was evidence to support that position.[28]

In early 2020, the COVID-19 pandemic struck. With nearly seven million workers applying for the Canada Emergency Response Benefit and schools closed for an indefinite period, the teachers accepted the 1 per cent increase and the government backed off on certain funding cuts and plans for degrading working conditions.[29] It was hard to call either side a winner, but teachers did not cave in at any point and could claim to have pushed the Ford government back on funding and class size, even if they'd lost on salary. Those were significant wins against a manifestly populist government shaping itself to replicate the Harris years.

Teachers became front-line workers in a COVID-19 world. Those tensions were played out by a generation of teachers who were experienced in work stoppages and picket signs. Overnight, they were immersed in circumstances none of them could have imagined. When it was elected, the Ford government appeared intent on strengthening the grip of neo-liberalism on the province. Despite that, the threat of the contagion reintroduced the state's responsibility for its citizens into the political discourse. How the elementary teachers and their amalgamated union navigate those contradictions is going to determine their future.

# Timeline of Key Events

| | |
|---|---|
| 1846 | Common School Act enacts public education in Canada West. |
| 1861 | The Ontario Educational Association (OEA) is formed. |
| 1871 | School Act establishes provincial inspectors and requires teachers to attend teachers' institute conferences. |
| 1885 | The first association of women teachers in Canada is formed in Toronto. |
| 1888 | The Lady Teachers' Association of Toronto is formed. |
| 1912 | Regulation 17 limits instruction in French to Grades 1 and 2. |
| 1918 | The Federation of Women Teachers' Associations of Ontario (FWTAO) is formed. |
| 1919 | The OEA supports equal pay for men and women. The Ontario Secondary School Teachers' Federation (OSSTF) is formed. |
| 1920 | The Ontario Public School Men Teachers' Federation (OPSMTF) is formed. |
| 1939 | L'Association des enseignants franco-ontariens (AEFO) is formed. |
| 1944 | Teaching Profession Act is passed. It creates the Ontario Teachers Federation (OTF) and provides for dues check-off at source. The Ontario English Catholic Teachers' Association (OECTA) is formed. |
| 1947 | Baby boom begins. |
| 1950 | Hope Commission tables its report. |
| 1951 | Joint FWTAO-OPSMTF salary committee is established. |
| 1953 | First grey letter is issued, against the Deseronto school board. |
| 1961 | The OPSMTF and the FWTAO agree upon one salary schedule. Robarts government begins building new schools. |

| 1962 | Premier Robarts relinquishes the education portfolio. Bill Davis is appointed minister of education. |
|---|---|
| 1963 | Most teachers resign from the Lakefield Public School Board. |
| 1966 | Baby boom ends. |
| 1967 | Hundreds of small boards of education are amalgamated into county boards of education.<br>Royal Commission on the Status of Women is created. |
| 1968 | The FWTAO forms the Young Married Women Teachers Committee.<br>Hall-Dennis Report is released. |
| 1969 | Davis, as minister of education, appoints the Reville Committee.<br>Qualifications Evaluation Council (QECO), through an agreement with the AEFO, FWTAO, OECTA, and OPSMTF, establishes salary scales based on qualifications.<br>Eleven amalgamated FWTAO and OPSMTF locals are active in the province. |
| 1971 | Bill Davis becomes premier.<br>Women are able to receive 15 weeks of paid maternity leave through unemployment insurance.<br>In December, the "90 factor" for pensions is brought in. |
| 1972 | National Action Committee on the Status of Women (NAC) is formed.<br>Reville Report is released.<br>Mary Hill, president of the Teachers' Federation of Carleton, becomes the first female voluntary member of OPSMTF. |
| 1973 | Over 5,000 Metro Toronto teachers gather in front of Queen's Park to protest the cutting of 1,145 teaching positions.<br>Bill 274, An Act to Amend the Ministry of Education Act, is introduced in the legislature, followed by Bill 275, An Act to Amend the Schools Administration Act.<br>On 18 December, all five unions join in a one-day, province-wide strike. |
| 1975 | Bill 100, School Boards and Teachers Collective Negotiations Act, is passed. |

Prime Minister Pierre Trudeau brings in federal wage and price controls and the Anti-Inflation Board (AIB).
*Formative Years* and *Education in the Primary and Junior Divisions* are released.

1977    The FWTAO Inter-mark poll on amalgamation is released.
        Jackson Commission (CODE) is established.

1978    Wage and price controls end.
        Final Jackson Report is released.
        Bette Stephenson is appointed minister of education.
        Lambton County teachers hold the first strike vote of elementary teachers under Bill 100.

1979    The boards of education are required to adopt formal affirmative action plans for the 1979–80 school year.
        Peel teachers strike for 13 days, the first elementary teacher strike under Bill 100.
        Brant teachers strike for 22 days.

1980    Matthews Commission Report is released.
        Bill 82, The Education Amendment Act, 1980, establishes special education classes.

1982    The OPSMTF removes "Men" from its name to become the OPSTF.
        Public Sector Compensation Restraint Act brings a second round of federal wage controls.
        Bill 179, Ontario Inflation Restraint Act, enacts provincial wage controls.
        Public Sector Coalition is formed.
        Bill 127, The Municipality of Metropolitan Toronto Amendment Act, amalgamates Metro Toronto school boards.
        "Exploding contracts" are ended.

1983    Bill 111, Public Sector Prices and Compensation Review Act, extends wage and price controls in Ontario for another year.

1984    The OPSTF begins the unionization of occasional teachers.
        Davis announces full funding for Roman Catholic separate schools system.
        Mary Hill is elected OPSTF president.
        Bette Stephenson launches the Affirmative Action Incentive Fund.

1985   Section 15, Equality Rights of the Charter of Rights and Freedoms comes into effect.
       Marg Tomen begins her court case to join the men's union.
       Liberals under David Peterson form the government.
       Ontario *Green Paper on Pay Equity* is released.

1986   Ontario Labour Relations Board grants OPSTF status as a trade union.
       Ontario Divisional Court dismisses Tomen's case.

1987   Metro Toronto teachers strike.
       Radwanski Report is released.
       Ontario Pay Equity Act is passed.
       Justice Ewaschuk dismisses Tomen's case.

1988   Linda Logan-Smith goes before the OTF Board of Directors.
       30,000 signatures on petitions requesting a change to the OTF's Bylaw 1, which kept women from joining the men's union, are delivered.
       Dr. Daniel Baum appointed to hear Tomen and Logan-Smith human rights cases.
       The OPSTF effort to unionize federal First Nation schools begins.

1989   Liberal government sets a goal of 50 per cent women school administrators.

1990   OPSTF begins to organize non-teaching workers in schools.
       Ottawa teachers strike.
       Lambton teachers strike.
       Boards of education are required to have affirmative action programs in place.
       NDP under Bob Rae form the government.

1991   Walpole Island teachers join OPSTF.
       A pension agreement is signed, giving teachers control of their pension fund.

1992   Fort Albany Band brings unionization of First Nation schools to a halt.
       $190 million is allocated for pay equity by the NDP government.
       The OPSTF claims 50 per cent of its members are women.

| | |
|---|---|
| 1993 | Social Contract is enacted.<br>East Parry Sound teachers strike.<br>Windsor teachers strike. |
| 1994 | Baum decision is handed down, ending the mandated division of the elementary teachers' unions by sex. |
| 1995 | Monique Bégin and Gerald Caplan release the Report of the Royal Commission on Learning.<br>Conservatives under Mike Harris form the government.<br>On 11 October, Bill 8, An Act to Repeal Job Quotas and to Restore Merit-based Employment Practices in Ontario, is tabled.<br>On 12 October, Bill 7, An Act to Restore Balance and Stability to Labour Relations and to Promote Economic Prosperity, is tabled. It permits replacement workers during a strike and layoffs without just cause.<br>On 29 November, Bill 26, the Savings and Restructuring Act, 1995, is tabled.<br>On 30 November 30, John Snobelen announces cuts to education.<br>On 14 December, Bill 31, An Act to Establish the Ontario College of Teachers, is tabled. |
| 1996 | Leon Paroian is appointed to conduct a review of Bill 100.<br>Elementary teachers join the Ontario Federation of Labour "Days of Action." |
| 1997 | The FWTAO and the OPSTF members vote 88 per cent and 92.5 per cent, respectively, in favour of amalgamation.<br>Bill 160, the Education Quality Improvement Act, is tabled.<br>On Monday, 27 October, the two-week, province-wide strike begins. |
| 1998 | Elementary Teachers' Federation of Ontario (ETFO) is formed. |
| 2014 | School Boards Collective Bargaining Act requires provincial bargaining for all monetary items. |
| 2018 | Doug Ford forms a Conservative provincial government. |
| 2020 | March 11, the World Health Organization declares COVID-19 a pandemic. |

# Notes

## Preface

1. The more common term "Conservative government" or "Conservatives" is used throughout the book.

2. Doug Hart and Arlo Kempf, *Public Attitudes Toward Education in Ontario 2015: The 19th OISE Survey of Educational Issues* (Toronto, Ontario Institute for Studies in Education (OISE), 2015), 16.

3. "Sex" and "gender" were binary terms under the legislation; more inclusive definitions had not yet been imagined. I found no case where an elementary teacher had attempted to have their union affiliation reassigned as a result of changing their gender identity.

4. York University, Clara Thomas Archives and Special Collections (hereafter YUCTA), OPSTF 2010-006/62, David Lennox, "As I See It: Time to Change," *OPSTF News*, October 1982, 3. The men's union made the name change in order to attract women into its ranks.

5. See Robyn Maynard, *Policing Black Lives: State Violence in Canada from Slavery to the Present* (Halifax & Winnipeg: Fernwood, 2017), 208–28, for a critical analysis of anti-Black racism in the school systems of Ontario, Quebec, and Nova Scotia. Also, Keren Brathwaite and Carle James, eds., *Educating African Canadians* (Toronto: James Lorimer, 1996). Neither book references teachers' unions being involved in anti-racist campaigns. Nor did I find any such programs in the archives of the two unions.

6. Thomas Fleming, *Worlds Apart: British Columbia Schools, Politics, and Labour Relations before and after 1972* (Mill Bay, BC: Bendall Books, 2011) is a Canadian example of a writer who takes a traditional view of historical development (sometimes called "whiggish") rather than a political economy viewpoint.

7. Thomas Picketty, *Capital in the Twenty-First Century* (Cambridge, MA: Harvard University Press, 2013), 237–335.

8. Andrea Levy, "In Conversation with Bhaskar Sunkara: The Trump Victory and the U.S. Left," *Canadian Dimension*, 51,1 (Winter 2017), 11. Sunkara is the editor and publisher of *Jacobin* magazine.

## Chapter 1: Constructing Public Education

1. Bruce Curtis, *Building the Educational State: Canada West, 1836–1871* (London, ON: Althouse, 1988), 24–25, 366–72.

2. Will Sloan, "New Plaque Next to Egerton Ryerson Statue Contextualizes Colonial Legacy," *Ryerson Today*, 10 July 2018, ryerson.ca.

3. James Miller, *Shingwauk's Vision: A History of Native Residential Schools* (Toronto: University of Toronto Press, 1996), 184.

4. Truth and Reconciliation Commission of Canada, *Final Report of the Truth and Reconciliation Commission of Canada: Volume One* (Toronto: James Lorimer and Company, 2015).

5. Bruce Curtis, "Educational Reform and the Construction of a Public in Upper Canada," in *The "Benevolent" State: The Growth of Welfare in Canada,* ed. Allan Moscovitch and Jim Albert (Toronto: Garamond Press, 1987), 51–54; Millie Morton, *Grace: A Teacher's Life, One-Room Schools, and a Century of Change in Ontario* (self-published, 2013), 112–14. Schools existed in Canada West before 1846, but they were locally controlled. The one-room school in Wellman, north of Stirling, was built in 1838.

6. Elizabeth Graham, "Schoolmarms and Early Teaching in Ontario," in *Women at Work: Ontario, 1850–1930,* ed. Janice Acton, Penny Goldsmith, and Bonnie Shepard (Toronto: Canadian Women's Educational Press, 1974), 170–74.

7. Bryan Palmer, *Working Class Experience: Rethinking the History of Canadian Labour, 1800–1991,* 2nd ed. (Toronto: McClelland and Stewart, 1992), 37–47; Alison Taylor, "Education for Industrial and 'Postindustrial' Purposes," *Educational Policy* 11,1 (March 1997), 5–6; Robert Kristofferson, "Craftsworkers and Canada's First Industrial Revolution: Reassessing the Context," *Journal of the Canadian Historical Society* 16,1 (2005), 116.

8. Egerton Ryerson, *Report on a System of Public Elementary Instruction for Upper Canada* (Montreal: Lovell and Gibson, 1847); Curtis, *Building the Educational State,* 101–7.

9. Louis Althusser, *On Ideology* (New York: Verso, 2008); Michael Apple, *Ideology and Curriculum* (New York: Routledge, 1990); Erik Olin Wright, *Class, Crisis and the State* (London: Verso, 1978).

10. Julian Kitchen and Diana Petrarca, "Teacher Preparation in Ontario: A History," *Teaching & Learning* 8,1 (2013/2014), 58; R.A. Hopkins, *The Long March* (Toronto: Baxter Publishing, 1969), 25.

11. Doris French, *High Button Bootstraps: Federation of Women Teachers' Associations of Ontario: 1918–1968* (Toronto: Ryerson Press, 1968), 17, 53, 63; Hopkins, *The Long March,* 72. After they formed, the FWTAO and the OPSMTF were both opposed to county model schools. By 1928, under pressure from both elementary teachers' unions, model schools had been discontinued.

12. Marta Danylewycz, Beth Light, and Alison Prentice, "The Evolution of the Sexual Division of Labour in Teaching: A Nineteenth-Century Ontario and Quebec Case Study," *Histoire sociale—Social History,* 16,31 (May 1983), 100–101; Marta Danylewycz and Alison Prentice, "Teachers' Work: Changing Patterns and Perceptions in the Emerging School Systems of Nineteenth- and Early Twentieth-Century Central Canada," *Labour / Le Travail* 17 (Spring 1986), 59–82.

13. Susan Gelman, "Stratford (Normal School) Teachers' College, 1908–1973," *Historical Studies in Education* 14,1 (2002), 115–16. "Normal" meaning that teachers were trained in the "principles and practice of teaching according to rules."

14. Ruth Childs and Barbara Bower, "Teacher Testing and Certification: An Historical Perspective from Ontario," *Journal of Educational Administration and History* 38,3 (December 2006); Alison Prentice, *The School Promoters: Education and Social Class in Mid-nineteenth Century Upper Canada* (Toronto: McClelland and Stewart, 1988), 18.

15. Harry Smaller, "Regulating the Regulators: The Disciplining of Teachers in Nineteenth-Century Ontario," in *Discipline, Moral Regulation, and Schooling*, ed. Kate Rousmaniere, Kari Dehli, and Ning de Coninck-Smith (New York: Garland, 1997), 102–5, 108–10.

16. Canada, An Act for the Better Establishment and Maintenance of Common Schools in Upper Canada, 23 May 1846, Statutes of Province of Canada, 9 Victoria, Chapter XX (1846), v.

17. G. Patrick O'Neill, "Teacher Education or Teacher Training: Which Is It?," *McGill Journal of Education* 21,3 (1986), 257.

18. R.D. Gidney, *From Hope to Harris: The Reshaping of Ontario's Schools* (Toronto: University of Toronto Press, 2002), 21, 53–55; Gelman, "Stratford (Normal School) Teachers' College," 120–21.

19. Ryerson, *Report*, 171–80.

20. Prentice, *The School Promoters*, 18.

21. John Abbot, "Accomplishing 'a Man's Task': Rural Women Teachers, Male Culture, and the School Inspectorate in Turn-of-the-Century Ontario," in *Gender and Education in Ontario: An Historical Reader*, ed. Ruby Heap and Alison Prentice (Toronto: Canadian Scholars' Press, 1991), 51–72.

22. Patrice Milewski, "Perilous Times: An Oral History of Teachers' Experience with School Inspection in the 1930s," *History of Education* 41,5 (September 2012). Milewski's oral history of the relationship between teachers and inspectors gives examples of the authoritarian pettiness and rigidity of the twice-yearly inspections.

23. YUCTA, FWTAO 1999-027/354, "Elementary and Secondary Education Integrated," *FWTAO Newsletter*, February 1965, 1.

24. Prentice, *The School Promoters*, 162–63.

25. Prentice, *The School Promoters*, 17–19; Graham, "Schoolmarms and Early Teaching," 175–82.

26. Hopkins, *The Long March*, 72. Hopkins notes that the rural boards were typically made up of three men. Robert Harris's famous painting hanging in the National Gallery of Canada, "A Meeting of the School Trustees," shows four men listening to a young woman teacher in PEI in 1885.

27. Rebecca Coulter and Christopher Greig, "The Man Question in Teaching: An Historical Overview," *Alberta Journal of Educational Research* 54,4 (Winter 2008), 421–22.

28. Susan Houston and Alison Prentice, *Schooling and Scholars in Nineteenth-Century Ontario* (Toronto: University of Toronto Press, 1988), 155–86.

29. Patrick Harrigan, "The Schooling of Boys and Girls in Canada," *Journal of Social History* 23,4 (Summer 1990), 811.

30. Mary Labatt, *Always a Journey: A History of the Federation of Women Teachers' Associations of Ontario, 1918–1993* (Toronto: Federation of Women Teachers' Associations of Ontario, 1993), 30–31.

31. French, *High Button Bootstraps*, 20–21; Sheila Cavanagh, "Female-Teacher Gender and Sexuality in Twentieth-Century Ontario, Canada," *History of Education Quarterly* 45 (Summer 2005), 250–52.

32. Danylewycz, Light, and Prentice, "The Evolution of the Sexual Division of Labour," 83–86, 96–101.

33. Patrice Milewski, "Teachers' Institutes in Late Nineteenth-Century Ontario," *Paedagogica Historica* 44,5 (2008), 610–14.

34. Ontario Educational Association, *Ontario Educational Association—1911* (Toronto: Ryerson Press, 1911), 34, 52–58, archive.org.

35. Elections Canada, "A History of the Vote in Canada," Chapter 2: From a Privilege to a Right: 1867–1919, elections.ca.

36. Toronto Women Teachers' Association, *The Story of the Women Teachers' Association of Toronto* (Toronto: Thomas Nelson and Sons, 1930), 7–16; Labatt, *Always a Journey*, 7.

37. Prentice, *The School Promoters*, 19, 148–51.

38. Gidney, *From Hope to Harris*, 11.

39. There is no evidence that teachers who were widows or who were the sole support for their family, and therefore permitted to teach, were treated any differently than other women teachers when it came to salaries.

40. Terry Wotherspoon, "From Subordinate Partners to Dependent Employees: State Regulation of Public School Teachers in Nineteenth-Century British Columbia," *Labour / Le Travail* 31 (Spring 1993), 77–78. Wotherspoon references British Columbia, the United States, Ontario, and Quebec.

41. Toronto Women Teachers' Association, *The Story of the Women Teachers' Association of Toronto*, 41.

42. Ontario Educational Association, *Ontario Educational Association, 1918* (Toronto: Ryerson Press 1918), 21–22.

43. YUCTA, FWTAO 1999-027/030, FWTAO Annual Meeting Minutes 1920, 7 April 1920, 30. Handwritten minutes.

44. Ontario Educational Association, *Ontario Educational Association—1920* (Toronto: Ryerson Press 1920), 17–18; YUCTA, OPSTF 2010-006/58, Research Papers, Articles & Miscellaneous file, unsigned, typewritten document. The origins of the OPSMTF are in dispute. R.F. Downey, a Peterborough principal, claims that he and Mr. Clark organized a meeting of the "male Public School Teachers of Peterborough" on 29 November 1918, established a constitution and sent it to the teachers in ten other cities for discussion. He contends that a first meeting of what was to become the OPSMTF was then held at the 1919 Ontario Educational Association meeting, but the Peterborough group was then usurped in 1920 by Chas Fraser and the Toronto teachers.

45. YUCTA, FWTAO 1999-027/289, *We the Teachers of Ontario*, 1944. The OTF reported approximately 24,500 teachers in the province in 1944, of whom

2,000 were OECTA members. The FWTAO had 12,000 members and was the largest of the teachers' unions at more than twice the membership of OSSTF. The OPSMTF reported 3,200 members.

46. Ontario Teachers' Federation (OTF), "About OTF: What We Do," otffeo.on.ca.

47. Labatt, *Always a Journey*; French, *High Button Bootstraps*, 112–14; Hopkins, *The Long March*, 141–52; Kristina Llewellyn, *Democracy's Angels: The Work of Women Teachers* (Montreal and Kingston: McGill-Queen's University Press, 2012), 108. In response to rumours of an unwritten agreement included in the negotiations for the Ontario Teacher Profession Act: none of the above writers references a "gentlemen's agreement" of any sort. Hopkins in particular, while relating his interview with one of the negotiating team members who was at the table with the ministry officials, never mentions an agreement to not engage in strikes or one that required that the two unions negotiate their collective agreements together. Nor did I find any reference in the fonds to such understandings.

48. Harry Smaller, "The Teaching Profession Act in Canada: A Critical Perspective," in *Labour Gains, Labour Pains: 50 Years of PC 1003*, ed. Cy Gonick, Paul Phillips, and Jess Vorst (Winnipeg: Society for Socialist Studies, 1995), 341–60.

49. Harry Smaller, "The Teacher Disempowerment Debate: Historical Reflections on 'Slender Autonomy,'" *Paedagogica Historica* 51,1–2 (2015), 136–51, 149.

50. Not all teachers were able to join the OTF as affiliates. Schools for First Nation children on reserves fell under federal jurisdiction with many, but not all, of those teachers represented by the Public Service Alliance of Canada (PSAC). The Ontario Teaching Profession Act did not cover private schools, which were largely exempt from provincial regulations and operated without unions. Teachers in schools for the deaf, blind, and other learning exceptionalities would not be given a specific designation under legislation until the passing of the Provincial Schools Negotiations Act in 1975. They would organize a sixth teachers' union, the Federation of Provincial Schools Authority Teachers (FOPSAT) outside of the OTF. FOPSAT would eventually merge with the secondary teachers to become its own local within the OSSTF (OSST, District 30, Provincial Schools Authority Teachers, d30.osstf.ca).

51. Mona Gleason, *Normalizing the Ideal: Psychology, Schooling, and the Family in Postwar Canada* (Toronto: University of Toronto Press, 1999), 31–36, 80–96, 119–25; Kari Dehli, "Doing Histories of Education and Psychology," *Encounters* 15 (2014), 109–13.

52. Jason Ellis, "Brains Unlimited: Giftedness and Gifted Education in Canada before *Sputnik* (1957)," *Canadian Journal of Education* 40,2 (2017), 11.

53. David Foot, *Boom, Bust and Echo: How to Profit from the Coming Demographic Shift* (Toronto: Macfarlane Walter and Ross, 1996), 18–22. Foot identifies the baby boom as the demographic increase in births between 1947 and 1966.

54. Cavanagh, "Female-Teacher Gender and Sexuality," 252–54.

55. Cavanagh, "Female-Teacher Gender and Sexuality," 114.

56. French, *High Button Bootstraps*, 134; OFL, "Submission of the Ontario Federation of Labour to the Royal Commission on the Status of Women," Appendix III. By 1967, 60 per cent of married women in Canada were in the labour force.

57. YUCTA, FWTAO 1999-027/1022, Motion passed at the March 20, 1968 Directors' Meeting.

58. YUCTA, FWTAO 1999-027/1022, Minutes of the Committee to Study the Problems of Young Married Women Teachers, 15 June 1968, 2.

59. YUCTA, FWTAO 1999-027/029, Annual Meeting Minutes 1981, 48. By 1980, 72 per cent of the membership of the FWTAO were married women.

60. Cavanagh, "Female-Teacher Gender and Sexuality," 266–67.

61. Danylewycz, Light, and Prentice, "The Evolution of the Sexual Division of Labour," 33–60.

62. YUCTA, OPSTF 2010-006/61, "Editorial: Selecting the New Principal," *OPSMTF News*, 1970–71, 2, 8.

63. French, *High Button Bootstraps*, 132.

64. French, *High Button Bootstraps*, 132. (Emphasis in the original.)

65. YUCTA, FWTAO 1999-027/162, Directors Meetings, Executive Meetings, Joint Meetings 1957–59 file, Minutes of Executive Meeting of the Federation of Women Teachers' Associations of Ontario, 22 August 1957, 1.

66. YUCTA, FWTAO 1999-027/283, Amalgamation-Miscellaneous (1&2), Beverly Brophy, "Amalgamation of the Federation of Women Teachers' Associations of Ontario and the Ontario Public School Men Teachers' Federation—Advantages and Disadvantages," 1974, 13. Paper for predoctoral study at University of Toronto; YUCTA, FWTAO 1999-027/162, Directors Meetings, Executive Meetings, Joint Meetings 1957–59 file, Minutes of Executive Meeting of the Federation of Women Teachers' Associations of Ontario, 2 November 1957, 2; 7 December 1957, 1.

67. Hopkins, *The Long March*, 209.

68. YUCTA, OPSTF 2010-006/61, "Formal Schooling and Income," *OPSMTF Newsletter*, February 1962, 2.

69. YUCTA, FWTAO 1999-027/008, Report of the Board of Directors 1976–77, 17–19; Qualifications Evaluation Council of Ontario, "Welcome to QECO," "History," qeco.on.ca.

70. YUCTA, FWTAO 1999-027/317, QECO 1969–72, Letter from Harvey R. Wilson to Miss Dorothy Martin, 21 April 1970.

71. YUCTA, FWTAO 1999-027/165, Federation of Women Teachers' Associations of Ontario's Response to the Ministry of Education's Position on Certification, n.d., 1–3; YUCTA, FWTAO 1999-027/024 (11C), 56th Annual Meeting of the Federation of Women Teachers' Associations of Ontario, minutes verbatim, 499.

72. YUCTA, FWTAO 1999-027/024, FWTAO Annual Meeting Minutes verbatim, 16–18 August 1972, 80–82.

73. YUCTA, FWTAO 1999-027/283(02), Letter from L. Dorothy Martin to R.H. Soward, Re: Amalgamation, 28 January 1971; YUCTA, OPSTF 2010-006/61 "Amalgamation, Phase One: At the Local Level," *OPSMTF News*, 1970–71, 6, 4.

74. YUCTA, FWTAO 1999-027/283(02), "(A Special Newsletter) Co-operation NOT Amalgamation," 1970, cover. Note: The legislation regarding education, unlike the Ontario Labour Relations Act, did not separate principals, as administrators, from classroom teachers.

75. YUCTA, FWTAO 1999-027/283(02), "(A Special Newsletter) Co-operation NOT Amalgamation," 1970, 2–6.

76. YUCTA, FWTAO 1999-027/283(02), "(A Special Newsletter) Co-operation NOT Amalgamation," 1970.

77. Judy Rebick, *Ten Thousand Roses: The Making of a Feminist Revolution* (Toronto: Penguin Canada, 2005), 27.

78. YUCTA, FWTAO 1999-027/333, Affirmative Action 1980–84 file, Memorandum from Thomas L. Wells to Chairmen of School Boards, "Equal Employment and Promotion Opportunities for Women," 2 January 1976, 1.

79. Ontario, Provincial Secretary for Social Development, *Equal Opportunity for Women in Ontario: A Plan for Action*, 1973.

80. YUCTA, FWTAO 1999-027/183, Minutes of the Board of Directors' Meeting, 15 June 1974, 8–11.

81. YUCTA, FWTAO 1999-027/270B, *About Face: Towards a More Positive Image of Women in Textbooks*, Ontario Status of Women Council, 1974; YUCTA, FWTAO 1999-027/183, Minutes of the Board of Directors' Meeting, 7 December 1974, 6; Minutes of the Board of Directors' Meeting, 7 February 1975, 2.

82. John Andrew Hope et al., *The Royal Commission on Education in Ontario* (Ontario, 1950), 575; Gidney, *From Hope to Harris*, 23–24, 29–30.

83. Kitchen and Petrarca, "Teacher Preparation in Ontario," 63; Gidney, *From Hope to Harris*, 53. John Robarts was premier of Ontario 1961–71.

84. YUCTA, OPSTF 2010-006/61, A.W. Robb, "Consolidation of School Boards," *OPSMTF Newsletter*, November–December 1967, 1; Ontario, Ministry of Education and Training, "For the Love of Learning," edu.gov.on.ca.

85. Peter Hennessy, *Schools in Jeopardy: Collective Bargaining in Education* (Toronto: McClelland and Stewart, 1979), 51–53.

86. Emmett Hall and Lloyd Dennis, *Living and Learning: Provincial Committee on Aims and Objectives of Education in the Schools of Ontario* (Toronto: Ontario Department of Education, 1968).

87. Gidney, *From Hope to Harris*, 70–77.

88. Nadeem Memon, "Contextualizing Hall-Dennis: The Rise of Progressive Educational Practices in Ontario, 1968–1972," OISE, M.A. thesis, 2006, 84.

89. Memon, "Contextualizing Hall-Dennis," 212.

90. Ontario Ministry of Education, "For the Love of Learning."

91. YUCTA, FWTAO 1999-027/030, Annual Meeting Minutes verbatim, August 1975, 294–99.

92.   The Department of Education was changed to the Ministry of Education in 1972.

93.   YUCTA, FWTAO 1999-027/030, Annual Meeting Minutes verbatim, August 1975, 294–95.

94.   YUCTA, FWTAO 1999-027/030, Annual Meeting Minutes verbatim, August 1975, 297.

95.   Canadian Teachers' Federation (CTF), "Teacher Strikes and Sanctions in Canada, 1919–1992."

96.   S.G.B. Robinson, *Do Not Erase* (Toronto: Ontario Secondary School Teachers' Federation, 1971). In 1950, prior to the Deseronto sanction by elementary teachers, the OSSTF local in Sudbury had issued a "pink letter" along with collecting teachers' resignations, effective January. The resignations were put before the courts. The local then withdrew both the pink letter and the resignations from the negotiations. Consequently, the CTF did not designate this series of actions as a workplace sanction.

97.   Ron Poste, OPSMTF past-president 1972–73, interview at his home in Trenton, ON, 21 November 2008. Those teachers who had continued to work for the Lakefield board were subsequently refused the support of their unions for the remainder of their careers.

98.   Linda Briskin, "In the Public Interest: Nurses on Strike," in *Public Sector Unions in The Age of Austerity*, ed. Stephanie Ross and Larry Savage (Halifax and Winnipeg: Fernwood, 2013); Linda Briskin, "Nurse Militancy and Strike Action," *Workers of the World* 1,2 (January 2013), 105–34.

99.   CTF, "Teacher Strikes and Sanctions in Canada."

100.   YUCTA, OPSTF 2010-006/61, "Minister's Cost Ceilings: How Will They Affect Education?," *OPSMTF News* 1970–71, 7, 1.

101.   For a full discussion of the 1960s and labour, see Bryan Palmer, *Canada's 1960s: The Ironies of Identity in a Rebellious Era* (Toronto: University of Toronto Press, 2008); YUCTA, OPSTF 2010-006/61, "Editorial," *OPSMTF News* 1970–71, 5, 8. The article opens with, "Like it or not, teacher militancy has arrived in Ontario."

102.   Rennie Warburton, "The Class Relations of Public School Teachers in British Columbia," *Canadian Review of Sociology and Anthropology / Revue canadienne de sociologie et d'anthropologie* 23,2 (Summer 1986), 213. See also Jennifer Ozga and Martin Lawn, *Teachers, Professionalism, and Class: A Study of Organized Teachers* (London: Falmer Press, 1981), v–x.

103.   Briskin, "In the Public Interest," 91–102.

104.   See Andrew Spaull, "Invoking Ghosts from the Past: The Formation of the Victorian Teachers' Union, Victoria, Australia, 1916–1926," *Historical Studies in Education / Revue d'histoire de l'éducation* 5 (Spring 1993) for his labour theory of teacher militancy.

105.   Gidney, *From Hope to Harris*, 117–18.

106. R.W. Reville, B.S. Onyschuk, and L. Hemsworth, *Professional Consultation and the Determination of Compensation for Ontario Teachers* (Toronto: The Committee of Inquiry, 1972), 2–3, 28–36, 54–56.

107. Gidney, *From Hope to Harris*, 119.

108. YUCTA, FWTAO 1999-027/355, "Reville Report Unfair to Teachers," *FWTAO Newsletter*, 1972–73, 2, 1; "Reville Report Is Anti-employee: FWTAO Brief Opposes Reville Report," *FWTAO Newsletter*, 1972–73, 3–5.

109. CTF, "Teacher Strikes and Sanctions in Canada."

110. YUCTA, FWTAO 1999-027/030, Annual Meeting Minutes verbatim, August 1975, 97–9; YUCTA, OPSTF 2010-006/61, "Teachers Need the Right to Strike Claims FWTAO," *OPSMTF News*, 1972–73, 6, 1.

111. YUCTA, OPSTF 2010-006/62, John Welch, "Provincial Executive Supports Queen's Park March by 6,000 Teachers from Metro Toronto Area, May 14," *OPSMTF News* 1972–73, 8, 1.

112. Ron Poste, interview, 21 November 2008.

113. YUCTA, FWTAO 1999-027/024, Annual Meeting Minutes verbatim, August 1973, 38, 189–94.

114. YUCTA, OPSTF 2010-006/61, "Editorial," *OPSMTF News*, 1972–73, 8.

115. YUCTA, FWTAO 1999-027/024, Annual Meeting Minutes verbatim, August 1973, 192.

116. YUCTA, FWTAO 1999-027/024, Annual Meeting Minutes verbatim, August 1973, 189–98.

117. YUCTA, OPSTF 2010-006/41, Provincial Assembly Minutes, August 1973, G6–8. Still, 28 per cent of the OPSMTF delegates voted against the right to strike, while only one vote went against the previous motion that compulsory arbitration be included as one of the alternatives.

118. YUCTA, FWTAO 1999-027/348, Special Meeting of FWTAO Directors and Association Presidents, 15 December 1973, 2–4.

119. Ontario, Bill 274, An Act to Amend the Ministry of Education Act, 1973.

120. Ontario, Bill 275, An Act to Amend the Schools Administration Act, 1973.

121. Ron Poste, interview, 21 November 2008.

122. YUCTA, FWTAO 1999-027/384, FWTAO, "An Analysis of Bill 275," *FWTAO Newsletter,* January 1974, 4, 8.

123. N. John Adams, "Administrators Oppose Bill 275: York Starts Push for Settlement," *Globe and Mail*, 9 February 1974, 4.

124. YUCTA, FWTAO 1999-027/348, Ontario Teachers' Federation, G.P. Wilkinson, "Open Letter to the Members of the Legislative Assembly of Ontario on Behalf of the Teachers of Ontario," 13 December 1973, 1.

125. Ted Blachar, "Ontario Doctors Back Teachers in Dispute with Wells," *Toronto Star*, 13 December 1973, A1, A6.

126. Peter Mosher, "Wells Changes Terms of Teachers' Resignations, Says They Cannot Be Effective until Aug 31," *Globe and Mail*, 13 December 1973, 1.

127. YUCTA FWTAO 1999-027/348, Memorandum from Florence Henderson to Key Teachers, "Bargaining Legislation at Last," 10 December 1973, 2.

128. Andy Hanson, "When Education and Legislation Meet: Teacher Collective Bargaining in Canada," Canadian Teachers' Federation, 2013, 2.

129. YUCTA, FWTAO 1999-027/348, Bill 274-275 1975 file, "The Diary of Thirteen Days and Bill 274," 2; YUCTA, FWTAO 1999-027/348, Special Meeting of FWTAO Directors and Association Presidents, 15 December 1973, 8.

130. YUCTA, FWTAO 1999-027/348, Bill 274-275, 1975 file, Telegram to Directors of Education of Ontario School Boards, 13 December 1973; Telegram to Principal of Every Elementary and Junior High School in Ontario, 13 December 1973.

131. YUCTA, FWTAO 1999-027/348, Special Meeting of FWTAO Directors and Association Presidents, 15 December 1973, 3-4.

132. Bill Davis became minister of education when Premier Robarts gave up the position in his second year as premier. Up until that time the premier also held the office of minister of education. Davis became premier in 1971.

133. Margaret Wilson, interview with author, Marlbank, ON, 7 February 2009. Margaret Wilson was the OSSTF president at the time of the strike. In her interview, she stated that a tentative resolution had been achieved the night of 17 December 1973, but because the strike had already been put in motion, the unions proceeded with the march the next day as a demonstration of strength. It should be noted that there would have been no way of contacting teachers who were already in transit.

134. YUCTA, FWTAO 1999-027/348, Bill 274-275, OTF Memorandum, "For Immediate Release," 20 December 1973. Announcing the resolution to Bill 274.

135. YUCTA, FWTAO 1999-027/024, Annual Meeting Minutes verbatim, August 1974, 109.

136. YUCTA, FWTAO 1999-027/024, Annual Meeting Minutes verbatim, August 1974, 105.

137. YUCTA, FWTAO 1999-027/183, Minutes of the Board of Directors' Meeting, 10 February 1973, 11; YUCTA, FWTAO 1999-027/348, "Needed: One Million Dollars," *FWTAO Newsletter*, 1973-74, 4, 2.

## Chapter 2: Structuring Collective Action

1. YUCTA, OPSTF 2010-006/62, "Editorial: Thank You, Mr. Wells for Your Help . . .," *OPSMTF News*, 1973-74, 4, 12.

2. N. John Adams, "Toronto Trustees Oppose Wells Bill, Plan No Penalties," *Globe and Mail*, 14 December 1973, 1.

3. Adams, "Administrators Oppose Bill 275."

4. Donna Dilschneider, "Toronto Trustees Support Walkout," *Toronto Star*, 14 December 1973, A6.

5. ETFO Government Relations Officer Vivian McCaffrey's office records (not archived) (hereafter ETFO GRO), Ontario Association of Education Administrative Officials, "Report to the Members: Area Meetings February 6th, 1974," 12 February 1974.

6. YUCTA, FWTAO 1999-027/024, Annual Meeting Minutes verbatim, August 1974, 270–72.

7. Ontario, Bill 100, School Boards and Teachers Collective Negotiations Act, 1975.

8. YUCTA, FWTAO 1999-027/348, N. John Adams, "Strike Rights Gained by Ontario Teachers: Lockout by Boards Allowed," *Globe and Mail*, 30 May 1975.

9. Robert Hebdon and Robert Stern, "Tradeoffs Among Expressions of Industrial Conflict: Public Sector Strike Bans and Grievance Arbitrations," *Industrial and Labor Relations Review* 51,2 (January 1998), 204, 207; Craig Heron, *The Canadian Labour Movement: A Short History* (Toronto: J. Lorimer, 1989), 107.

10. Ontario, School Boards and Teachers Collective Negotiations Act.

11. Ontario, School Boards and Teachers Collective Negotiations Act, Part VIII.

12. YUCTA, FWTAO 1999-027/030, Annual Meeting Minutes verbatim, August 1975, 104, 122, 127.

13. Viewed at the ETFO offices, copies available from the author (hereafter ETFO-caa), FWTAO and OPSMTF Policy Re Strike and Arbitration, 28 August 1975.

14. Jeremy Gilbert, "What Kind of Thing Is 'Neoliberalism'?," *New Formations: A Journal of Culture/Theory/Politics* 80–81 (2013), 7. Gilbert points out that Chilean dictator Augusto Pinochet received assistance devising his campaign of union repression from students of the Chicago School.

15. David Harvey, *A Brief History of Neoliberalism* (Oxford, GB: Oxford University Press, 2007), 13, 87. Harvey writes that the political changes that enabled neo-liberalism to emerge were evident by the mid-1970s.

16. Leo Panitch and Donald Swartz, "The Continuing Assault on Public Sector Unions," in *Public Sector Unions in The Age of Austerity*, ed. Ross and Savage, 31–45.

17. Jim Stanford, "Canada's Transformation Under Neoliberalism" *Canadian Dimension* (29 March 2014), canadiandimension.com.

18. Leo Panitch and Donald Swartz, *The Assault on Trade Union Freedoms: From Wage Controls to Social Contract* (Toronto: Garamond, 1988), 24–25.

19. Allan Maslove and Gene Swimmer, *Wage Controls in Canada, 1975–1978* (Ottawa: Institute for Research on Public Policy, 1980), 34.

20. Jean-Luc Pepin, "Canada and the Anti-inflation Program: One Year Later, an Address by the Honourable Jean-Luc Pepin, P.C., M.P., Chairman, Anti-Inflation Board, Federal Government of Canada at the Empire Club," speeches.empireclub.org.

21. YUCTA, OPSTF 2010-006/61, "Tough Times for Teachers," *OPSMTF News*, May 1976, 2.

22. Margaret Wilson, interview, 7 February 2009; Dave Lennox, email interviews with author, from Haines City, FL, February 2010. Lennox was the OPSTF president between 1982 and 1984 and the OPSTF general secretary from 1987 to 1998.

23. *Toronto Star*, "Day of Protest Inspiring Victory Labor Claims," 15 October 1976, A1, A11.

24. YUCTA, OPSTF 2010-006/61, "Taking AIM at the AIB," *OPSMTF News*, January 1977, 10–13.

25. YUCTA, FWTAO 1999-027/029, Annual Meeting Minutes, August 1976, 43.

26. Statistics Canada, Table 278-0009, "Person-days Not Worked in Canada as a Result of Work Stoppages, by Industry Based on the North American Industry Classification System (NAICS) and Region," statcan.gc.ca.

27. CTF, "Teacher Strikes and Sanctions in Canada."

28. YUCTA, FWTAO 1999-027/333, Papers on Status of Women, "Memorandum from Thomas Wells to Chairmen of School Boards, Re: Equal Employment and Promotion Opportunities for Women," 2 January 1976.

29. YUCTA, FWTAO 1999-027/2333, Ida Hill, "Chronology of Affirmative Action Activities of the Ministry of Education," Ministry of Education Affirmative Action Memo, 8 February 1989. The FWTAO archives indicate that FWTAO was working with the Ontario Women's Directorate 1979–81.

30. YUCTA, FWTAO 1999-027/029, Annual Meeting Minutes 1980, FWTAO Official Minutes, Appendix I, Statement of Priorities for 1980–81 as Adopted by the Board of Directors, 12 August 1980, 2.

31. YUCTA, FWTAO 1999-027/767, "LEAF Honours FWTAO," *FWTAO Newsletter*, December 1992–January 1993, inside cover; Ontario Women's Directorate, "30 Years." LEAF was founded in 1985.

32. Speech given by Joan Westcott at the FWTAO Reunion, Kingston, Ontario, 4 April 2008. The Judy Erola LEAF Award was given to the FWTAO in 1992.

33. YUCTA, OPSTF 2010-006/61, Ron Stephen, "My Brother's Keeper," *OPSTF News*, January 1977, 3.

34. Kathryn McMullen, Jason Gilmore, and Christel Le Petit, "Women in Non-traditional Occupations and Fields of Study," Statistics Canada, 29 April 2010, statcan.gc.ca.

35. Gidney, *From Hope to Harris*, 162–63.

36. YUCTA, 1999-027/029, 1980 Annual General Meeting of the Federation of Women Teachers' Associations of Ontario, Tuesday evening, August 12, 1980, 10.

37. YUCTA, FWTAO 1999-027/767, Minister of Education Marion Boyd, "A Message from the Minister of Education," Pat Kincaid, "Ministry of Education Family Violence Initiatives," *FWTAO Newsletter*, December 1990 / January 1991, 64; Elaine Batcher and Vicki Wright, "Readers Teach Sex Stereotypes," 54–57. The latter article reviewed readers for young children following the murder of the fourteen young women at the École Polytechnique in Montreal on 6 December 1989.

38. YUCTA, FWTAO 1999-027/2333, Affirmative Action, Equal Opportunity Resolution of OPSMTF, Passed at the Ontario Public Men Teachers' Federation August Assembly 1981, 23 November 1981.

39. YUCTA, OPSTF 2010-006/59, Dave Lennox, "Fair Play," *OPSTF Newstoday*, 20 April 1984, 1.

40. YUCTA, FWTAO 1999-027/029, Annual Meeting Minutes, 13–16 August 1974, 37–42. The May-June 1968 OPSMTF Newsletter, "Progress Towards Unity," 1, references the formation of the Toronto Teachers' Federation as the third amalgamated local. Mississauga and Nepean township locals were the first to amalgamate.

41. YUCTA, FWTAO 1999-027/283, "Women to Be Polled on Merger," *FWTAO Newsletter*, 1, 1.

42. YUCTA, FWTAO 1999-027/283(07), Letter from Jeanne Frolick, President to Federation Member, n.d.

43. YUCTA, FWTAO 1999-027/283, "Is Larger Better?," *FWTAO Newsletter*, Special Edition, 1976–77; YUCTA, FWTAO 1999-027/283 (05), Jeanne Frolick, "More Male Teachers Urged for Elementary System," *FWTAO Newsletter*, February 1977, 2.

44. YUCTA, FWTAO 1999-027/283, Amalgamation 1976 file, Amalgamation: Issues Raised in Group Sessions at the Presidents' Conference, November 20, 1976.

45. YUCTA, FWTAO 1999-027/283, Amalgamation 1976 file, Statement by Margaret Beckingham, for *FWTAO Newsletter*, 1975–76, 6.

46. YUCTA, OPSTF 2010-006/41, Provincial Assembly Minutes, August 1972, G-13.

47. YUCTA, FWTAO 1999-027/283, Amalgamation Research Survey, Canadian Inter-mark, *A Research Survey on Attitudes of FWTAO Members Toward Amalgamation* (Toronto, July 1977).

48. Canadian Inter-mark, *A Research Survey on Attitudes of FWTAO Members*, 4.

49. Canadian Inter-mark, *A Research Survey on Attitudes of FWTAO Members*, 4. (Emphasis in the original.)

50. YUCTA, FWTAO 1999-027/029, Annual Meeting Minutes, August 1977, 4.

51. YUCTA, OPSTF 2010-006/61, "Where Do We Go From Here?," *OPSMTF News*, October 1977, 3.

52. YUCTA, FWTAO 1999-027/029, Annual Meeting Minutes, August 1977, 6.

53. YUCTA, FWTAO 1999-027/283, Amalgamation 1976 file, After Discussion of Opinion Poll, 16 August 1977.

54. YUCTA, OPSTF 2010-006/41, Minutes of the Provincial Assembly 1977, H11.

55. YUCTA, OPSTF 2010-006/41, Minutes of the Provincial Assembly 1977, F6, F7.

56. YUCTA, OPSTF 2010-006/41 Provincial Assembly Minutes, August 1974, G20.

57. YUCTA, OPSTF 2010-006/62, "Up Front with Promissory Notes," *OPSMTF News*, October 1975, 6.

58.  YUCTA, FWTAO 1999-027/348, Bill 274-275, Memorandum to Key Teachers, "Civil Rights Fund," 1 February 1974.

59.  YUCTA, FWTAO 1999-027/348, Bill 274-275, FWTAO, "Needed: One Million Dollars," *FWTAO Newsletter*, January 1974, 1–2.

60.  YUCTA, FWTAO 1999-027/183, Directors' Meeting, 9 February 1974, 2; YUCTA, FWTAO 1999-027/024, Annual Meeting Minutes verbatim 1975, 505.

61.  YUCTA, FWTAO 1999-027/183, Florence Henderson, Directors' Meeting, 9 February 1974, 1.

62.  YUCTA, FWTAO 1999-027/024, Annual Meeting Minutes verbatim, 1974, 411–15, 502–20, 523–4.

63.  YUCTA, FWTAO 1999-027/356, *FWTAO Newsletter*, 1974–75, 1, 8.

64.  YUCTA, OPSTF 2010-006/61, David Dunnill, "Strike and Arbitration Policy Examined," *OPSMTF News*, January 1976.

65.  YUCTA, FWTAO 1999-027/183, Directors' Meeting, 11 August 1975, Evening Session, 3–6.

66.  YUCTA, FWTAO 1999-027/030, Annual Meeting Minutes verbatim, August 1975, 34–5, 186.

67.  YUCTA, FWTAO 1999-027/030, Annual Meeting Minutes verbatim, August 1975, 175.

68.  YUCTA, FWTAO 1999-027/030, Annual Meeting Minutes verbatim, August 1975, 101.

69.  YUCTA, OPSTF 2010-006/41, Minutes of the Provincial Assembly, 17–20 August 1976, B5.

70.  YUCTA, OPSTF 2010-006/61, Ron Stephen, "The Sixth Affiliate," *OPSMTF News*, October 1975, 8.

71.  YUCTA, OPSTF 2010-006/61, Neil Davis, "Straight Talk about Principals," *OPSMTF News*, September 1975, 3.

72.  YUCTA, OPSTF 2010-006/61, Ron Stephen, "The Sixth Affiliate," *OPSMTF News*, September 1975, 8.

73.  YUCTA, OPSTF 2010-006/61, Duncan Jewell, "Study Results Revealing Member Militancy Low," *OPSMTF News*, September 1975,9.

74.  YUCTA, OPSTF 2010-006/61, Howard Moscoe, "Standardized Curriculum = Standardized Children," *OPSMTF News*, January 1977, 18.

75.  YUCTA, OPSTF 2010-006/61, Bill Davis, "Premier Davis Discusses Evaluation," *OPSMTF News*, January 1977, 4.

76.  Alan Sears, *Retooling the Mind Factory: Education in a Lean State* (Aurora, ON: Garamond Press, 2003), 90.

77.  Memon, "Contextualizing Hall-Dennis," 90–96.

78.  YUCTA, OPSTF 2010-006/61, Peter McLaren, "Teaching and the Language of Possibility: An Interview with Jeanne Brady Giroux," *OPSMTF News*, October 1985, 13; Henry Giroux and Peter McLaren, "Can Teachers Be Transformative Intellectuals?," *OPSMTF News*, December 1985, 7; Henry Giroux and Peter McLaren, "Critical Pedagogy: New Directions for Educational Reform," *OPSMTF News*, April 1986, 9.

79. Ontario Ministry of Education, "For the Love of Learning"; Ontario, Ministry of Education, *The Formative Years: Provincial Curriculum Policy for the Primary and Junior Divisions of the Public and Separate Schools of Ontario*, 1975; Ontario Ministry of Education, *Education in the Primary and Junior Divisions*, 1975.

80. Martin Friedland, *The University of Toronto: A History* (Toronto: University of Toronto Press, 2002), 472; Ontario Ministry of Education, "For the Love of Learning."

81. William Davis, "The Making of a World-Class Institution: The Honourable William Davis on Conceiving and Implementing OISE," in *Inspiring Education: A Legacy of Learning, 1907–2007: Celebrating 100 Years of Studies in Education at the University of Toronto*, 2006, oise.utoronto.ca, 20, 50.

82. YUCTA, OPSTF 2010-006/61, Robert Jackson, "My Gut Feeling Right Now Is That We Are in Trouble," *OPSMTF News*, February 1978, 1.

83. The smaller reports published by the Commission on Declining School Enrolments in Ontario (CODE) are available at OISE. In all there were 42 studies, 18 information bulletins, and 12 mini-studies commissioned.

84. ETFO-caa, FWTAO, and OPSMTF Policies and Procedures for Redundancy, 17 January 1979.

85. YUCTA, OPSTF 2010-006/61, Stuart Smith, "Liberal Education Policy Outlined," *OPSMTF News*, January 1977, 6; Robert Jackson, *The Final Report of the Commission on Declining School Enrolments in Ontario* (Toronto: Commission on Declining School Enrolments in Ontario, 1978).

86. YUCTA, FWTAO 1999-027/792, Responses to Various Reports file, "Some Comments on *Issues and Directions*," 1981, 5.

87. Dr. Bette Stephenson served as the first woman board member and the first woman chair of the Ontario Medical Association. She left her position as minister of labour to accept her new appointment to minister of education in August 1978.

88. YUCTA, FWTAO 1999-027/792, Responses to Various Reports file, "Some Comments on *Issues and Directions*," 1981, 4.

89. YUCTA, OPSTF 2010-006/61, Duncan Jewell, "College of Teachers: An Idea Whose Time Has Come," *OPSMTF News*, December 1980, 30.

90. YUCTA, FWTAO 1999-027/008, Report of the Board of Directors 1968–1969, 8. In this school year, professional improvement loans amounted to $17,362; Report of the Board of Directors 1971–1972, 24. A total of $29,000 in scholarships was granted for the 1972–73 school year. See Susan Ferguson, *Women and Work: Feminism Labour and Social Reproduction* (Toronto: Between the Lines, 2020), 30–39, 58, for a theoretical discussion of "equality feminism," women having access to the workplace and equal wages.

91. John King, "Wage, Price Controls to Ease after April 14: Most Taxpayers Get a $100 Break," *Globe and Mail*, 21 October 1977, 1.

92. YUCTA, FWTAO 1999-027/029, Annual Meeting Minutes 1978, FWTAO Official Minutes, 61.

93. YUCTA, OPSTF 2010-006/61, "George Meek Wins Second Term as President, Doug McAndless First Full-time 1st VP," *OPSMTF News*, October 1978, 1.

94. YUCTA, FWTAO 1999-027/029, Report of the Board of Directors, Annual Meeting Minutes 1973, FWTAO Official Minutes, 1; YUCTA, FWTAO 1999-027/183, Directors' Meeting, Friday Evening, 17 August 1973, 1.

95. YUCTA, FWTAO 1999-027/024, Annual Meeting Minutes verbatim, August 1973, 194–95.

96. YUCTA, OPSTF 2010-006/41, Doug McAndless, "Address to the 1979 Provincial Assembly," Provincial Assembly Minutes, August 1979, AE1–2.

97. YUCTA, FWTAO 1999-027/029, Annual Meeting Minutes 1978, FWTAO Official Minutes, 45–46.

98. YUCTA, OPSTF 2010-006/61, "Where Have All the Babies Gone," *OPSMTF News*, February 1978, 10–12.

99. ETFO-caa, FWTAO, "The Reality of Declining Enrolment," handout for the Collective Bargaining Representative (CBR) Workshop, 8–9 December 1978.

100. Robert Jackson, *The Challenge of Declining Enrolments: Critical Emerging Problems and Recommendations for Immediate Action (Interim Report No. 2)* (Toronto: Commission on Declining School Enrolments in Ontario, 1978), x.

101. YUCTA, FWTAO 1999-027/008, Annual Meeting, Report of the Board of Directors, 1978–79, 5–9, 13–14.

102. ETFO-caa, letter from F.L. Showler to Edith Butlin, 7 September 1971; letter from Edith Butlin to W.C. Lech, 16 September 1971; letter from Edith Butlin to R.J. Linton, 1 October 1971.

103. YUCTA, OPSTF 2010-006/61, Bill Menagh, "Teachers and Seniority," *OPSMTF News*, March 1979, 9.

104. YUCTA, OPSTF 2010-006/61, Bill Menagh, "Teachers and Seniority," *OPSMTF News*, March 1979, 9.

105. ETFO-caa, FWTAO, Minutes of the Joint Executive Meeting of the Federation of Women Teachers' Associations of Ontario and the Ontario Public School Men Teachers' Federation, 10 February 1979, 1–2.

106. Barbara Richter, Margaret Tomen v. Ontario Teachers' Federation (OTF) and the Ontario Public School Teachers' Federation (OPSTF), *FWTAO Witness: Ontario Human Rights Commission*, Vol. 41 (Toronto: Nethercut, 13 November 1990). Barbara Richter, as a witness in the Ontario Human Rights Commission proceedings, confirmed that joint voting was the practice for the two teachers' unions. E. Lennon, for the FWTAO, confirmed "about half" of the chief negotiators for the Economic Policy Committees were from the FWTAO.

## Chapter 3: First Strikes

1. YUCTA, FWTAO 1999-027/015, attachment to letter from Kathleen Dyson to W. Wood, 4 June 1970, 3.

2. ETFO-caa, George Ferguson, "In the Matter of the Arbitration Between the Windsor Board of Education and District No. 1, The Ontario Secondary

School Teachers' Federation," 16 July 1973, 9. The arbitrator awarded a retroactive settlement to secondary teachers where the grid showed a $7,600 starting salary and a top salary of $16,600.

3. YUCTA, OPSTF 2010-006/61, "Marie MacGregor, FWTAO Provincial President and a Lambton County Teacher," *OPSMTF News*, June 1978, photo, 8. Marie MacGregor was the 1977–78 FWTAO president.

4. YUCTA, OPSTF 2010-006/61, "Lambton: Story of a Strike That Almost Was," *OPSMTF News*, June 1978, 8–9.

5. YUCTA, FWTAO 1999-027/045, Special Executive Meeting in Joint Session, 9 June 1979; YUCTA, FWTAO 1999-027/045, FWTAO Executive Meeting, FWTAO and OPSMTF Items of Mutual Concern, 3 November 1979.

6. YUCTA, FWTAO 1999-027/045, FWTAO Executive Meeting, FWTAO and OPSMTF Items of Mutual Concern, 3 November 1979, 7/5.

7. YUCTA, FWTAO 1999-027/045, FWTAO Executive Meeting, FWTAO and OPSMTF Items of Mutual Concern, 3 November 1979, 7/13. (Emphasis in the original.)

8. Linda Briskin, "Equity Bargaining / Bargaining Equity," Restructuring Work and Labour in the New Economy (Initiatives on the New Economy) Working Papers Series, 2006-01, genderwork.ca, 12–13.

9. YUCTA, FWTAO 1999-027/045, FWTAO Executive Meeting, 15 April 1978, Minutes of the Joint Executive Meeting of Federation of Women Teachers Associations of Ontario and the Ontario Public School Men Teachers' Federation, 6 April 1978, 2.

10. YUCTA, OPSTF 2010-006/36, Provincial Executive Minutes, March 1989, 13–19. In the 1987 Metropolitan Toronto strike, the OPSTF disciplined 42 principals and vice-principals who did not forward the required contribution to their union.

11. YUCTA, FWTAO 1999-027/045, FWTAO Executive Meeting, 15 April 1978, Minutes of the Joint Executive Meeting of Federation of Women Teachers Associations of Ontario and the Ontario Public School Men Teachers' Federation, 6 April 1978, 1–3; ETFO-caa, Memo from Shirley Stokes and Robert Lamb to Brant County Members of FWTAO and OPSMTF, Re: Your Superannuation Benefits and the Strike, 6 February 1980. The "last seven years" referred to those people who intended to retire within seven years of the date of the strike.

12. YUCTA, FWTAO 1999-027/029, Annual Meeting Minutes 1979, FWTAO Official Minutes, 52; YUCTA, OPSTF 2010-006/41, Provincial Assembly Minutes, August 1979, AE-1.

13. YUCTA, OPSTF 2010-006/61, Burleigh Mattice, "Peel: One Refusal Too Many," *OPSMTF News*, November 1979, 2.

14. YUCTA, OPSTF 2010-006/61, Burleigh Mattice, "Retirement Gratuity: Myth and Reality," *OPSMTF News*, November 1978, 2.

15. Caroline Alphonso, "Sick Days Costing Ontario School Boards $1-Billion a Year," *Globe and Mail*, 28 March 2016.

16.    Robert Anthony, D. James Christie, and Rodney E. Smart, *Sick Leave Gratuities and Resultant Liabilities* (Toronto: Ministry of Education, 1976).

17.    ETFO-caa, Box marked OPS 11, Kristian John Kirkwood, *Report on the Survey on Teacher Absenteeism*, Toronto: OPSMTF, 1977.

18.    YUCTA, OPSTF Box 61, Burleigh Mattice, "Peel: One Refusal Too Many," *OPSMTF News*, November 1979, 2.

19.    YUCTA, FWTAO 1999-027/357, "The Peel Strike: 13 Days That Shook the Region," *FWTAO Newsletter*, 1979–80, 2, insert; Board of Directors' Report 1979–80, August 1980, 5.

20.    YUCTA, FWTAO 1999-027/357, "The President Says," *FWTAO Newsletter*, 1979–80, 2, 2.

21.    Zuhair Kashmeri, "Demand Arbitration: Parents, Children Picket Peel Board," *Globe and Mail*, 5 October 1979, 8.

22.    "Teachers' Negotiators Accept Mediation Report on Peel Strike," *Globe and Mail*, 17 October 1979, 9.

23.    "2-Year Pact Is Accepted by Teachers," *Globe and Mail*, 23 October 1979, 8.

24.    YUCTA, FWTAO 1999-027/357, "Peel Strike Ends," *FWTAO Newsletter*, 1979–80, 2, 1.

25.    YUCTA, OPSTF 2010-006/45, Minutes of the Executives of the Federation of Women Teachers' Associations of Ontario and the Ontario Public School Men Teachers' Federation Meeting in Joint Session, 3 November 1979.

26.    Paul Knox, "Brant Aids Teachers: It's the Union Way," *Globe and Mail*, 22 November 1979, 13.

27.    YUCTA, FWTAO 1999-027/357, "What Makes Brant Different," *FWTAO Newsletter*, 1979–80, 3,1.

28.    "Brant Teachers' Walkout Affects 11,200 Students," *Toronto Star*, 14 November 1979, A23.

29.    YUCTA, FWTAO 1999-027/357, "Brant Strike Ends," *FWTAO Newsletter*, 1979–80, 4,1.

30.    YUCTA, FWTAO 1999-027/357, "Peel Surplus Transfer Policy Settled in Committee," *FWTAO Newsletter*, 1979–80, 4, 1. As the Brant strike ended, the Peel trustees agreed to seniority provisions for their teachers.

31.    YUCTA, FWTAO 1999-027/008, Board of Directors' Report 1979–80, August 1980, 6.

32.    YUCTA, OPSTF 2010-006/40, Provincial Executive Meeting Minutes, 4–5 January 1980, 1.

33.    B.C. Matthews and John Crispo, *The Report of a Commission to Review the Collective Negotiation Process Between Teachers and School Boards* (Toronto: Ministry of Education, June 1980), 17.

34.    CTF, "Teacher Strikes and Sanctions in Canada."

35.    YUCTA, FWTAO 1999-027/775, Letter from M.P. Hyndman, Blackwell, Law, Spratt, Armstrong and Grass. to Miss Jean Stubley, "By-law 6, 1980, 1979," 12 November 1980, 2.

36. YUCTA, FWTAO 1999-027/775, Letter from M.P. Hyndman, Blackwell, Law, Spratt, Armstrong and Grass, to Miss Jean V. Stubley, 17 February 1981.

37. YUCTA, FWTAO 1999-027/775, Letter from Ross Andrew, OPSMTF Secretary, to Mr. W.A. Jones, Secretary-Treasurer OTF, 15 December 1980, 2.

38. YUCTA, OPSTF 2010-006/59, "Metro Strike Discipline Concluded," *OPSTF Newstoday*, 1 March 1989, 1. The OPSTF published the names of 15 teachers and 73 principals and vice-principals. The teachers had crossed their own picket line, while the principals and vice-principals had not forwarded their pay during the strike.

39. YUCTA, FWTAO 1999-027/008, Report of the Board of Directors 1981–82, 13.

40. YUCTA, OPSTF 2010-006/61, "Hello, I'm Mary. I've Joined OPSMTF," *OPSMTF News*, 1972–73, 1, 3. Two other women became OPSMTF voluntary members that year. They were B. Marion Axford, chief supervisor of guidance for the Scarborough Board, and Fran Cooper, vice-principal with the Carleton Board.

41. YUCTA, OPSTF 2010-006/58, Letters file, Application for Membership in O.P.S.M.T.F., Mary Carol Hill, signed 18 August 1972. The two notes written on the application identify her as the "1st Female from FWTAO" and "1st to join from FWTAO."

42. YUCTA, OPSTF 2010-006/41, 1974 Provincial Assembly Minutes, A8.

43. YUCTA, OPSTF 2010-006/61, "TLC at TFC [Teachers' Federation of Carleton]," *OPSMTF News*, March 1977, 5.

44. YUCTA, OPSTF 2010-006/62, "Passive Bystander or Political Activist," *OPSTF News*, October 1982.

45. YUCTA, OPSTF 2010-006/62, *Ottawa Citizen*, "Women Teachers Out of Date," in *OPSTF News*, October 1982, 40.

46. YUCTA, OPSTF 2010-006/62, "The Many Moods of Mary," *OPSTF News*, October 1984, cover. No president in the past had been labelled with "moods," nor would any future president; only the OPSMTF's first woman president had her authority diminished on the front page of the newsletter.

47. ETFO GRO, Teachers and the Canadian Economy, Information Memo, from Donald J. Heimbecker to Chief Teacher Welfare Officers, CTF Teacher Welfare Committee and CTF Economics of Education Committee, 27 September 1982, 1.

48. Ronald Anderson, "Controls Imminent Despite Harmfulness," *Globe and Mail*, 24 August 1982, B2.

49. Morningstar, *Andex Chart*, 2019.

50. Canada, Public Sector Compensation Restraint Act (S.C. 1991, c. 30).

51. ETFO-caa, Ed Finn, "Bill C-124—Anti-Union Legislation: It Seeks to Destroy Unions, Not Just Control Wages," *The Facts*, August–September 1982, 12.

52. ETFO GRO, Memorandum from R.D. Mosher to Members of the CTF Board of Directors, Presidents, et al., "CTF Campaign Re Wage Controls

and the Canadian Economy," 30 August 1982; "Teachers and Wage Controls," OPSTF Bulletin 3, 8 October 1982.

53. ETFO GRO, Information Memo, from Wilfred Brown to Chief Teacher Welfare Officers, CTF Teacher Welfare Committee and CTF Economics of Education Committee, 8 April 1983, 11–12; Ontario, Bill 179, An Act Respecting the Restraint of Compensation in the Public Sector of Ontario and the Monitoring of Inflationary Conditions in the Economy of the Province, 1982.

54. ETFO GRO, Letter from Howard Goldblatt, Sack, Charney, Goldblatt and Mitchell, to Bill Getty, OSSTF District 16, "Re: Inflation Restraint Act," 24 September 1982; Memo: Re Bill 179—Inflation Restraint Act, 1982, From Sack Charney, Goldblatt and Mitchell, 28 September 1982.

55. ETFO GRO, Wage Controls—Bill 179, Negotiations, Implications for Ontario Teachers—The Inflation Restraint Act, 21 September 1982.

56. ETFO-caa, Ontario Ministry of Treasury and Economics, "Ontario Government Wage Restraint and Administered Prices Program: An Overview," 21 September 1982.

57. Canadian Press, "Davis Appoints 5 Members to Inflation Restraint Board," Globe and Mail, 24 December 1982, 12.

58. Maslove and Swimmer, Wage Controls in Canada, 46.

59. ETFO GRO, Wage Control—Bill 179, Ontario Teachers Federation (Draft) Understandings, 14 October 1982, 1.

60. ETFO GRO, D.A.L. Auld, "School Board Salary Settlements in the Context of Public and Private Wage Change" (revised version), 5 June 1982, 17.

61. ETFO GRO, Wage Control—Bill 179, "OTF Plans Action to Fight Wage Controls," OTF/FEO Interaction, October 1982, 1–2.

62. YUCTA, FWTAO 1999-027/357, "Bill 179 Denies Rights and Discriminates Against Public Employees," FWTAO Newsletter, November 1982, 1.

63. ETFO-caa, "Teachers Oppose Discriminatory Wage Controls," FWTAO Bulletin, 1982–83, 1.

64. ETFO GRO, Wage Control—Bill 179, "Teachers and Wage Controls," FWTAO Bulletin, October 1982, 1.

65. YUCTA, FWTAO 1999-027/830, Memo from Kathleen O'Neil to K. Sigurjonsson and CB Staff, Re: $35,000 Rule and Part-time Teachers, 6 September 1983, 1; ETFO GRO, Wage Controls, Memo from Liz Coome to Members of the Provincial Executive, Re: Impact of the Inflation Restraint Act, 31 August 1983, 3.

66. YUCTA, FWTAO 1999-027/349, Inflation Restraint Act (Bill 179) Synopsis for Teachers, January 1983.

67. YUCTA, FWTAO 1999-027/357, "Teachers Protest Bill 179," FWTAO Newsletter, November 1982, 3–5; ETFO GRO, Wage Controls—Bill 179, "Government Attack on Teachers Unfair, Unjust, Unacceptable," OPSTF Bulletin, 15 October 1982, 1.

68. YUCTA, FWTAO 1999-027/829, Sample Letter to be Sent by Provincial Presidents of FWTAO and OSSTF to Membership, n.d.; YUCTA, FWTAO

1999-027/828, Memorandum to Marilyn Dickson from Kay Sigurjonsson, 27 October 1982.

69. YUCTA, FWTAO 1999-027/349, Bill 179, Book 3, "Teachers' Rights Disappear in Bill 179," *OTF Insight*, November 1982, 1.

70. YUCTA, FWTAO 1999-027/349, Bill 179, Teachers, Come to a Mass Rally to Protest Bill 179 [on 10 November 1982], n.d.; ETFO GRO, Wage Control—Bill 179, OPSTF Press Release, Re: Teachers to Hold Meeting in Windsor on Wage Restraint Legislation, 8 November 1982.

71. YUCTA, FWTAO 1999-027/349, Possible Activities Related to Government Imposition of Wage Controls, 13 October 1983, 3.

72. ETFO GRO, Teachers—Wage Control, OPSTF, Urgent Action Requested, 3 October 1983.

73. YUCTA, FWTAO 1999-027/349, Letter from Susan Hildreth to Robert Welch, 26 September 1983.

74. ETFO GRO, Teachers—Wage Control file, Letter to the Honourable Larry Grossman from David J. Lennox, 28 October 1983, 1.

75. YUCTA, FWTAO 1999-027/828, Memos to Staff, Memorandum from Kay Sigurjonsson to David Aylsworth, letter attached, Casualties of the Inflation Restraint Act, 7 September 1983, 1–4.

76. ETFO-caa, Letter from R.M. McKay, Acting Director Policy Analysis and Legislation Branch [on Ministry of Education letterhead], to Mr. Rae J. Linton, Director of Education, The Peterborough County Board of Education, 20 July 1982.

77. ETFO GRO, Bill 111, Compensation Restraint Act, Memo from Ontario Inflation Restraint Board to All Compensation Plan Administrators, Re: Public Sector Prices and Compensation Review Act, 29 December 1983; ETFO GRO, Bill 111, Compensation Restraint Act, Fact Sheets on the Public Sector Wage and Price Restraint Program, 8 November 1983.

78. Wayne Ross and Rich Gibson, *Neoliberalism and Education Reform* (Cresskill, NJ: Hampton, 2007), 107–18.

79. Michael Howlett and Keith Brownsey, "The Old Reality and the New Reality: Party Politics and Public Policy in British Columbia, 1941–1987," *Studies in Political Economy* 25 (Spring 1988), 1–2; Bryan Palmer, *Solidarity: The Rise and Fall of an Opposition in British Columbia* (Vancouver: New Star Books, 1987). While Howlett and Brownsey claim Bennett presented 23 bills in one day, Palmer, in *Solidarity*, counts 26 bills, as do others.

80. Neo-liberalism was both an economic plan for restructuring economies to maximize profit and a political ideology to minimize resistance from below, but it was never a unified political program. See Kean Birch and Vlad Mykhnenko, eds., *The Rise and Fall of Neoliberalism: The Collapse of an Economic Order?* (London: Zed Books, 2010).

81. E.P. Thompson, *The Making of the English Working Class* (London: Penguin Books, 1991), 8–9.

82. Ernest B. Akyeampong, "A Statistical Portrait of the Trade Union Movement," *Perspectives* (Statistics Canada, Winter 1997), 45–54, statcan.gc.ca.

## Chapter 4: Defining Priorities

1. Learning Disabilities Association of Ontario, *Learning Disabilities: A New Definition*, 2001, 4–5, ldao.ca.

2. YUCTA, FWTAO 1999-027/177, Submission to the Social Development Committee Regarding Bill 82, August 1980, 14.

3. Ontario, Bill 82, The Education Amendment Act, 1980, c 61.

4. YUCTA, FWTAO 1999-027/177, Submission to the Social Development Committee Regarding Bill 82, August 1980, 3–9.

5. YUCTA, FWTAO 1999-027/177, Submission to the Social Development Committee Regarding Bill 82, August 1980, 3.

6. Ontario Ministry of Education, "For the Love of Learning."

7. Regina Bussing, Bonnie Zima, Amu Perwien, Thomas Belin, and Mel Widawski, "Children in Special Education Programs: Attention Deficit Hyperactivity Disorder, Use of Services, and Unmet Needs," *American Journal of Public Health* 6 (June 1998), 883.

8. Regina Bussing, Bonnie Zima, Faye Gary, and Cynthia Garvan, "Barriers to Detection, Help-Seeking, and Service Use for Children with ADHD Symptoms," *Journal of Behavioral Health Services and Research* 30,2 (April–June 2003), 184–86.

9. Ontario, The Education Amendment Act, 1980.

10. Heather-jane Robertson, Great Expectations: Essays on Schools and Society, *Our Schools / Our Selves*, Special Issue, 16,4 (Summer 2007), 43–48.

11. ETFO-caa, Ontario Ministry of Education, "Provision of Health Support Services in School Settings," Policy Memorandum 81, 19 July 1984.

12. ETFO-caa, FWTAO, Provision of Health Support Services in School Settings, Questionnaire, 15 January 1985.

13. YUCTA, FWTAO 1999-027/008, 1984-85-9A, Report of the Board of Directors 1984–85, 16; ETFO-caa, Position Papers, September 1985, 25.

14. Dave Lennox, email interview with author, 14 March 2010. See chapter 1, note 47.

15. YUCTA, FWTAO 1999-027/1088, "Notes from the Work Group on Collective Bargaining," 17 September 1981, 1.

16. ETFO-caa, Memorandum from G.B. Mattice to R.R. Andrew, Negotiations Policy, 20 January 1986.

17. *Hansard,* 23 February 1983.

18. Ontario, Bill 127, The Municipality of Metropolitan Toronto Amendment Act, 1982.

19. Ontario, Bill 127, 130j (2)a.

20. YUCTA, FWTAO 1999-027/348, Bill 127, 1982, 1983, 1988, "What Can We Do?" poster.

21. Panitch and Swartz, "The Continuing Assault on Public Sector Unions," 31–32.

22. Gidney, *From Hope to Harris*, 124–41.

23. Ontario, Bill 30, An Act to Amend the Education Act, 1985.

24. YUCTA, FWTAO 1999-027/349, FWTAO, Submission to the Social Development Committee of the Ontario Legislature on the Subject of the Education Amendment Act 1985, July 1985, 6–7, 16; YUCTA, OPSTF 2010-006/62, Joe Hueglin, "Living Together, Learning Apart," *OPSTF News*, October 1985, 30–31.

25. Trevor Harrison and Jerrold L. Kachur, eds., *Contested Classrooms: Education, Globalization, and Democracy in Alberta* (Edmonton, University of Alberta Press, 1999), 107–18.

26. Crawford Kilian, *School Wars: The Assault on B.C. Education* (Vancouver: New Star Books, 1985).

27. Bernard Shapiro, *The Report of the Commission on Private Schools in Ontario* (Toronto: Ontario, October 1985), 205.

28. YUCTA, FWTAO 1999-027/349, FWTAO, Submission to the Social Development Committee of the Ontario Legislature on the Subject of the Education Amendment Act 1985, July 1985, 12, 22.

29. The FWTAO reported 1.6 per cent of its members were principals and vice-principals.

30. YUCTA, FWTAO 1999-027/851, Affirmative Actions in School Boards 1984 file, Office of the Deputy Premier, Ontario Women's Directorate, for Release August 21, 1984, 10:30 am.

31. YUCTA, FWTAO 1999-027/010, Joan Westcott, "Affirmative Action Ministry Priority Too," *FWTAO Newsletter*, February–March 1987, 33.

32. While it has been argued with some merit that the NDP agreement to support Peterson's Liberals was not a true coalition government, no legislation could move forward unless it was endorsed by both parties. Although it was a temporary alliance, to all appearances it was a coalition.

33. YUCTA, FWTAO 1999-027/2333, Chris Ward, Minister of Education, Remarks: Focus on Leadership Conference, 30 March 1989.

34. YUCTA, FWTAO 1999-027/008, Report of the Board of Directors 1988–89, August 1989, 8.

35. Florence Bird, *Report of the Royal Commission on the Status of Women in Canada* (Ottawa: Canada, 1970).

36. Canada, Canadian Human Rights Act, 1977, s.11.

37. YUCTA, FWTAO 1999-027/348, Pay Equity in Ontario, 9 February 1987.

38. Sandro Contenta, "Trustees Want Teachers Left Out of Equal Pay Law," *Toronto Star*, 22 February 1987, A3.

39. YUCTA, FWTAO 1999-027/0271, Brief Concerning Bill 154, Pay Equity in the Broader Public Sector and in the Private Sector, February 1987, 24.

40. Florence Henderson, Margaret Tomen v. Ontario Teachers' Federation (OTF) and the Ontario Public School Teachers' Federation (OPSTF),

*FWTAO Witness: Ontario Human Rights Commission*, Vol. 19 (Toronto: Neth-ercut, 12 April 1990), 2227–57. On 2257, Henderson responds, "Yes, it was the summer of 1950 and it had been begun in 1946 and been dealt with at almost every meeting of the Board of Governors [of the OTF] in those intervening four years."

41.   YUCTA, FWTAO 1999-027/0271, "Teachers Ask for Pay Equity Soon," news release, 25 February 1987.

42.   Rosemary Warskett, "The Politics of Difference and Inclusiveness within the Canadian Labour Movement," *Economic and Industrial Democracy* 17,4 (November 1996), 617.

43.   Jill Vickers, Pauline Rankin, and Christine Appelle, *Politics as if Women Mattered: A Political Analysis of the National Action Committee on the Status of Women* (Toronto: University of Toronto Press, 1993); Judy Rebick, *Ten Thousand Roses*. These two accounts give a fuller discussion of the part played by feminists.

44.   Canada, Constitution Act, 1982, *Canadian Charter of Rights and Freedoms*, 32(2).

45.   YUCTA, FWTAO 1999-027/008, 1984-85-9A, 1984–85 Report of the Board of Directors, 36.

46.   "Highlights from the Government of Ontario's 'Green Paper on Pay Equity," *Canadian Women Studies / Les Cahiers de la femme* 6,4 (Winter 1985), 106.

47.   Ontario, *Green Paper on Pay Equity*, 1985, 10.

48.   YUCTA, FWTAO 1999-027/767, "Pay Equity Activities," *FWTAO News-letter*, November/December 1988, inside cover; Ontario, Pay Equity Act, RO 1990.

49.   ETFO GRO, Teachers—Pay Equity file, Letter from Sack, Charney, Goldblatt, and Mitchell to Ms. Kate Hughes, 29 July 1988, 1 of the attached "Complaint."

50.   Patricia McDermott, "Pay Equity in Ontario: A Critical Legal Analysis," *Osgoode Hall Law Journal* 28,2 (1990), 383–84, 388.

51.   YUCTA, FWTAO 1999-027/357, "Bargain on Women's Issues, Delegates Urged," *FWTAO Newsletter*, 4, 1. The article included comments on the presentation by Shelly Acheson, human rights director with the OFL, and a film produced by the Women's Bureau, Ontario Ministry of Labour entitled *Affirmative Action Update*.

52.   McDermott, "Pay Equity in Ontario," 394.

53.   YUCTA, FWTAO 1999-027/348, Pay Equity in Ontario, 9 February 1987.

54.   ETFO GRO, Memorandum from Bill Getty to John Telford, Pre-degree Category, 15 April 1987, 3.

55.   ETFO GRO, Bill 154, The Pay Equity Act, 1987, June 1987, 9.

56.   ETFO GRO, Teachers—Pay Equity, Memorandum from H.J. Cooney to the Provincial Executive, 2 November 1988.

57.   YUCTA, OPSTF 2010-006/67, Pay Equity Job Rate file, attached to Memorandum from Liz Coome to Collective Bargaining Staff, Regional Coor-

dinators, Collective Bargaining Consultants, 27 September 1988, Pre-Degree Categories.

58. ETFO-caa, Memorandum from Liz Coome to Dave Lennox, Non Degree Teachers, 28 January 1988.

59. YUCTA, FWTAO 1999-027/767, "Pay Equity Review," *FWTAO Newsletter*, October/November 1991, inside cover.

60. Gidney, *From Hope to Harris*, 183.

61. CTF, "Teacher Strikes and Sanctions in Canada."

62. YUCTA, FWTAO 1999-027/010, Joan Westcott, "Priorities Mean Action," *FWTAO Newsletter*, September/October 1986, 41.

63. YUCTA, OPSTF 2010-006/58, Dave Lennox, "The Changing Face of Elementary Teachers," *OPSTF News*, March 1987, 5.

64. ETFO-caa, Memorandum from Victoria Corbett to Kay Sigurjonsson and CB Staff, Lanark Tentative Agreement, 16 February 1987.

65. ETFO-caa, Special Provincial Assistance Peel, Bulletin 2, 22 April 1987.

66. ETFO-caa, Full Provincial Assistance, Dryden, Bulletin 7, 25 May 1987.

67. YUCTA, FWTAO 1999-027/008, Board of Directors Report, 1986–87, 26.

68. ETFO-caa, Extracts from the Metropolitan Toronto Elementary Teachers' Rationale to the Fact Finder Dr. William Marcotte, October 6, 1986.

69. YUCTA, FWTAO 1999-027/008, Board of Directors Report, 1986–87, 26.

70. ETFO-caa, Full Provincial Assistance, Metropolitan Toronto, Bulletin 8, June 4, 1987.

71. ETFO-caa, Full Provincial Assistance, Metropolitan Toronto Full Provincial Assistance Bulletin 10, 16 June 1987, 2.

72. YUCTA, FWTAO 1999-027/012, Metropolitan Toronto Elementary Teachers' Rationale to the Factfinder, 1985–86, Collective Bargaining Workshop, 17–18 January 1986.

73. ETFO-caa, Extracts from the Metropolitan Toronto Elementary Teachers' Rationale to the Fact Finder Dr. William Marcotte, October 6, 1986, 39–45.

74. Shelly Page, "Public Elementary Teachers Give Leaders a Strike Mandate," *Toronto Star*, 19 June 1987, A7.

75. ETFO-caa, Full Provincial Assistance, Metropolitan Toronto, Bulletin 14, 14 September 1987.

76. CTF, "Teacher Strikes and Sanctions in Canada."

77. YUCTA, FWTAO 1999-027/008, Report of the Board of Directors 1987–88, 22.

78. YUCTA, FWTAO 1999-027/010, "Collective Bargaining Representatives 1987/88," *FWTAO Newsletter*, January 1988, 34–39.

79. YUCTA, OPSTF 2010-006/58, "London District: Hard Bargaining Improves Staffing and Working Conditions," *OPSTF News*, December 1989, 9.

80. YUCTA, FWTAO 1999-027/008, Report of the Board of Directors 1989–90, 17.

81. YUCTA, FWTAO 1999-027/795, Job Hunting, Bargaining Priorities file, Bargaining Priorities 1992–93.

82. ETFO GRO, OPSTF, Submission to the Legislature's Select Committee on Education with Respect to the Funding of Education, September 1989, 9.

83. Angela Mangiacasale, "OBE STRIKE: Deep Labor Woes at Root?: There's No Consensus on Cause of Conflict Between Teachers, Board," *Ottawa Citizen*, 14 May 1990, C1; YUCTA, OPSTF 2010-006/59, Dave Lennox, "Negotiations," *OPSTF News*, June 1990, 5.

84. "Ottawa: OBE Asks Teachers to Agree to Arbitration," *Ottawa Citizen*, 4 April 1990, B3.

85. Bruce Ward, "Money Just a Symptom of OBE Teachers Woes: Irritants Have Been Growing during the Past 10 Years," *Ottawa Citizen*, 21 April 1990, B5.

86. Gidney, *From Hope to Harris*, 148–49.

87. Ontario, "Documents des comité: Comité permanent des affaires sociales, 1990 décembre 18, Bill 13, Ottawa-Carleton French-Language School Board Amendment Act, 1990"; Education Relations Commission, *Annual Report 1991–92*, 26.

88. YUCTA, FWTAO 1999-027/008, 1989–90 Report of the Board of Directors, August 1990, 17; CTF, "Teacher Strikes and Sanctions in Canada."

89. YUCTA, FWTAO 1999-027/767, "Ottawa Strike Settled," *FWTAO Newsletter*, August/September 1990, 11.

90. Sears, *Retooling the Mind Factory*, 1–2.

91. YUCTA, FWTAO 1999-027/029, Minutes of the 69th Annual Meeting, 18 August 1987, 27–28; ETFO-caa, Address by Elsie McMurphy, President, B.C. Teachers' Federation to the Ontario Public School Teachers' Federation, 1987 Provincial Assembly Minutes, 18 August 1987.

92. Wendy Poole, "Neo-liberalism in British Columbia Education and Teachers' Union Resistance: Changes in Teachers' Work and the Challenges Facing Teacher Unions," *International Electronic Journal for Leadership in Learning* 11 (2007).

93. YUCTA, FWTAO 1999-027/029, Annual Meeting Minutes, August 1987, 28.

94. Statistics Canada, "Socio-demographic Factors in the Current Housing Market," *Daily*, 18 October 2005, statcan.gc.ca.

95. Foot, *Boom, Bust and* Echo, 23–25. Foot identifies the "baby-boom echo" as those born between 1980 and 1995.

96. YUCTA, OPSTF 2010-006/58, "Teacher Shortage," *OPSTF News*, February 1989, 5.

97. Glen Tunney, Ontario Teachers' Pension Plan. Email exchange with the author.

98. Malcolm Rowan, chair, Task Force on the Investment of Public Sector Pension Funds, *In Whose Interest?* (Toronto: Queen's Printer, 1987), 1, 8, 143–45.

99. YUCTA, OPSTF 2010-006/58, David Kendall, "It's Our Pension, Mr. Nixon!," *OPSTF News*, April 1989, 32.

100. Ontario, Teachers' Superannuation Act, Ontario: Revised Statutes: Vol. 1970: Iss. 5, Article 48; YUCTA, FWTAO 1999-027/008, Report of the Board of Directors, 1988–89, 27–28.

101. YUCTA, FWTAO 1999-027/767, Joan Byrne "Retirement in the 1990s," *FWTAO Newsletter*, April/May 1990, insert.

102. YUCTA, FWTAO 1999-027/767, "FWTAO Speaks for Women in Pension Dispute," *FWTAO Newsletter*, January 1990, inside cover.

103. YUCTA, FWTAO 1999-027/2333, Remarks by Chris Ward, Minister of Education, Focus on Leadership Conference, Affirmative Action Memo April 1989, 30 March 1989, 4; Memorandum from Ada Hill to Status Conveners, Presidents and Directors, April 1989, Re: Affirmative Action in School Boards, 1.

104. ETFO GRO, Teachers—Pay Equity file, Memorandum from H.J. Cooney to Provincial Executive, Recommendations re Pay Equity Implementation, 2 November 1988, 1.

105. ETFO-caa, Education Relations Commission, "Scattergrams of Teachers Employed and Length of Service," 2 November 1988, 4, 17.

106. YUCTA, FWTAO 1999-027/008, Report of the Board of Directors 1985–86, 9.

107. ETFO GRO, Teacher-Pay Equity, Letter from Kathleen Martin to Kate Hughes, Sack, Charney, Goldblatt and Mitchell, 29 July 1988.

108. YUCTA, FWTAO 1999-027/008, Report of the Board of Directors 1989–90, 20.

109. YUCTA, FWTAO 1999-027/1011, Pay Equity Bulletin, 5 September 1990, 1.

110. YUCTA, FWTAO 1999-027/008, Report of the Board of Directors 1989–90, 18.

111. YUCTA, FWTAO 1999-027/1011, Pay Equity Bulletin, 5 September 1990, 1.

112. ETFO GRO, Memorandum from Sean Conway to Chairpersons of School Boards, Pay Equity Act, 13 July 1990, 2.

113. Richard Mackie, "Opposition to Pay-Equity Bid Dropped: Rae Asks Ministry to End Intervention in Case That Would Expand Scope of Law," *Globe and Mail*, 20 September 1990, A7.

114. YUCTA, FWTAO 1999-027/767, "Pay Equity Success in the Wentworth-Perth Judicial Review," *FWTAO Newsletter*, June 1991, inside cover; YUCTA, FWTAO 1999-027/008, Report of the Board of Directors 1990–91, 11.

115. YUCTA, FWTAO 1999-027/767, FWTAO, "Pay Equity Update," *FWTAO Newsletter*, December 1991 / January 1992, inside cover. "There are now pay equity plans in 57 boards. That leaves 20 boards to be done."

116. Vickers, Rankin, and Appelle, *Politics as if Women Mattered*.

117. YUCTA, OPSTF 2010-006/69, 1988–89 Bulletins file, Pat McAdie, "The Case for Pay Equity," *Pay Equity Bulletin*, 6 February 1989, 3.

118. ETFO-caa, Memorandum from Liz Coome to Dave Lennox, Non Degree Teachers, 28 January 1988.

119. ETFO-caa, FWTAO, "Bargaining for Women in the Eighties." Used in June 1987 collective bargaining training.

120. YUCTA, FWTAO 1999-027/012, Collective Bargaining Workshop, 17–18 January 1986, Introduction. This document reports that 70.6 per cent of FWTAO members were married.

121. *Globe and Mail*, "House Approves Boost of 10 Cents an Hour to Increase Federal Minimum Wage to $1.75," 18 June 1971, 4.

122. YUCTA, FWTAO 1999-027/767, "Do Not Resign Because of Pregnancy," *FWTAO Newsletter*, January 1990, inside cover.

123. Gøsta Esping-Andersen, *The Three Worlds of Welfare Capitalism* (Princeton, NJ: Princeton University Press, 1990), 66, 164–65.

124. YUCTA, FWTAO 1999-027/767, FWTAO, "Settlement News," *FWTAO Newsletter*, October/November 1990, inside cover.

125. YUCTA, FWTAO 1999-027/767, FWTAO, "Advances Towards Paid Pregnancy Leave," *FWTAO Newsletter*, April/May 1991, inside cover.

126. YUCTA, FWTAO 1999-027/767, FWTAO, "Gains in Maternity Leave SUB Plans," *FWTAO Newsletter*, February/March 1992, inside cover.

127. ETFO GRO, Teachers—Pay Equity file, Memorandum from Dave Lennox to Executive Members, Re: Pay Equity Legislation, 26 July 1988, 9.

128. ETFO GRO, Teachers—Pay Equity file, June Executive Meeting No. 7:15, June 1987.

129. Nancy Fraser, *Unruly Practices: Power, Discourse, and Gender in Contemporary Social Theory* (Minneapolis: University of Minnesota Press, 1989), 201.

130. YUCTA, OPSTF 2010-006/62, Dave Lennox, "As I See it: Time to Change," *OPSTF News*, October 1982, 7.

131. YUCTA, FWTAO 1999-027/801, Ontario Public School Teachers Federation Documents and Correspondence file, In the Supreme Court of Ontario Divisional Court: Southey, Kever and Smith JJ, In the Matter of the Corporations Act, R.S.O. 1980, c. 95, released 8 June 1984, 16–21.

132. YUCTA, FWTAO 1999-027/008, Report of the Board of Directors 1983–84, 42.

133. YUCTA, FWTAO 1999-027/801, Ontario Public School Teachers Federation Documents and Correspondence file, Tory, Tory, DesLauriers, and Binnington, Letter from H. Lorne Morphy to Florence Henderson, 22 June 1983.

134. YUCTA, OPSTF 2010-006/62, "Second Term for Hill: Queen Mary and Her Court Poised for Another Year of Action," *OPSTF News*, October 1985, 1.

135. YUCTA, OPSTF 2010-006/35, Provincial Assembly Minutes, August 1985, Motions passed, Thursday afternoon, Session G3.

136. YUCTA, OPSTF 2010-006/35, Mary Hill, Report of the President, Provincial Assembly Minutes, August 1985, I2.

137. YUCTA, OPSTF 2010-006/35, Report of the Executive Task Force on Unionization of Occasional Teachers, Provincial Assembly Minutes, August 1985, G64–66.

138. YUCTA, OPSTF 2010-006/55, Membership Extension Task Force file, The Unionization of Occasional Teachers, June 1984, Membership Extension Task Force, i–6.

139. YUCTA, OPSTF 2010-006/55, OSSTF/FEESO 1990–91 file, *OSSTF/FEESO Handbook 1990–91*, Bylaw 2.1.1.2.

140. YUCTA, OPSTF 2010-006/59, "OPSTF Wins Trade Union Status," *OPSTF Newstoday*, 28 March 1986, 1.

141. YUCTA, OPSTF 2010-006/35, Provincial Assembly Minutes, August 1985, G64–66.

142. YUCTA, OPSTF 2010-006/35, Provincial Assembly Minutes, August 1985, Motions Passed, Session E, 14 August 1985, 3.

143. YUCTA, OPSTF 2010-006/37, Report of the Status of Women Committee (ad hoc), Minutes and File of Reports of the Provincial Assembly, August 1986, E12.

144. YUCTA, OPSTF 2010-006/37, Dave Lennox, Report of the Secretary, Provincial Assembly Minutes, August 1987, F3–4.

145. YUCTA, OPSTF 2010-006/58, Linda Markle, "Breaking the Mold," *OPSTF News*, June 1989, 32.

146. YUCTA, OPSTF 2010-006/58, Charlotte Morgan, "An Occasion to Be Treasured: The OPSTF Assembly," *OPSTF News*, October 1992, 22; ETFO-caa, "Imagine What We Can Achieve Together: District Homework Assignment," 1992, 52.

147. Canada, Constitution Act, 1982, *Canadian Charter of Rights and Freedoms*, 15.

148. Mary Eberts, Florence I. Henderson, Kathleen A. Lahey, Catharine A. MacKinnon, Sheila McIntyre, and Elizabeth J. Shilton, *The Case for Women's Equality: The Federation of Women Teachers' Associations of Ontario and the Canadian Charter of Rights and Freedoms* (Toronto: Federation of Women Teachers' Associations of Ontario, 1991), 19–25.

149. YUCTA, OPSTF 2010-006/62, Mary Hill, "Time to Review and Recommit," *OPSTF News*, June 1986, 3.

150. YUCTA, OPSTF 2010-006/37, Minutes and File of Reports of the Provincial Assembly, August 1986, AB8.

151. Mario Spagnuolo and Larry Glassford, "Feminism in Transition: The Margaret Tomen Membership Case and the Formation of the Elementary Teachers' Federation of Ontario," *Historical Studies in Education* 20,2 (Fall 2008), 64–65.

152. YUCTA, FWTAO 1999-027/008 1987-88-9A, Report of the Board of Directors, 1987–88, 48–49.

153. Eberts et al., *The Case for Women's Equality*, 25.

154. YUCTA, FWTAO 1999-027/767, Joan Westcott, "Supreme Court Rules in Favour of FWTAO," *FWTAO Newsletter*, August/September 1991, 33.

155. ETFO-caa, Gail Emmerson, "Perspectives," *Tabloyd*, 28 September 1987, np.

156. ETFO-caa, "The Ayatollah Approves," *Nugget*, 21 September 1987, np.

157. ETFO-caa, "An Ironic Setback for Ontario Women," *Ottawa Citizen*, A8.

158. YUCTA, FWTAO 1999-027/008, Report of the Board of Directors 1987–88, August 1988, 48–49.

159. YUCTA, OPSTF 2010-006/62, "Thirty Thousand Teachers Protest Bylaw 1," *OPSTF Newstoday*, 20 April 1988, 1.

160. Donn Downey, "Teachers Ask Board to Probe Union Bias," *Globe and Mail*, 9 April 1988, A6.

161. Robert Brehl, "Teachers' Union Demands Inquiry into 'Biased' Rules," *Toronto Star*, 10 April 1988, A6.

162. YUCTA, OPSTF 2010-006/58, Dave Lennox, "Secretary" *OPSTF News*, April 1988, 5.

163. YUCTA, OPSTF 2010-006/62, Dave Lennox, "Human Rights Commission Convenes Board of Inquiry," *OPSTF Newstoday*, 30 September 1988, 1.

164. YUCTA, FWTAO 1999-027/767, Joan Westcott, "The Challenge to FWTAO Membership," *FWTAO Newsletter*, November/December 1988, 33.

165. Morris Wernick, "Finances and Politics Control the Classroom," *Globe and Mail*, 26 April 1988, A7.

166. *Globe and Mail*, "Former Editor of Toronto Star Hired to Do Study on Dropouts," 21 February 1987, A7.

167. George Radwanski, *Ontario Study of the Relevance of Education and the Issue of Dropouts* (Toronto: Ontario Ministry of Education, 1987), 123–26, 142–47, 152–59.

168. Sandro Contenta, "Standards for Grades 3 to 6 May Be Set by '89, Ward Says," *Toronto Star*, 15 September 1988, A4; Sandro Contenta, "Standard Testing on Way for Elementary Pupils," *Toronto Star*, 22 February 1989, A1.

169. Sandro Contenta, "Ontario Teachers Reject Standard Tests for the 3 Rs," *Toronto Star*, 23 February 1989, A7.

170. Ian Macdonald, *Report of the Commission on the Financing of Elementary and Secondary Education in Ontario* (Toronto: Ontario Ministry of Education, 1985), 39–43.

171. YUCTA, OPSTF 2010-006/59, Bill Martin, "Fall 1989: A Woeful Litany for Education," *OPSTF News*, February 1990, 3.

## Chapter 5: Social Democracy in a Neo-liberal Era

1. YUCTA, OPSTF 2010-006/59, Bill Martin, "A New Political Ball Game," *OPSTF News*, October 1990, 3.

2. YUCTA, OPSTF 2010-006/59, Dave Lennox, "Pay Equity," *OPSTF News*, October 1990, 5.

3. James Rinehart, *Tyranny of Work: Alienation and the Labour Process* (Toronto: Nelson, 2006), 55–57.

4. Ontario, Premier's Council, *Competing in the New Global Economy: Report of the Premier's Council* (Toronto: The Council, 1988); Ontario, Premier's Council, *People and Skills in the New Global Economy: Premier's Council Report* (Toronto: The Council, 1990).

5. Taylor, "Education for Industrial and 'Postindustrial' Purposes," 19.

6. Gidney, *From Hope to Harris*, 216–7.

7. Tanya Talaga, "Ex-NDP Minister Tony Silipo Dead at 54," *Toronto Star*, 11 March 2012.

8. Gidney, *From Hope to Harris*, 218–24.

9. Bruce Curtis, D.W. Livingstone, and Harry Smaller, *Stacking the Deck: The Streaming of Working-Class Kids in Ontario Schools* (Our Schools Our Selves, 1992), 89.

10. Stephen E. Anderson and Sonia Ben Jaafar, "Policy Trends in Ontario Education," Working Paper, Sub-project 2 of "The Evolution of Teaching Personnel in Canada," SSHRC Major Collaborative Research Initiatives Project, 2002–2006, ICEC Working Paper #1, Toronto: Ontario Institute for Studies in Education, September 2003, 8–14, oise.utoronto.ca.

11. Susan Walker, "Education Critics Slam New Curriculum Policy," *Toronto Star*, 24 October 1992, A1, A28.

12. Duncan MacLellan, "Neoliberalism and Ontario Teachers' Unions: A 'Not-So' Common Sense Revolution," *Socialist Studies / Études socialistes* 5 (August 2009), 58.

13. Michael Wiener, Letter to the Editor, *Montreal Gazette*, 12 May 1998, B2.

14. YUCTA, FWTAO 1999-027/767, "Lambton on Strike," *FWTAO Newsletter*, October/November 1990, inside cover; YUCTA, OPSTF 2010-006/59, Dave Lennox, "Lambton Elementary Teachers' Strike," *OPSTF News*, December 1990, 5.

15. CTF, "Teacher Strikes and Sanctions in Canada."

16. YUCTA, OPSTF 2010-006/61, "OPSMTF Endorses Earlier Policies to Cover Possibility of Staff Cuts," *OPSMTF News*, 1971–72, 5, 1.

17. YUCTA, OPSTF 2010-006/59, Dave Lennox, "Lambton Elementary Teachers' Strike," *OPSTF News*, December 1990, 5.

18. CTF, "Teacher Strikes and Sanctions in Canada."

19. YUCTA, FWTAO 1999-027/767, "Lambton Strike Settled in November," *FWTAO Newsletter*, February/March 1991, inside cover.

20. YUCTA, FWTAO 1999-027/336, Memorandum from Bet Kagayama to Mary Pattinson, Metro Strike—Pension Payment, 14 January 1992, 1, 2, 4–5, in History of FWTAO Practices (Re: Financial Matters), n.d. In 1979, the waiting period for receiving $25 strike pay had been 11 days.

21. ETFO-caa, Memorandum from Christine Brown to Provincial Executive, Staff Officers, re: The New Ontario Labour Relations Act, 31 March 1993; Panitch and Swartz, *Assault on Trade Union Freedoms*, 165–7.

22. ETFO-caa, Unionization of Occasional Teachers Organizer's Manual, 7 September 1989, ii; Part of the Family, 20 February 1990; Memorandum from Louise Ewing to Duncan Jewell, December OPSTF Executive Motions, 6 December 1988.

23. ETFO-caa, Memorandum from Bill Martin to Provincial Executive, Non-statutory Membership within OPSTF, 7 September 1989. (Emphasis in the original.)

24. YUCTA, OPSTF 2010-006/55, Teachers with Indian Band Councils (TIBC) file, Memorandum from Duncan Jewell to David Lennox, Unionization of Private School Teachers, 18 July 1988.

25. YUCTA, OPSTF 2010-006/36, Provincial Executive Minutes, 14 September 1988, 37; YUCTA, OPSTF 2010-006/55, Membership Extension Task Force file, Letter from Dave Lennox to Bill Markle, Legal Opinion—Extension of Membership, 25 October 1989; TIBC file, Memorandum from Duncan Jewell to Provincial Executive, Unionization of Teachers Teaching for Indian Bands, 25 November 1988.

26. YUCTA, OPSTF 2010-006/55, TIBC file, 1985–86 Collective Agreement Between Nelson House Education Authority Inc. and Nelson House Teachers' Association; 1979–81 Collective Agreement Between the Peguis School Board and the Peguis Teachers' Association #2648 of the Manitoba Teachers' Society; 1981 Collective Agreement Between the School Board of Sandy Bay and The Sandy Bay Teachers' Association of The Manitoba Teachers' Society; Canadian Labour Relations Board, Syndicat des travailleurs de l'enseignement de Louis-Hémon, applicant, and Conseil des Montagnais du Lac St-Jean, employer, Board File 555-1577, 23 December 1982.

27. YUCTA, OPSTF 2010-006/55, TIBC file, Memorandum from Louise Ewing to Duncan Jewell, December Executive Motions, 6 December 1988.

28. Ontario Labour Relations Board File No: 2842-88-R, Ontario Public School Teachers and the Muskoka Board of Education, 19 July 1989, canlii.org; ETFO Coordinator of Protective Services Christine Brown's office records (hereafter ETFO CPS), Christine Brown, The State of the Unions, April OPSTF Executive 8:16, March 19, 1997.

29. YUCTA, OPSTF 2010-006/36, Provincial Executive Minutes, 9 July 1990, 24.

30. YUCTA, OPSTF 2010-006/36, Provincial Executive Minutes, 15 September 1990, 12.

31. YUCTA, OPSTF 2010-006/55, TIBC file, Letter from Wilhelmina Patzer to Ontario Public School Teachers' Federation, 4 September 1988; Letter from Duncan Jewell to Mrs. Wilhelmina Patzer, 21 September 1988.

32. ETFO-caa, Memorandum from Harold Vigoda to OPSTF Provincial Executive and Secretary, September Executive Motion (4) Organizing First Nation Indian Bands, 28 September 1992, 1.

33. YUCTA, OPSTF 2010-006/59, Table of Contents, OPSTF News, April 1991, 1.

34. Bernard Schissel and Terry Wotherspoon, *The Legacy of School for Aboriginal People: Education, Oppression, and Emancipation* (Don Mills ON: Oxford University, 2003), 101.

35. Schissel and Wotherspoon, *The Legacy of School for Aboriginal People*, 6; Truth and Reconciliation Commission, *Final Report*, 147–48.

36. Clive Hocking, "Native Leaders, BCTF Begin Dialogue," *Teacher: Newsmagazine of the B.C. Teachers' Federation*, June 1988, 1, bctf.ca.

37. YUCTA, OPSTF 2010-006/59, "George Erasmus Speaks . . ." *OPSTF News*, April 1991, 6–8.

38. ETFO-caa, Memorandum from Duncan Jewell to Provincial Executive, Unionization of Education Staff at Lakeview School, 10 July 1991, and attached letter from Albert (Bud) Debassige.

39. ETFO-caa, Letter from Peter Suchanek to Harold Vigoda, In the Matter of the Canada Labour Code (Part I—Industrial Relations) and an application for certification as bargaining agent pursuant to Section 24 thereof concerning the Ontario Public School Teachers' Federation, applicant, and The Mundo Peetabeck Education Authority, employer, file 555-3392 (hereafter Canadian Labour Code file 555-3392), 4 December 1991; ETFO-caa, Memorandum from Harold Vigoda to Provincial Executive, Re: September Executive Motion (4) Organizing First Nation Indian Bands, 28 September 1992.

40. ETFO-caa, Letter from Carol Garrow to Chief Alex Metatawabin and Andre Reuben, Canadian Labour Code file 555-3392, 30 January 1992; 9 March 1992; 11 March 1992.

41. ETFO-caa, Letter from Chief Ed Metatawabin to Peter Suchanek, Mundo Peetabeck Education Authority, 22 January 1992.

42. ETFO-caa, Memorandum from Harold Vigoda to Provincial Executive and Secretary, September Executive Motion (4) Organizing First Nation Indian Bands, 28 September 1992, 1–5.

43. ETFO-caa, Letter from Herold Vigoda to Canadian Labour Relations Board, Attention Mr. Peter T. Suchanek, 10 October 1992.

44. Rebecca Coulter, Professor Emerita and Adjunct Research Professor, Faculty of Education, Western University, London, ON, 30 October 2016, personal communication.

45. ETFO-caa, Letter from Gene Lewis to Mundo Peetabeck Education Authority, Attention Mr. Earl Whelan, Principal, St. Ann's School, 27 October 1992.

46. ETFO-caa, Letter from Gary Fick to Dave Lennox, 23 September 1991. The letter was requesting support to organize educational assistants.

47. YUCTA, FWTAO 1999-027/767, "First Pay Equity Plan," *FWTAO Newsletter*, October/November 1990, inside cover.

48. YUCTA, OPSTF 2010-006/67, Pay Equity Information Model Plans file, Pay Equity Settlement Between the 40 Participating OPSBA Boards of Education and FWTAO, OPSTF and AEFO Representing the Elementary Teachers Employed by Those Boards, 25 February 1991.

49. YUCTA, FWTAO 1999-027/767, "Pay Equity Victory," *FWTAO Newsletter*, April/May 1991, inside cover.

50. Ontario, Pay Equity Act, Ontario Regulation 491/93.

51. ETFO GRO, Teacher-Pay Equity file, Memorandum to Directors of Education from Mariette Carrier-Fraser to Directors of Education, Pay Equity Funding for 1993, 1993: B8, 22 November 1993.

52. ETFO GRO, Teacher-Pay Equity file, Pay Equity Survey 1993.

53. YUCTA, FWTAO 1999-027/767, Joan Westcott, "Pay Equity Achievements," *FWTAO Newsletter*, October/November 1991, 41.

54. ETFO GRO, Teacher-Pay Equity file, Memorandum from H. Cooney to G. Lewis, Occasional Teacher Pay Equity Plans, 14 December 1993.

55. ETFO GRO, Teacher-Pay Equity file, Memorandum from Burt Cottenden and Burleigh Mattice to Collective Bargaining Staff, Status of Pay Equity Plans for Occasional Teacher Branches, 27 March 1995.

56. YUCTA, FWTAO 1999-027/767, "Pay Equity Nearing Completion," *FWTAO Newsletter*, October/November 1992, inside cover.

57. YUCTA, FWTAO 1999-027/767, Joan Westcott, "Employment Equity a Ministry Mandate," *FWTAO Newsletter*, April/May 1990, 41; Peter Small, "Job Equity Priority for Women Teachers," *Toronto Star*, 19 August 1992, A20.

58. YUCTA, FWTAO 1999-027/767, Joan Westcott, "Equity Legislation Vital to Women," *FWTAO Newsletter*, December 1991–January 1992, 33; "Pay Equity Update," inside cover.

59. Ontario, Bill 79, Employment Equity Act, 1993.

60. Reg Whitaker, "The Cutting Edge of Ontario's Bad Law," *Globe and Mail*, 6 January 1994, A19. This was one example.

61. Nancy Hartsock, *The Feminist Standpoint Revisited, and Other Essays* (Boulder, CO: Westview Press, 1998).

62. ETFO-caa, Equity, 16 February 1994. Prepared for an OPEN Meeting.

63. ETFO-caa, Memorandum from Ada Hill and Bev Saskoley to FWTAO Directors, Employment Equity Regional Meetings, 5 May 1994; Letter from Juanita Westmoreland-Traoré, Employment Equity Commissioner, to Dear Friend, 11 April 1994.

64. ETFO-caa, FWTAO, Seniority / Collective Bargaining and Employment Equity, 7 June 1994, 1.

65. YUCTA, FWTAO 1999-027/1058, Affirmative Action, Employment Equity Report, 1997, 10.

66. ETFO-caa, Letter from Monica Woodley to Dear Friends, 2 June 1994.

67. YUCTA, FWTAO 1999-027/1058, Affirmative Action Employment Equity Report, 1993, 25, 34.

68. Margaret Wilson, interview, 7 February 2009.

69. YUCTA, FWTAO 1999-027/250, Affirmative Action, Employment Equity Report, 1997, 10–11.

70. YUCTA, OPSTF 2010-006/59, Burleigh Mattice, "Is Your Pension Life in Order?," *OPSTF News*, June 1991, 34.

71. Statistics Canada, *Canada's Retirement Income Programs: A Statistical Overview, 1900–2000*, Minister of Industry, 2003, 67–82.

72. Susan Sayce and Michael Gold, "Revisiting Industrial Democracy and Pension Trusteeship: The Case of Canada," *Economic and Industrial Democracy* 32,3 (2011), 487–88; Finkel Alvin, "The State of Writing on the Canadian Welfare State: What's Class Got to Do with It?," *Labour / Le Travail* 54 (Fall 2004), 161.

73. YUCTA, OPSTF 2010-006/59, Dave Lennox, "Pensions: A New Reality," *OPSTF News*, October 1991, 5.

74. YUCTA, OPSTF 2010-006/59, "Agreement Reached on Pension Plan," *Newstoday*, 13 September 1991.

75. YUCTA, FWTAO 1999-027/1045, FWTAO Pension Committee 1994–95 file, Teachers' Pension Plan Board, Plan at a Glance, 1994. The OTF reported assets of $33 billion.

## Chapter 6: The Social Contract

1. Morningstar, *Andex Chart*, 2019.

2. Philip Cross, "How Did the 2008–2010 Recession and Recovery Compare with Previous Cycles?," *Canadian Economic Observer*, January 2011, statcan.gc.ca.

3. Patrick Monahan, *Storming the Pink Palace; The NDP in Power: A Cautionary Tale* (Toronto: Lester Publishing, 1995), 169–74; Thomas Walkom, *Rae Days* (Toronto: Key Porter Books, 1994), 144–45.

4. YUCTA, OPSTF 2010-006/58, Dave Lennox, "Weak Staffing Clauses Leave Teachers Vulnerable," *OPSTF News*, June 1992, 5.

5. ETFO GRO, Briefing Notes, March 1992, 2.

6. George Martell, *A New Education Politics: Bob Rae's Legacy and the Response of the Ontario Secondary School Teachers' Federation* (Toronto: James Lorimer 1995), 74.

7. Larry Savage, "Contemporary Party-Union Relations in Canada," *Labor Studies Journal* 35,1 (2010); Stephen McBride, "The Continuing Crisis of Social Democracy: Ontario's Social Contract in Perspective," *Studies in Political Economy* 50 (1996).

8. Walkom, *Rae Days*, 1–8; Mel Watkins, "Ontario: Discrediting Social Democracy," *Studies in Political Economy* 43 (1994), 143.

9. YUCTA, FWTAO 1999-027/988, Social Contract (1 of 2) file, Jobs and Services: A Social Contract for the Ontario Public Sector, 23 April 1993, 1, 7.

10. YUCTA, FWTAO 1999-027/988, Social Contract Update, 22 April 1993.

11. Yonatan Reshef and Sandra Rastin, *Unions in the Time of Revolutions: Government Restructuring in Alberta and Ontario* (Toronto: University of Toronto Press, 2003), 137. The supportive unions included the United Steelworkers of America, United Food and Commercial Workers Union, International Association of Machinists and Aerospace Workers, and Service Employees International Union.

12.   Derek Fudge and John Brewin, *Collective Bargaining in Canada: Human Right or Canadian Illusion?* (Nepean, ON: National Union of Public and General Employees and United Food and Commercial Workers Canada, 2005), 48–51; William Walker, "Tories Vote for NDP's Pay-Cut Law," *Toronto Star*, 24 June 1993, A2.

13.   ETFO-caa, E.S. Lavender, "Report of the Fact Finder, The East Parry Sound Women Teachers' Association and The Ontario Public School Teachers' Federation East Parry Sound," 23 November 1992, 1, 14.

14.   YUCTA, OPSTF 2010-006/58, Dave Lennox, "Weak Staffing Clauses Leave Teachers Vulnerable," *OPSTF News*, June 1992, 5.

15.   YUCTA FWTAO, 199-027/988, Social Contract (2 of 2) file, Fax from Joan Westcott to WTA Presidents and Board of Directors, Re: Education Sector Social Contract Talks, 21 May 1993; ETFO CPS, Memorandum from Gene Lewis to District Presidents, Branch Presidents, Social Contract Update, 21 May 1993; Memorandum from Gene Lewis to District Presidents, Branch Presidents, Re: Social Contract Update, 27 May 1993.

16.   ETFO CPS, Social Contract Agitprop file, Memorandum from Social Contract Team to FWTAO Directors WTA Presidents, Social Contract Update, 30 September 1993, 9; YUCTA, OPSTF 2010-006/59, Gene Lewis, "The Social Contract: An Infamous Act That Will Go Down in History," *Newstoday*, 30 August 1993.

17.   ETFO-caa, Paula Knopf, Education Relations Commission, "In the Matter of an Inquiry Pursuant to the East Parry Sound Board of Education and Teachers Dispute Settlement Act, Determination," July 1994 (Hereafter ETFO-caa, Knopf, Inquiry East Parry Sound), 109–10.

18.   ETFO GRO, Bill 100 Review file, Changes in the Terms and Conditions of Expired Collective Agreements Undertaken Pursuant to Section 10 (3) (b) of the *School Boards and Teachers Collective Negotiations Act*: An Historical Summary, 18 November 1993.

19.   ETFO GRO, Bill 100 Review file, Memorandum from Vivian McCaffrey to Gene Lewis, Re: The 60 Day Provision in Bill 100, 24 November 1993.

20.   Ontario, School Boards and Teachers Collective Negotiations Act, S10(3).

21.   Martell, *A New Education Politics*, 86–87.

22.   ETFO GRO, Bill 100 Review file, Memorandum from Vivian McCaffrey to Gene Lewis, Re: The 60 Day Provision in Bill 100, 24 November 1993, 2–4.

23.   YUCTA, FWTAO 1999-027/348, "Trustees Support Strike Right," *FWTAO Newsletter*, 1973–74, 5, 1.

24.   Anne Jarvis, "Little-Known Provision of Law Fuels Ontario Teacher Strikes," *Windsor Star*, 11 November 1993, A3.

25.   ETFO-caa, Knopf, Inquiry East Parry Sound, 108.

26.   ETFO-caa, Letter from Barbara Sargent and Gene Lewis to Bob Rae, 19 October 1993.

27. ETFO-caa, Letter from P.V. Pasco to Director of Education Norm Mason, Local FWTAO President Eileen McGowan (mistakenly), Local OPSTF President Jim Johnson, and Local OSSTF President Stephen Todoroff, 29 October 1993; Letter from Marg Beswitherick and Jim Johnston to Nancy Woodruff, Home and School Association Secretary Nancy Woodruff, 1 November 1993; Letter from Gary Hammond to Herb Cooney, and Carol Zavitz, 27 October 1993; Letter from G.B. Mattice to Tim Hainsworth, South River and Area Chamber of Commerce President, 27 October 1993.

28. ETFO-caa, Letter from Carol Zavitz and Herb Cooney to Janette Rawn, 29 October 1993; and Media Release, Teachers Ready to Meet Public, n.d.

29. ETFO-caa, Letter from John Stopper to Norm Mason, 10 November 1993.

30. ETFO-caa, FWTAO and OPSTF, Two Panels out Today, Picket Captains News, 10 November 1993.

31. ETFO-caa, Letter from the East Parry Sound Principals' Association to Barbara Sargent and Gene Lewis, 3 November 1993.

32. ETFO-caa, Letter from Barbara Sargent and Gene Lewis to Norm Mason, 5 November 1993.

33. ETFO-caa, Letter from East Parry Sound Board of Education Chair Art Osburn to Jim Johnson and Marg Beswitherick, 15 November 1993.

34. ETFO-caa, Letter from Marg Beswitherick and Jim Johnson to Dave Cooke, 19 November 1993.

35. ETFO-caa, FWTAO and OPSTF press release, Late Breaking News, 19 November 1993.

36. ETFO-caa, Memorandum from G. Burleigh Mattice, Strike Pay, 15 November 1993.

37. ETFO-caa, Knopf, Inquiry East Parry Sound, 118.

38. YUCTA, OPSTF 2010-006/58, "East Parry Sound Teachers Win at Arbitration," OPSTF News, April 1994, 23.

39. ETFO-caa, Knopf, Inquiry East Parry Sound, 120–21.

40. ETFO-caa, Windsor Board of Education press release, Fact Finder Releases Report Regarding Elementary Teacher Negotiations, 29 July 1993.

41. ETFO-caa, M.G. Mitchnick, "In the Matter of an Arbitration Between the Board of Education for the City of Windsor and FWTAO and OPSTF, pursuant to the Windsor Teachers Dispute Settlement Act, 1993," 16 May 1994, 3–6.

42. ETFO-caa, Strike Headquarters binder, Jane Sparrow, "Statement by the Chair of the Board, Re: Is Our Contract Dispute with Elementary School Teachers a Local Battle in a Provincial War?," 27 October 1993.

43. ETFO-caa, Strike Headquarters binder, Sparrow, "Statement by the Chair of the Board," 27 October 1993, 2.

44. ETFO-caa, FWTAO and OPSTF, fax, Why Are the Elementary Teachers on Strike?, 16 November 1993.

45. ETFO-caa, Strike Headquarters binder, Letter from [FWTAO] Barbara Sargent to Gene Lewis, 15 November 1993, 2.

46. ETFO-caa, handwritten letter from Lynn Moir [Peterborough County Occasional Teachers Local] to Harold [Vigoda], 27 November 1993.

47. Anne Jarvis, "School Strike: 5 Days Lost: Parent Meets Board Boss to Address the Issues," *Windsor Star*, 12 November 1993, A3.

48. Rob Hornberger, "Board Feels Heat as Parents Strike Back," *Windsor Star*, 11 November 1993, A1.

49. ETFO-caa, FWTAO and OPSTF, Media Advisory, Windsor Elementary Teachers Move Their Protest to Essex County, 25 November 1993.

50. ETFO-caa, Media Release, Premier Rae Tells Windsor Elementary Teachers the Playing Field Isn't Level, 26 November 1993.

51. ETFO-caa, Letter from Barbara Sargent and Gene Lewis to elementary teachers, Dear Colleague, 22 November 1993.

52. ETFO-caa, FWTAO report, Meeting with ERC Called by Minister of Education, n.d.

53. YUCTA, FWTAO 1999-027/767, "Two Fall Strikes Important," *FWTAO Newsletter*, January/February 1994, inside cover.

54. Anne Jarvis, "Strike's Legacy Anger, Distrust," *Windsor Star*, 18 December 1993, A1.

55. Anne Jarvis, "Teachers' Bitterness Tempers Relief Over New Contract," *Windsor Star*, 28 June 1994, A3.

56. ETFO GRO, Bill 100 Review file, Letter from Dave Cooke to Barbara Sargent, filed 19 April 1994.

57. George Ehring and Wayne Roberts, *Giving Away a Miracle: Lost Dreams, Broken Promises, and the Ontario NDP* (Oakville ON: Mosaic 1993), 28–31.

58. YUCTA, OPSTF 2010-006/58, Ron Poste, "How Do You Like Socialism—So Far?," *OPSTF News*, June 1993, 36.

59. Dr. Daniel Jay Baum, email exchange with the author, 29 October 2009.

60. Karen Schucher, "Contesting Women's Solidarity: Human Rights Law and the FWTAO Membership Case," York University, Magistrate of Laws thesis, 2006, 94–7.

61. Lynne Ainsworth, "Woman's Fight to Be Member of Male Union Gets Hearing," *Toronto Star*, 25 October 1989, A28.

62. Eberts et al., *The Case for Women's Equality*, 667.

63. YUCTA, FWTAO 1999-027/767, Barbara Sargent and Joan Westcott, "A Blow to Human Rights," *FWTAO Newsletter*, May/June 1994, 2–5.

64. Sargent and Westcott, "A Blow to Human Rights," 5.

65. Sargent and Westcott, "A Blow to Human Rights," 5.

66. Eberts et al., *The Case for Women's Equality*, 91–93.

67. Schucher, "Contesting Women's Solidarity," 1.

68. Rosalie Abella in Schucher, "Contesting Women's Solidarity," 145.

69. Ontario Human Rights Commission, Margaret Tomen v. Ontario Teachers' Federation (OTF) and the Ontario Public School Teachers' Federation (OPSTF) (Toronto: Nethercut, 13 November 1990), 41, 102.

70. Tomen v. OTF and OPSTF, 44–46, 51, 61–62.

71. Tomen v. OTF and OPSTF, 61.

72. Tomen v. OTF and OPSTF, 67.

73. YUCTA, FWTAO 1999-027/767, Joan Westcott, "Membership Issue Clarified," *FWTAO Newsletter*, September/October 1994, 41.

74. YUCTA, FWTAO 1999-027/971, Joan Westcott, "Working Towards a Smooth Transition," *FWTAO Newsletter*, May/June 1998, 32.

## Chapter 7:
## Mike Harris and the "Common Sense" Counterrevolution

1. Sears, *Retooling the Mind Factory*, 225–28.

2. Monique Bégin and Gerald Caplan, *For the Love of Learning: Report of the Royal Commission on Learning, Volume IV, Making It Happen* (Toronto: Queen's Printer, 1995), Recommendation 166.

3. Bégin and Caplan, *For the Love of Learning*, Recommendations 96–97.

4. ETFO-caa, "OTF Action Plan," OTF *Communiqué*, 30 January 1996.

5. YUCTA, OPSTF 2010-006/58, "Redesigning Ontario Education: Minister Responds to Report of Royal Commission on Learning," *OPSTF News*, April 1995, 5–14.

6. YUCTA, FWTAO 1999-027/767, "Sweeping Educational Reforms: Some Questions and Concerns," *FWTAO Newsletter*, March/April 1995, 8–11.

7. YUCTA, FWTAO 1999-027/767, Joan Westcott, "Are New Reforms Really New Foundations?," *FWTAO Newsletter*, March/April 1995, 33.

8. YUCTA, OPSTF 2010-006/58, Gene Lewis, "Meeting with the Minister," *OPSTF News*, February 1995, 32; MacLellan, "Neoliberalism and Ontario Teachers' Unions," 58–60.

9. YUCTA, OPSTF 2010-006/58, Reg Ferland, "The Common Sense Revolution," *OPSTF News*, December 1994, 3.

10. YUCTA, OPSTF 2010-006/58, Reg Ferland, "Get Ready to Vote," *OPSTF News*, April 1995, 3.

11. Progressive Conservative Party of Ontario, "The Common Sense Revolution," 11, scribd.com.

12. ETFO GRO, OPSTF Briefs file, Submission to the Finance and Economic Affairs Committee with Respect to the 1996 Provincial Budget, February 1996, 5–6.

13. Rinehart, *Tyranny of Work*, 148–75.

14. Samuel Bowles and Herbert Gintis, *Schooling in Capitalist America: Educational Reform and the Contradictions of Economic Life* (New York: Basic Books, 1976), 131–41.

15. ETFO-caa, Memorandum from Duncan A. Jewell to Negotiation Officers, Re: Rob Fairley's Speech to the Provincial Meeting of Negotiation Officers, 3 November 1995. (Emphasis in the original.)

16. Marcella Munro, "Ontario's 'Days of Action' and Strategic Choices for the Left in Canada," *Studies in Political Economy* 53 (1997), 138.

17. Miro Cernetig, "Out of the West They Rode, the Anti-Tax Gang," *Globe and Mail*, 17 April 1993, D3; Alison Taylor, "'Re-culturing' Students and Selling Futures: School-to-Work Policy in Ontario," *Journal of Education and Work* 18,3 (Fall 2005), 334.

18. YUCTA, OPSTF 2010-006/58, Ben Andrews, Keith Balfour, and Nancy Stitch, "Taxpayers' Federation 'Study' Misleading," *OPSTF News*, June 1995, 12–13.

19. Gidney, *From Hope to Harris*, 237–8.

20. ETFO-caa, Memorandum from Reg Ferland to Participants at the Council of Presidents, Ministry Document on Funding Cutbacks, 30 January 1996.

21. Ontario was the only province to have Grade 13.

22. ETFO-caa, Ontario Public School Boards' Association, Ontario Separate School Trustees' Association, Association française des conseils scolaires de l'Ontario, Association franco-ontarienne des conseils d'écoles catholiques, and Ontario Ministry of Education and Training, *Restructuring: New Realities, New Beginnings*, 1994, 18–19.

23. Progressive Conservative Party of Ontario, "The Common Sense Revolution," 12.

24. Alfie Kohn, *The Case Against Standardized Testing: Raising the Scores, Ruining the Schools* (Portsmouth, NH: Heinemann, 2000).

25. Ardavan Eizadirad, *Decolonizing Educational Assessment: Ontario Elementary Students and the EQAO* (Cham, Switzerland, 2019), 33.

26. YUCTA, OPSTF 2010-006/58, Charlotte Morgan, photograph, *OPSTF News*, October 1996, 1.

27. Gidney, *From Hope to Harris*, 264.

28. YUCTA, FWTAO 1999-027/971, "Safeguarding Employment Equity," *FWTAO Newsletter*, November/December 1995, inside cover.

29. ETFO CPS, Memorandum from Christine Brown to Executive et al., Changes to Labour Law, 12 October 1995; ETFO CPS, Ontario Ministry of Labour, "Background: Labour Relations Amendments," 4 October 1995.

30. Ontario, Bill 8, An Act to Repeal Job Quotas and to Restore Merit-Based Employment Practices in Ontario, 1995.

31. ETFO CPS, Memorandum from Christine Brown to Employment Equity Contacts et al., Repeal of Employment Equity Act, 25 October 1995.

32. Mary Cornish, "Canadian Compliance with Beijing Platform for Action Pay and Employment Equity Requirements," presentation to International Seminar on Women's Rights, London, UK, September 1999, 9–12, cavalluzzo.com.

33. YUCTA, FWTAO 1999-027/250, Affirmative Action, Employment Equity Report, 1997, 11.

34. YUCTA, OPSTF 2010-006/53, Provincial Executive Minutes, 22 November 1995, 1.

35. YUCTA, FWTAO 1999-027/971, Joan Westcott, *FWTAO Newsletter*, November/December 1995, 30; YUCTA, FWTAO 1999-027/630, Memorandum from Cavalluzzo, Hayes, Shilton, McIntyre, and Cornish regarding intervener status in case of Ontario Regulation 384/95 and 385/95.

36. YUCTA, FWTAO 1999-027/971, Cecilia Reynolds and Harry Smaller, "Economic Downturns Affect Women and Men Differently," *FWTAO Newsletter*, January/February 1996, 50–57.

37. YUCTA, FWTAO 1999-027/1026 B, Letter from Sheryl Hosizaki to Giles Bisson, 21 November 1995.

38. YUCTA, FWTAO 1999-027/971, Joan Westcott, "When $400 Million Is Really $800 Million," *FWTAO News*, March/April 1996, 30; ETFO-caa, Memorandum from John C. Snobelen to Chairs of School Boards, Directors of Education, General Legislative Grants, 1996–97, 30 November 1995.

39. Paul Kellogg, "Workers Against Austerity—Lessons from Canada's 'Days of Action,' 1995–1998," AUSpace: Athabasca University, 3 May 2011, athabascau.ca.

40. YUCTA, OPSTF 2010-006/58, Charlotte Morgan "Cutback Calendar," *OPSTF News*, April 1996, 6–7.

41. Morgan, "Cutback Calendar," *OPSTF News*, April 1996, 6–9; James Rusk, "Mass Ontario Labour Strike Fails to Shut Down London: Organizers of Anti-Tory Protest Satisfied as Major Plants Closed," *Globe and Mail*, 12 December 1995, A3.

42. YUCTA, OPSTF 2010-006/58, Dave Lennox, "Solidarity or Apathy," *OPSTF News*, December 1995, 5.

43. YUCTA, FWTAO 1999-027/971, Sheryl Hoshizaki, "Speaking Back to Media Myths," *FWTAO Newsletter*, November/December 1995, 31–4.

44. YUCTA, FWTAO 1999-027/971, Sheryl Hoshizaki, "Care of a Federation: A Personal Journey," *FWTAO Newsletter*, May/June 1996, 32–3.

45. Kristen Kozolanka, *The Power of Persuasion: The Politics of the New Right in Ontario* (Montreal: Black Rose Books, 2007), 54, 94, 250–51.

46. ETFO-caa, Sack Goldblatt Mitchell, Memorandum on the Omnibus Savings and Restructuring Act, 1995 (Bill 26), 11 December 1995.

47. ETFO-caa, Memorandum from Reg Ferland to Participants at the Council of Presidents, 30 January 1996. The memorandum included a copy of a document stamped confidential: "Measures to Address the $400 Million Reduction in the General Legislative Grants," 9 January 1996.

48. Memorandum from Ferland to Council of Presidents, 30 January 1996, 11.

49. Memorandum from Ferland to Council of Presidents, 30 January 1996, 10, 13.

50. ETFO-caa, "Take 2 Aspirins: Articulating the Argument for Sick Days," February 1996, i.

51. YUCTA, FWTAO 1999-027/971, FWTAO, "FWTAO Participates in Protest Against Education Cuts," *FWTAO Newsletter*, January/February 1996, inside cover; Sears, *Retooling the Mind Factory*, 239.

52. ETFO-caa, "OTF Action Plan," *OTF Communiqué*, 30 January 1996.

53. YUCTA, OPSTF 2010-006/59, "Historic Meeting Brings OTF Affiliate Presidents Together," *OPSTF Shock Absorber*, 22 February 1996.

54. ETFO-caa, "OTF Action Plan," *OTF Communiqué*, 30 January 1996.

55. ETFO-caa, Government Initiatives Report Form (numbers 1 through 10), 23–29 January 1996.

56. MacLellan, "Neoliberalism and Ontario Teachers' Unions," 52.

57. YUCTA, OPSTF 2010-006/53, Provincial Executive Minutes, 7 February 1996, 2–5.

58. YUCTA, FWTAO 1999-027/971, "Historic Presidents' Meeting," *FWTAO Newsletter*, March/April 1996, inside cover; YUCTA, OPSTF 2010-006/53, Provincial Executive Minutes, 7 February 1996, 9.

59. YUCTA, FWTAO 1999-027/971, "Hamilton Day of Action," *FWTAO Newsletter*, March/April 1996, inside cover; William Shields, "Kingston Workers Will Demonstrate in Hamilton," *Kingston Whig-Standard*, 23 February 1996, 8.

60. Bryan Palmer, "Nine Hour Movement," *Canadian Encyclopedia* (Historica Canada, 2006), thecanadianencyclopedia.ca. The Nine Hour Movement of 1872 brought together unionized and non-unionized workers to demand shorter workdays. In Canada, it began in Hamilton.

61. Richard Brennan, "Harris Dismisses Labor Protestors," *Kingston Whig-Standard*, 26 February 1996, 6.

62. Jack Lakey, "Day 2: Labor Turns Up the Heat," *Toronto Star*, 25 February 1996, A1, A14.

63. Kellogg, "Workers Against Austerity."

64. YUCTA, OPSTF 2010-006/53, Provincial Executive Minutes, 7–9 April 1996, 20.

65. David Rapaport, *No Justice, No Peace: The 1996 OPSEU Strike Against the Harris Government in Ontario* (Montreal: McGill-Queen's University Press, 1999), 143, 216.

66. YUCTA, OPSTF 2010-006/58, Charlotte Morgan, "Cutback Calendar," *OPSTF News*, April 1996, 8–9.

67. Gidney, *From Hope to Harris*, 242–43.

68. ETFO CPS, Memorandum from Christine Brown to Provincial Executive et al., Key Components of 1996 General Legislative Grants, 14 March 1996.

69. YUCTA, OPSTF 2010-006/58, Reg Ferland, "Traitors and Heroes—The Struggle Continues," *OPSTF News*, April 1996, 3.

70. ETFO-caa, Status of Restoration of Increments, 1 September 1996.

71. YUCTA, FWTAO 1999-027/1088, Renfrew 1996–97 file, FWTAO and OPSTF, Information Bulletin to the Members of the Federation of Women Teachers' Associations of Ontario and The Ontario Public School Teachers' Federation, Renfrew County Board of Education.

72. YUCTA, FWTAO 1999-027/971, Joan Westcott, "Electing the First Council of the College of Teachers," *FWTAO Newsletter*, September/October 1996, 24.

73. ETFO GRO, Submission to the Social Development Committee with Respect to Bill 31, The Ontario College of Teachers Act, 1995, April 1996, 9–10.

74. Gidney, *From Hope to Harris*, 243.

75. ETFO CPS, Memorandum from Christine Brown to District Presidents, Follow-up to Survey on Lay-offs, 16 May 1996.

76. YUCTA, OPSTF 2010-006/58, Dave Lennox, "Shadows and Night Sounds," *OPSTF News*, June 1996, 5.

77. Sears, *Retooling the Mind Factory*, 239–40.

78. Lisa Wright, "Teachers May Face Strike Ban: Ministry Won't Rule Out Anything in Bill 100 Review," *Toronto Star*, 24 August 1996, A1.

79. Ontario, Ministry of Education and Training, "Province to Review Outdated School Board / Teacher Bargaining Rules," News Release Communiqué, 23 August 1996.

80. Leon Paroian, *Review of the School Boards' / Teachers' Collective Negotiations Process in Ontario, 1996* (Ontario, 1996), 10–13, 17, 19, 20–6, 29.

81. YUCTA, FWTAO 1999-027/971, Margaret Gee, "Teachers Are Heroes," *FWTAO Newsletter*, September/October 1996, 25–6.

82. YUCTA, OPSTF 2010-006/52, Provincial Executive Minutes, November 1996, 2.

83. YUCTA, OPSTF 2010-006/58, Bill Martin, "OTF News," *OPSTF News*, October 1996, 36.

84. YUCTA, FWTAO 1999-027/971, "Metro Days of Action," *FWTAO Newsletter*, November/December 1996, inside cover.

85. YUCTA, FWTAO 1999-027/971, Joan Westcott, "The Importance of Speaking Out," *FWTAO Newsletter*, November/December 1996, 28.

86. Julio Gomes, "Trustees Slam Provincial Education Cuts," *Thunder Bay Chronicle-Journal*, 19 October 1996, A3.

87. ETFO-caa, Ontario Public School Boards' Association, OPSBA Clearinghouse for Local Public Awareness Activities, 15 November 1996.

88. ETFO-caa, Ontario Public Supervisory Officials' Association, "Our Future Together: A Message to the Premier from the Directors of Education of Ontario's Public School Boards," 18 November 1996, 1.

89. Stephen Lawton, Mark Ryall and Teresa Menzies, *A Study on Costs: Ontario Public Elementary/Secondary Education Costs as Compared to Other Provinces* (Ontario Institute for Studies in Education 1996).

90. ETFO-caa, Wilf Brown, "Ontario Ministry of Education Study on Cost of Education," Canadian Teachers' Federation, 30 September 1996; YUCTA, OPSTF 2010-006/58, Christine Brown, "A Web Well Spun: Education Costs and the Big Lie," *OPSTF News*, October 1996, 26–27.

91. Sears, *Retooling the Mind Factory*, 236.

## Chapter 8: Fighting Back

1. Jennifer Brown, "Ready to Strike?: Elementary Teachers Move Toward Strike," *Richmond Hill / Thornhill Liberal*, 26 January 1997, 1.

2. ETFO-caa, York Region Teachers on Line, 24 March 1997, 1.

3. ETFO-caa, FWTAO and OPSTF, Can the Message Be More Obvious??!!, Bulletin 10, 25 February 1997.

4. ETFO-caa, FWTAO and OPSTF, York Region Elementary Teachers Vote 87.1% to Strike!, Media Release, 21 February 1997. The percentage of approval in the strike vote varied in different reports.

5. Gidney, *From Hope to Harris*, 246–47.

6. Ontario, Bill 104, Fewer School Boards Act, 1997.

7. YUCTA, OPSTF 2010-006/58, Dave Lennox, "What a Mess," *OPSTF News*, December 1996, 5.

8. YUCTA, OPSTF 2010-006/58, Charlotte Morgan, "Days of Action," *OPSTF News*, December 1996, 7.

9. ETFO CPS, Memorandum from Christine Brown to Fellow Collective Bargaining Staff Officers, Law for Activists, 15 November 1996.

10. YUCTA, FWTAO 1999-027/250, 1997 Report of the Board of Directors, August 1997, 9–10.

11. YUCTA, FWTAO 1999-027/971, "The Future of Education Campaign," *FWTAO Newsletter*, November/December 1996, inside cover, "The Importance of Speaking Out," *FWTAO Newsletter*, November/December 1996, 28.

12. Mel Watkins, "Politics in the Time of Space and Globalization," in *Changing Canada: Political Economy as Transformation*, ed. Wallace Clement and Leah F. Vosko (Montreal: McGill-Queen's University Press, 2003).

13. YUCTA, FWTAO 1999-027/1022 (197D), Pres. Forum Joint Session file, FWTAO and OPSTF, Minister Delivers Another Blow to Education, 8 February 1997.

14. ETFO-caa, Memorandum from Christine Brown to Provincial Executive, Staff Officers, The State of the Unions, 19 March 1997, 1.

15. YUCTA, FWTAO 1999-027/1037, FWTAO, "Paroian's Recommendations," 1; Kathy Schaffer, "Principal and Vice-Principal Status as Teachers," *PAR Newsletter*, February 1997, 2.

16. YUCTA, OPSTF 2010-006/58, "Survey of Fundraising in Public Elementary Schools," "Very Important Report Card: Moving Ontario Students Back to the 1950s," "Are Government Cuts Affecting Your Classroom?" *OPSTF News*, February 1997, inserts.

17. YUCTA, FWTAO 1999-027/1050, Provincial Protest 1997, Campaign Against Bill 160 (2 of 2) file, Memorandum from Kathleen Loftus to AER Staff, Re: Inquiries from you, members, public, etc., 7 October 1997; YUCTA, OPSTF 2010-006/52, Provincial Executive Minutes, March 1997, 15.

18. YUCTA, OPSTF 2010-006/58, Bill Martin, "Education Under Seige [*sic*]," *OPSTF News*, April 1997, 32.

19. YUCTA, FWTAO 1999-027/971, Joan Westcott, "What's in Store for 1997?," *FWTAO Newsletter*, January/February 1997, 28.

20. YUCTA, OPSTF 2010-006/52, Provincial Executive Minutes, April 1997, 4.

21. YUCTA, FWTAO 1999-027/971, "A System in Peril," *FWTAO Newsletter*, September/October 1997, 11, 16.

22. ETFO CPS, Memorandum from Jeff Holmes to OPSTF District Presidents et al., Labour Legislation, 3 June 1997.

23. ETFO CPS, Jeff Holmes, "Teachers to Resist Anti-Labour Government," media release, 28 July 1997.

24. YUCTA, FWTAO 1999-027/29, Annual Meeting Minutes, 13 August 1997, 40–1.

25. YUCTA, OPSTF 2010-006/27, Provincial Assembly Minutes, August 1997, 2–4.

26. ETFO GRO, OPSTF Briefs file, Sack Goldblatt Mitchell, Summary of Bill 136, The Public Sector Transition Stability Act, 1997, as amended, 2 October 1997 1–2.

27. Gidney, *From Hope to Harris*, 257.

28. ETFO GRO, OPSTF, Presentation on Bill 160, *The Education Quality Improvement Act, 1997* to the Administration of Justice Committee, 21 October 1997, 2–3, 10, 11–14, 27.

29. YUCTA, FWTAO 1999-027/029, 1997 FWTAO Annual Meeting, 13 August 1997, 39–41; YUCTA, OPSTF 2010-006/58, "Creating a Crisis," *OPSTF News*, December 1997, 12–13.

30. Peter Small and Donovan Vincent, "24,000 Rally to Back Protesting Teachers: Show of Strength before Talks with Snobelen," *Toronto Star*, 7 October 1997, A1, A4.

31. YUCTA, OPSTF 2010-006/58, Memorandum from FWTAO/OPSTF Picketing Workshop to WTA Presidents et al., Information Picketing, 23 October 1997.

32. YUCTA, OPSTF 2010-006/58, OTF, Key Messages for Local Presidents, 27 October 1997.

33. Daniel Girard and Joel Ruimy, "'Mr. Fixit' Set to Deal with Teachers: Johnson Willing to Compromise as He Takes Over Education Hot Seat," *Toronto Star*, 11 October 1997, A1, A32.

34. Daniel Girard, "Eves Denies Plan to Chop $1 Billion from Schools," *Toronto Star*, 17 October 1997, A1.

35. Daniel Girard, "Teachers' Talks Collapse: Both Sides Meet Again Today but There's Little Hope and a Strike Could Come as Early as Thursday," *Toronto Star*, 21 October 1997, A1.

36. Ron Bull, "Grim Outlook," Photograph, *Toronto Star*, 21 October 1997, A1.

37. Daniel Girard and Joel Ruimy, "Strike Will Punish Parents and Children: Harris: 126,000 Teachers Set to Walk Off the Job on Monday," *Toronto Star*, 23 October 1997, A1, A35.

38. Daniel Girard, Joel Ruimy, and Peter Small, "School's Out!: Teachers' Picket Lines Go Up Today at Schools in Ontario and There Is Little Hope the 2.1 Million Students Will Be Back in Classrooms Soon," *Toronto Star*, 27 October 1997, A1, A22.

39. YUCTA, OPSTF 2010-006/58, Charlotte Morgan, "The Battle of Bill 160," *OPSTF News*, December 1997, 9.

40. YUCTA, OPSTF 2010-006/58, OTF News Releases, Communiqué file, Eileen Lennon et al., "Letter from the Presidents," *OTF Communiqué*, 26 October 1997; OTF, "Teachers Will Not Be in Their Classrooms on Monday, October 27, 1997," *OTF Communiqué*, 26 October 1997.

41. YUCTA, OPSTF 2010-006/58, "Solidarity/Solidarité," *OTF Communiqué*, 27 October 1997.

42. YUCTA, FWTAO 1999-027/1050, Provincial Protest 1997, Campaign Against Bill 160 (1 of 2) file, OTF "Key Messages for Local Presidents."

43. YUCTA, OPSTF 2010-006/58, OTF, "OTF and Affiliates' Five Point Plan to Resolve the Impasse Regarding Bill 160," 30 October 1997.

44. YUCTA, OPSTF 2010-006/58, OTF, "Solidarity Continues to Be Our Strength," *OTF Communiqué*, 31 October 1997.

45. YUCTA, OPSTF 2010-006/58, Dave Lennox, "Victory Delayed," *OPSTF News*, December 1997, 5.

46. Douglas James Nesbitt, "Days of Action: Ontario's Extra-parliamentary Opposition to the Common Sense Revolution, 1995–1998," Queen's University, Ph.D. thesis, 2018, 279–83.

47. Kellogg, "Workers Against Austerity," 17.

48. YUCTA, FWTAO 1999-027/1050, Provincial Protest 1997, Campaign Against Bill 160 (1 of 2) file, October 30 OTF and Affiliate Key Media Messages for Local Presidents.

49. Nesbitt, "Days of Action," 320.

50. Nesbitt, "Days of Action"; Christie Blatchford, "Judges Ruling Boosts Teachers," *Toronto Sun*, 4 November 1997.

51. YUCTA, FWTAO 1999-027/1050, Memorandums, News Releases & Media (2 of 3) file, "Moral Victory for Teachers," *OTF Communiqué*, 3 November 1997; "Injunction Application Dismissed," *OTF Communiqué*, 4 November 1997.

52. Harry Glasbeek, "Class War: Ontario Teachers and the Courts," *Osgoode Hall Law Journal* 37 (Spring and Summer 1999), 816–18.

53. YUCTA, OPSTF 2010-006/58, "Only 36% of Ontarians Support Government Positions," *OTF Communiqué*, 5 November 1997.

54. YUCTA, FWTAO 1999-027/1050, Memorandums, News Releases & Media (2 of 3) file, "Teachers Meet Government's Objective; Still Not Enough," *OTF Communiqué*, 4 November 1997; Daniel Girard, "Teachers' Strike: No End in Sight," *Toronto Star*, 4 November 1997, A1.

55. Daniel Girard, Joel Ruimy, and Peter Small, "Teachers Ponder Ending Walkout: Union Leaders Eye Different Tactics after Talks Break Down Again," *Toronto Star*, 5 November 1997, A1, A4; YUCTA, FWTAO 1999-027/1050, Memorandums, News Releases & Media (2 of 3) file, Thane Burnett, "Metro Folks Back Teachers," *Toronto Sun*, 4 November 1997; Provincial Protest 1997, Campaign Against Bill 160 (1 of 2) file, November 4 OTF and Affiliate Key Media Messages for Local Presidents.

56. YUCTA, FWTAO 1999-027/1050, Protecting Quality Education: We Won't Back Down (coloured file), n.d.

57. YUCTA, FWTAO 1999-027/1050, Memorandums, News Releases & Media (2 of 3) file, OTF Action Plan Memorandum from the OTF to Branch Affiliate Presidents, Provincial Rally sponsored by Teacher Supporters, 5 November 1997.

58. YUCTA, OPSTF 2010-006/58, Memorandum from Dave Kendall to Staff Officers, Survey of OPSTF Presidents, 6 November 1997.

59. Barb Gunning, Hastings Women Teachers' Association President 1996–97, interview by author, Thomasburg, ON, 20 February 2009. She was clear that she did not receive any survey by mail or phone from the provincial FWTAO office.

60. Joel Ruimy and Jane Armstrong, "It's Back to School: One Million Students in Class Monday, the Rest Could Follow," *Toronto Star*, 7 November 1997, A1.

61. YUCTA, FWTAO 1999-027/1050, Provincial Protest 1997, Campaign Against Bill 160 (1 of 2) file, Letter from AEFO President Diane Chénier, FWTAO President Maret Sädam-Thompson and OPSTF President Phyllis Benedict to teachers, 6 November 1997.

62. Barb Gunning, interview, 20 February 2009.

63. Peter Small and Joel Ruimy, "Back to School?: Not So Fast, Some Teachers Warn," *Toronto Star*, 8 November 1997, A1, A9.

64. Girard, Ruimy, and Small, "Teachers Ponder Ending Walkout."

65. Barb Gunning, interview, 20 February 2009.

66. Briskin, "In the Public Interest," 93–99.

67. Rebecca Coulter, "School Restructuring Ontario Style: A Gendered Agenda," in *Teacher Activism in the 1990s*, ed. Susan Robertson and Harry Smaller (Toronto: James Lorimer, 1996), 90.

68. YUCTA, FWTAO 1999-027/1050, Memorandums, News Releases & Media (2 of 3) file, OTF and Affiliate Key Media Messages for Local Presidents, 4 November, 4:30 p.m.

69. YUCTA, OPSTF 2010-006/58, Charlotte Morgan, "The Battle of Bill 160," *OPSTF News*, December 1997, 6–7.

70. Glasbeek, "Class War," 838–41.

71. YUCTA, OPSTF 2010-006/58, Memorandum from Phyllis Benedict, to District Presidents, Branch Presidents, Provincial Executive, Staff, Re: Principals/Vice-Principals in Federation from Jan. 1st to March 31st, 6 December 1997.

72. YUCTA, OPSTF 2010-006/58, Charlotte Morgan, "The Battle of Bill 160," *OPSTF News*, December 1997, 11.

73. ETFO-caa, Ontario Court of Justice (General Division), Court File No. 97-CV-137709, "Ontario Teachers' Federation ('OTF'), et al., and The Attorney General of Ontario," 17 March 1998.

74. YUCTA, FWTAO 1999-027/971, Joan Westcott, "Overview of 1998," *FWTAO Newsletter*, January/February 1998, 24.

75.  YUCTA, OPSTF 2010-006/58, Elementary Principals' and Vice-Principals Association of Ontario (EPVPAO), Supporting Professionalism and Protecting Rights, n.d.

76.  Ontario Principals' Council, principals.ca.

77.  Hugh Mackenzie, "Reading Rozanski: A Guide to the Report of the Education Equality Task Force 2002" (Canadian Centre for Policy Alternatives, 11 December 2002), 1, policyalternatives.ca.

78.  Hugh Mackenzie, *No Time for Complacency: Education Funding Reality Check* (Ottawa: Canadian Centre for Policy Alternatives, November 2009).

79.  YUCTA, FWTAO 1999-027/801, Ontario Teachers' Federation, *We the Teachers of Ontario*, 1980, 2.

80.  Judy Fudge and Eric Tucker, *Labour Before the Law: The Regulation of Workers' Collective Action in Canada, 1900–1948* (Toronto: Oxford University Press, 2001), 2–3.

81.  Thomas Walkom, "Striking Teachers Triumph Despite Fracture of Unions," *Toronto Star*, 7 November 1997, A6.

82.  The factor, age plus years of service, is used by pension plans in calculating the age at which an individual worker can retire without a penalty.

83.  YUCTA, FWTAO 1999-027/1053, *OTF Communiqué*, "Pension Negotiations . . . Update," *OTF Communiqué*, 20 February 1998.

84.  YUCTA, OPSTF 2010-006/58, James Daw, "Smart Money: Teachers Weigh Retirement Odds," *OPSTF News*, May 1998, 26.

85.  YUCTA, FWTAO 1999-027/971, Margaret Gee, "Teachers as Agents of Change," *FWTAO Newsletter*, November/December 1996, 30.

86.  Sara Jean Green, "Women Teachers' League Fades into Co-ed Federation," *Globe and Mail*, 18 August 1998, A3.

87.  Nicolass Van Run, "Coping with the Strike," *Toronto Star*, 27 October 1997, A6.

88.  ETFO-caa, District Fee Rebate Voluntary Members 1995–96, Account 1005, June 1996. The total number of voluntary members in June 1996 was 3,884. Carleton local had 568 voluntary members, with the London local next at 233 voluntary members.

89.  YUCTA, FWTAO 1999-027/971, FWTAO, "Protecting Teachers' Rights," *FWTAO Newsletter*, May/June 1997, inside cover.

90.  YUCTA, OPSTF 2010-006/58, Dave Lennox, "Secretary," *OPSTF News*, June 1997, 5.

91.  YUCTA, FWTAO 1999-027/1058, Model Constitution for the Locals of the Elementary Teachers' Federation of Ontario, March 1998; Joint FWTAO and OPSTF Presidents' Meeting Agenda, 30 April 1998.

92.  YUCTA, OPSTF 2010-006/56, Meeting between OPSTF and FWTAO, 22 July 1994.

93.  YUCTA, FWTAO 1999-027/029, Annual Meeting Minutes 1998, 5–6.

## Chapter 9: Finding a Voice

1. Through most of the twentieth century, fluid gender identities were not part of the public consciousness. Gender was assigned by physical characteristics observed at birth. While same-sex relationships were talked and written about during this period (often derisively), they challenged existing ideas of sexual orientation, not gender.

2. YUCTA, FWTAO 1999-027/767, "FWTAO Bargaining Priorities 1993–94," *FWTAO Newsletter*, April/May 1993, inside cover. Priorities for collective bargaining included: "physical safety, seniority, discrimination, harassment and parental rights [paid maternity leave]."

3. Nancy Christie, "By Necessity or By Right: The Language and Experience of Gender at Work," *Labour / Le Travail* 50 (Fall 2002).

4. Warskett, "The Politics of Difference and Inclusiveness," 598.

5. One male teacher I talked with told me of the men teachers at the school regularly having lunch in the local "strip club" during the 1970s. In two schools, one in northern Ontario and one in the southeast of the province, I was told of the men, including teachers, custodians, and at least one senior administrator, gathering after school to watch pornographic movies, again in the 1970s. While this may or may not have been pervasive across the province, in those elementary schools, "stag" behaviour after hours was an accepted constituent of male comradery. A number of women spoke of buying their alcohol in another town where they would not be recognized, or of getting a man to buy liquor for them. While the social significance of the men's proclivities can be debated, the weight of social sanctions clearly fell heavier on women teachers.

6. Joan Sangster, *Earning Respect: The Lives of Working Women in Small-Town Ontario, 1920–1960* (Toronto: University of Toronto Press, 1995), 112.

7. Warskett, "The Politics of Difference and Inclusiveness," 617 (previously quoted).

8. YUCTA, FWTAO 1999-027/1058, Report of the Board of Directors 1990–91, 15.

9. Joan Sangster, *Through Feminist Eyes: Essays on Canadian Women's History* (Edmonton: AU Press, 2011), 129.

10. Sangster, *Through Feminist Eyes*, 136–39.

11. Gender-based tensions that existed between the two unions are still very much alive within the ETFO. These two items come up for debate regularly at the annual general meetings.

12. YUCTA, FWTAO 1999-027/971, Joan Westcott, "It's Elementary!," *FWTAO Newsletter*, March/April 1997, 28.

13. YUCTA, FWTAO 1999-027/971, Maret Sädem-Thompson, "Unity: Strength and Action," *FWTAO Newsletter*, September/October 1997, 29.

14. T.H. Marshall and Tom Bottomore, *Citizenship and Social Class* (London: Plato, 1992), 8, 27–43; Esping-Andersen, *The Three Worlds of Welfare Capitalism*, 9–23.

15. Harvey, *A Brief History of Neoliberalism*, 7, 19–27, 33, 54, 64–8, 75–7, 119–20, 161, 169–78, 205.

16. This is also true of the other teachers' unions in the province—the OSSTF, OECTA, and AEFO.

17. E.P. Thompson, "The Moral Economy of the English Crowd in the Eighteenth Century," *Past and Present* 50 (Spring 1971), 76–136.

18. Although, as Spaull and Mann note when examining Australian teachers' unions, "trade unionism is not the same as working class consciousness." Andrew Spaull and Susan Mann, "Teacher Unionism in Australia: The Case of Victoria," in *The Politics of Teacher Unionism: International Perspectives*, ed. Martin Lawn (Beckenham, UK: Croom Helm, 1985), 27.

19. YUCTA, FWTAO 1999-027/971, Maret Sädem-Thompson, "From Anger to Activism," *FWTAO Newsletter*, November/December 1997, 29.

20. YUCTA, OPSTF 2010-006/58, Charlotte Morgan, "The Battle of Bill 160," *OPSTF News*, December 1997, 6–12.

21. Elementary Teachers' Federation of Ontario, "Building a Just Society," etfo.ca.

22. Elementary Teachers' Federation of Ontario, "Guide to Pregnancy and Parental Leave," etfo.ca.

23. Barbara Richter, Executive Assistant FWTAO and Staff Officer ETFO, email exchange with the author. Richter quoted from the "FWTAO Handbook."

24. See Tim McCaskell, *Race to Equity: Disrupting Educational Inequity* (Toronto: Between the Lines, 2005), for a historical view of anti-racism, anti-homophobic, and other equity battles in the Toronto Board of Education. McCaskell points to the involvement of the OSSTF local.

25. Such sentiments were much in evidence at the FWTAO reunion, Kingston, ON, 4 April 2008.

26. Barbara Richter, *It's Elementary: A Brief History of Ontario's Public Elementary Teachers and Their Federations* (Elementary Teachers' Federation of Ontario, 2008), 12.

27. Christine Brown, "ETFO Celebrates 10 Years of Success: Ten Years of Collective Bargaining," *ETFO Voice*, December 2008.

28. "Striking Teachers Claim Parents, Kids on their Side in Education Fight," *Windsor Star*, 14 February 2020, windsorstar.com.

29. Caroline Alphonso, "Ontario Elementary Teachers' Union Reaches Tentative Deal with Province," *Globe and Mail*, 20 March 2020, theglobeandmail.com.

# Index

**Andy Hanson** retired from teaching to write labour history. He lives in Toronto with his partner. In the 1997 campaign against Premier Mike Harris, he was a member of the local consolidated committee of five teachers' unions organizing marches and rallies, co-ordinating picket lines, and communicating with members. After the men's and women's elementary teachers amalgamated, he was elected ETFO local vice-president and held that position for twelve years. Hanson received his PhD in Canadian Studies from Trent University in 2013.